Society of Biblical Literature
Monograph Series 18

Published for the Society of Biblical Literature

Glory at the Right Hand

Psalm 110 in Early Christianity
David M. Hay

Nashville   ABINGDON PRESS   New York

GLORY AT THE RIGHT HAND

Library of Congress Cataloging in Publication Data

HAY, DAVID M. 1935-   Glory at the right hand.
  (Society of Biblical Literature. Monograph series, 18)
  A revision of the author's thesis, Yale, 1965.
  Includes bibliographical references.
  1. Bible. O.T. Psalm CX—Criticism, interpretation, etc.—History—Early
church.
  I. Title. II. Series.
  BS1430.2.H33 1973   223′.2   73-297

ISBN: 0-687-20633-2

MANUFACTURED BY THE PARTHENON PRESS AT
NASHVILLE, TENNESSEE, UNITED STATES OF AMERICA

To Mary Cam, with gratitude

Preface

This book has grown out of a doctoral dissertation completed in 1965 at Yale University. I received invaluable encouragement and criticism from Yale professors Paul W. Meyer (the thesis advisor), Erwin R. Goodenough, Paul S. Minear, and Paul Schubert. The subject of the investigation was suggested by Professor Nils A. Dahl, and his comments after reading a revised form of the study two years ago gave major impetus toward publication. The editor of the Society of Biblical Literature Monograph Series, Professor Robert A. Kraft, has contributed many improvements in content as well as format. Finally I am indebted to the library staffs at Yale and at Princeton Theological Seminary for indispensable efficiency in providing materials, and to Miss Emily Kletzien for expert typing of a messy manuscript.

DAVID M. HAY
Cedar Rapids, Iowa
20 June 1972

Contents

Abbreviations

Apcr Jas	Apocryphon of James
Apoc Pet	Apocalypse of Peter
ATANT	Abhandlungen zur Theologie des Alten und Neuen Testaments
b	Babylonian Talmud (also = ben [son of] in names)
BCE	before the common era
BEvT	Beiträge zur evangelischen Theologie
BHT	Beiträge zur historischen Theologie
BKAT	Biblischer Kommentar: Altes Testament
BNTC	Black's New Testament Commentary
BZNW	Beihefte zur ZNW
CE	common era
CNT	Commentaire du Nouveau Testament
Eus EH	Eusebius, *Ecclesiastical History*
ET	English translation (by)
FRLANT	Forschungen zur Religion und Literatur des Alten und Neuen Testaments
GCS	Die griechischen christlichen Schriftsteller der ersten drei Jahrhunderte
HAT	Handbuch zum Alten Testament
Heg (EH)	Hegesippus as cited in Eusebius, *Ecclesiastical History*
HKAT	Handkommentar zum Alten Testament
HNT	Handbuch zum Neuen Testament
H-S	E. Hennecke and W. Schneemelcher, *New Testament Apocrypha*, ET R. M. Wilson (Philadelphia: Westminster, 1963, 1965), 2 vols.
ICC	International Critical Commentary
JBL	*Journal of Biblical Literature*

JE	Jewish Encyclopedia
JTS	*Journal of Theological Studies*
LCL	Loeb Classical Library
Meyer	H. A. W. Meyer, Kritisch-exegetischer Kommentar über das Neue Testament
MNTC	Moffatt New Testament Commentary
MT	Masoretic text (Hebrew Bible)
NICNT	New International Commentary on the New Testament
NovT	*Novum Testamentum*
NT	New Testament
NtAbh	Neutestamentliche Abhandlungen (Münster: Aschendorff)
NTD	Das Neue Testament Deutsch
NTS	*New Testament Studies*
OG	Old Greek (Jewish scriptures in Greek)
par	(and) parallel (s)
PG	J. Migne, *Patrologia graeca*
PLACE	position at the right hand of God
Pol *Phil*	Polycarp, *Epistle to the Philippians*
RB	*Revue biblique*
RGG	Die Religion in Geschichte und Gegenwart
SBT	Studies in Biblical Theology
SESSION	session at the right hand of God
Sib Or	Sibylline Oracles
Str-B	H. L. Strack and P. Billerbeck, *Kommentar zum Neuen Testament aus Talmud und Midrasch* (Munich: Beck, 1922 ff)
TDNT	G. Kittel and G. Friedrich (eds.), *Theological Dictionary of the New Testament,* ET G. Bromiley (Grand Rapids: Eerdmans, 1964 ff)
TU	Texte und Untersuchungen
TWNT	G. Kittel and G. Friedrich, *Theologisches Wörterbuch zum Neuen Testament* (Stuttgart: Kohlhammer, 1932 ff)
VT	*Vetus Testamentum*
WMANT	Wissenschaftliche Monographien zum Alten und Neuen Testament
ZNW	*Zeitschrift für die neutestamentliche Wissenschaft*

Note: Other abbreviations of ancient Jewish and Christian writings (and transliteration of Hebrew and Greek) generally follow the form listed in JBL 90 (1971), 513-14. The abbreviations of Philo's works are taken from F. H. Colson and G. H. Whitaker, *Philo* 1 (LCL; Cambridge, Mass.:Harvard Univ., 1929), xxiii f.

Introduction

An oracle of Yahweh to my lord: "Sit at my right
hand until I make your foes a stool for your feet."
Yahweh has sworn and will not retract: "You are a
priest forever after the order of Melchizedek."

These two sentences in Ps 110 (vss 1 and 4) are among the Jewish
scriptural texts most often quoted or alluded to by early Christian
writers. Thirty-three quotations and allusions are scattered through the
NT, and seven more may be found in other Christian writings produced before the middle of the second century.[1] Many of these references to the psalm are set in passages of high theological consequence,
and certain phrases in the psalm have been linked with central Christian beliefs ever since. Yet up to now no full, systematic analysis of
early Christian interpretations of Ps 110 has appeared.

Recent progress along two paths of scholarly inquiry makes detailed
study of early Christian usage of the psalm especially desirable. The
burgeoning number of studies dealing with Christian interpretation
of Jewish scriptures in NT times suggest a variety of questions. Why
was this particular psalm cited so often by early Christians? Was their
exegesis of it simply an extension of Jewish messianic interpretation?
Does it imply the psalm's incorporation into a collection of scriptural
testimonies? Is C. H. Dodd right in supposing that early Christians
paid careful attention to context when interpreting the psalm and
derived their understanding of it from Jesus himself?[2] Barnabas
Lindars contends Christians first applied the psalm to Jesus as a literal
description of his resurrection, and he thinks it possible to trace the

[1] See list in Appendix.
[2] *According to the Scriptures* (Digswell Place: Nisbet, 1952), 110, 126.

15

logical or historical development of the psalm's interpretation within the church.[3] Jean Daniélou, in a series of publications, has emphasized the variety of meanings which the psalm took on for Christians of the first two centuries. But he urges that its use illustrates not only the unity of the NT writings but the unity of early Christian thought with the OT as well.[4]

On the other hand, studies of the evolution of NT christology have made certain questions pressing. Did application of the title "lord" to Jesus stem from Ps 110.1? How far did the psalm's fourth verse beget priestly ideas about him? What theological or existential significance did early believers attach to Jesus' SESSION at God's right hand? Oscar Cullmann maintains that the mere frequency of references to that SESSION proves that the primitive church generally proclaimed Jesus' present rule as king.[5] Ferdinand Hahn claims that Ps 110.1 decisively shaped convictions about Jesus' exaltation and the delay of his parousia.[6] Philipp Vielhauer sharply denies Hahn's contentions.[7]

These and other particular questions and judgments will be explored in this study. No single problem or hypothesis has dominated previous research in this area. Yet it would seem that one fundamental historical question should be faced: why was Ps 110 so popular among early Christians? It seems unlikely that the frequency of its utilization could be mere accident even if different users gave it different interpretations. Rather, the psalm was an unusually apt vehicle for expressing the ultimacy of Jesus, though not for describing his saving work.

From a methodological standpoint, all previous study suffers from incompleteness—from failure to analyze all Christian uses of the psalm in the NT period, and from failure to examine with sufficient breadth

[3] *New Testament Apologetic* (London: SCM, 1961), 45-51.

[4] "La session à la droite du Père (Ps. 109, 1-2)," 42-49 in J. Daniélou, *Etudes d'exégèse judéo-chrétienne* (*Théologie historique* 5; Paris: Beauchesne, 1966). An earlier form of the same article appeared (under the same title) in K. Aland, F. L. Cross et al. (eds.) *Studia Evangelica* 1 (TU 73, 1959), 689-98. A briefer discussion appears in J. Daniélou, *The Bible and the Liturgy* ET (Notre Dame: Univ. Press, 1956), 307-11, where the following characteristic statement relating to Ps. 110 occurs (p. 307): "We might say that it was in the categories of the Old Testament that the first Fathers thought about the fact of Christ."

[5] *The Christology of the New Testament,* ET S. Guthrie and C. Hall (Philadelphia: Westminster, 1959), 223.

[6] *The Titles of Jesus in Christology,* ET H. Knight and G. Ogg (London: Lutterworth, 1969), 129-35.

[7] *Aufsätze zum Neuen Testament* (*Theologische Bücherei* 31; Munich: Kaiser 1965), 167-75.

the traditions and associations behind those uses. In addition, most writers have tended to make dubious assumptions about a uniformity of meaning in the various quotations and allusions. Apart from their sheer number, the most remarkable feature of early Chrisian references to Ps 110 is the wide diversity of meanings.

This study aims at comprehensiveness and discrimination of the different hues of meaning in individual references to the psalm. Part 1 surveys the history of interpretations in ancient Judaism and early Christianity (down to the fourth century). The texts of early Christian quotations and allusions are scrutinized to determine what form or forms of the psalm's text were current. Part 2 is a detailed analysis of Christian interpretations to the time of Justin Martyr, organized according to the different meanings or functions assigned to the psalm. Since the same quotation or allusion may have multiple meanings in a given passage, Part 2 necessarily contains some repetition of basic exegetical observations. An important advantage of such repetition is that it shows continuity as well as discontinuity between various authors' interpretations.

I shall limit myself to direct quotations and "definite allusions." The latter term will usually[8] indicate references either to a position at the right hand of God or to a priest of Melchizedek's order. Ps 110 is the only significant pre-Christian literary source which expressed either conception.[9] It is not demonstrable that Christians before the time of Justin Martyr referred to any portions of the psalm other than its first and fourth verses, although it is possible that there are deliberate allusions to other sections of the psalm in the extant literature. The "mighty scepter" phrase in Ps 110.2 *might* lie beneath several declarations about the divine Word (e.g. Heb 1.3; 4.12; Rev 19.15); Justin Martyr so interprets the phrase, and he may have been following older Christian practice.[10] Yet such allusions, if they exist at all, lie so far below the surface of our documents that they cannot be recognized with any confidence.

[8] For reasons to be given later, Eph 2.6 and Rev 3.21 will be regarded as allusions to Ps 110.1.

[9] Cf Hahn, *Titles*, 130 and 134 n. 7. The reference to a heavenly right-hand throne in T Job 33 (see below, pp. 22 f) can hardly have been a significant influence (primitive Christian literature never clearly refers to the Testament). On the other hand, the idea of Jesus' right-hand session seems to have early become an established theologoumenon; probably some early Christian references to the idea were written without conscious allusion to Ps 110.1. See below, pp. 43 f.

[10] Thus Daniélou asks if the sequence of ideas in Ps 110.1-2 does not underlie Acts 2.33 and Mk 16.19 (*Etudes,* 49).

17

Part 1
A Survey of Ancient Exegesis of Psalm 110

CHAPTER 1
Origin, and Interpretations in Jewish Tradition

The Original Meaning of Psalm 110

When and under what circumstances the psalm was composed are still matters of scholarly controversy. The majority opinion today is that it is a pre-exilic royal psalm, composed for a Davidic monarch in Jerusalem.[1] The relative simplicity of its thought and the directness of its language support such a view.[2] Some scholars, however, still advocate a post-exilic origin; the favorite theory for this side of Babylon has been one supposing the psalm a piece of Hasmonean propaganda. An acrostic for "Simon" has been detected, and the whole composition has undeniable suitability as an oracular legitimation for priestly rulers in Jerusalem.[3]

Since vss 1 and 4 are the only ones definitely used by Christians in the NT period, we may concentrate our attention on them. The orig-

[1] See, e.g., A. Weiser, *The Psalms,* ET H. Hartwell (Philadelphia: Westminster, 1962), 693; S. H. Hooke, *Alpha and Omega* (Welwyn: Nisbet, 1961), 106; R. de Vaux, *Ancient Israel: Its Life and Institutions,* ET J. McHugh (New York: Mc-Graw-Hill, 1961), 402; H. J. Kraus, *Psalmen* 2 (BKAT; Neukirchen: Neukirchener Verlag, 1960), 755 f.

[2] So H. Gunkel, *Einleitung in die Psalmen* (Göttingen: Vandenhoeck & Ruprecht, 1933), 169; E. R. Hardy, "The Date of Psalm 110," JBL 64 (1945), 385-90; de Vaux, *Ancient Israel,* 109.

[3] The Hasmonean theory, including the acrostic, was advanced by B. Duhm (*Die Psalmen,* 2nd ed. [Tübingen: Mohr, 1922], 398, 400) and others. Recent advocates include R. H. Pfeiffer, *History of New Testament Times* (New York: Harper, 1949), 19. J. C. Dancy (*A Commentary on I Maccabees* [Oxford: Blackwell, 1954], 34) feels that the acrostic argument is "extremely weak" but that the psalm may nonetheless have been written for Simon. R. Tournay ("Le Psaume CX," RB 57 [1960], 5-41) argues that the psalm is post-exilic but pre-Maccabean, expressive of the messianic dreams of the ruling priests in Jerusalem during the Persian or early hellenistic period. While not impossible, the theory depends largely on guesses about a period for which we have little pertinent evidence.

inal sense of 110.1 was evidently that a particular Israelite monarch reigned with the power and authority of Yahweh himself. Possibly it alludes to the physical situation of the king's throne to the right (or south) of Solomon's temple, where God was believed to be enthroned.[4] In any case the right-hand position certainly symbolizes highest honor and closeness to Yahweh. Ps 110.1c promises that God will defeat all the monarch's enemies, an idea developed vividly in vss 5-6.[5] The king is Yahweh's earthly vicegerent, and his throne depends on Yahweh.[6]

Ps 110.4 announces an irrevocable divine decree that someone, presumably the king addressed in vs 1,[7] is a priest "after the order of Melchizedek." Ancient kings, including those of Israel, sometimes performed priestly functions.[8] The precedent of Melchizedek was invoked both because he had combined the offices of king and priest and because he had reigned in pre-Israelite Jerusalem; the psalmist evidently sought to fuse the religious traditions of that earlier period with those of the Davidic monarchy.

Once composed and accepted by the community of Israel as a part of sacred tradition, Ps 110 had to be interpreted meaningfully by succeeding generations. Before reviewing the limited evidence on how Jews after the Babylonian exile did interpret it, we may usefully pause to note major problems which the psalm must have presented for any serious exegete. The first question must always have been: about whom does it speak? In periods when Jews lacked political independence, interpreters might naturally think of great leaders of the past, of a future messiah, or of some heavenly personage. In any case, how would the SESSION at God's right be taken? Did it imply active government or passivity? If vs 3 of the psalm was taken to affirm that the one addressed was God's Son, how would the divine begetting be understood? What associations would readers have with

[4] W. Grundmann, TWNT 2,38 n. 9 (=TDNT 2,39 n. 9) ; H. J. Kraus, *Worship in Israel*, ET G. Buswell (Richmond: Knox, 1966) , 223.

[5] For biblical and extra-biblical parallels to the image of making a footstool of one's foes, see Kraus, *Psalmen* 2,757 f.

[6] Cf 1 Chr 17.14; 28.5; 29.23; 2 Chr 9.8; 13.8. The king sits on God's throne.

[7] H. H. Rowley offers an ingenious but highly conjectural theory that vs 4 is addressed to Zadok and vs 1 to David ("Melchizedek and Zadok [Gen 14 and Ps 110]," *Festschrift Alfred Bertholet*, ed. W. Baumgartner et al. [Tübingen: Mohr, 1950], 461-72) .

[8] See, e.g., 1 Sam 13.9-10; 2 Sam 6.14,18; 24.25; 1 Kgs 3.4,15; 8.14, 52-65; 9.25; 2 Kgs 16.12-15. Cf Jer 30.21. See G. von Rad, *Old Testament Theology* I, ET D. M. G. Stalker (New York: Harper, 1962) , 323.

Melchizedek and how would they conceptualize a priesthood identified with him rather than with Aaron or Zadok? How literally would the psalm's fierce war language be construed? The psalm was probably never just an arsenal from which polemical weapons could be drawn. It was part of the religious tradition that each new generation had to confront and assess in the light of its own experiences and aspirations.

Pre-Christian Interpretations: Actual and Possible

The Old Greek Version (OG).—This translation of Ps 110 probably dates from somewhere between the third and first centuries BCE and represents the earliest known interpretation.[9] There are relatively few significant textual variants.[10] In vs 1, a simple *eipen* renders *neûm*, which bears a special aura of prophetic revelation (cf Num 24.3; 2 Sam 23.1; Isa 56.8; Ps 36.2). But the OG represents the command to be seated as a divine oracle no less plainly than does the MT. Whereas early Christian quotations of the verse represent both God and the one addressed with the common title *kyrios*, it seems certain that originally the OG did not translate the divine name as *kyrios* but retained the tetragrammaton in Hebrew or Greek letters instead.[11] Christian authors, beginning with Justin Martyr, often saw profound significance in the use of *kyrios* for both God and the one addressed by God in Ps 110.1. Presumably this "discovery" did not impress many Jews.

A major difference between MT and OG appears only in vs 3. Here the Hebrew is virtually unintelligible, while the Greek distinctly describes the birth of a divine child:

[9] On the date of the translation, see S. Jellicoe, *The Septuagint and Modern Study* (Oxford: Clarendon Press, 1968), 69. The use of "OG" instead of "LXX" in the present study is meant to underline the fact that increasingly scholars are inclined to emphasize the fact that there was no *single unified* Greek translation of the Jewish scriptures in the pre-Christian era. Cf R. A. Kraft, "Jewish Greek Scriptures and Related Topics," NTS 16 (1969-70), 387 n. 2, and the note in R. F. Zehnle, *Peter's Pentecost Discourse* (SBL Monograph 15, Nashville: Abingdon, 1971), 9. It may also be noted here that our psalm will in this study be consistently referred to as "Ps 110" although it is number 109 in the OG and, following the Vulgate, is often so designated in Christian literature. This decision is taken purely for the sake of convenience and brevity.

[10] See A. Rahlfs, *Septuaginta: Psalmi cum Odis* (Göttingen: Vandenhoeck & Ruprecht, 1931=1967), on which all references to OG are based. Vss 1 and 4 of the psalm in the OG and MT (quoted from R. Kittel, *Biblia Hebraica* [Stuttgart: Württ. Bibelanstalt, 1951]) are reproduced in the Appendix.

[11] See P. E. Kahle, *The Cairo Genizah*, 2nd ed. (Oxford: Blackwell, 1959), 222. Cf Vielhauer, *Aufsätze*, 148-50.

עמך נדבת   μετὰ σοῦ ἡ ἀρχὴ
ביום חילך   ἐν ἡμέρᾳ τῆς δυνάμεώς σου
בהדרי־קדש   ἐν ταῖς λαμπρότησιν τῶν ἁγίων
מרחם משחר   ἐκ γαστρὸς πρὸ ἑωσφόρου
לך טל ילדתיך   ἐξεγέννησά σε.

S. Mowinckel and many other OT scholars think that the OG is close to the sense of the original Hebrew text;[12] if so, the corruption of the present Hebrew text may have resulted from deliberate efforts by scribes to conceal the meaning.[13] From the apparent absence of any allusion to vs 3 in the NT, H. J. Kraus has concluded that probably its meaning was unknown.[14] Yet at least by Justin Martyr's day Christians were finding rich meaning in the verse. Perhaps, then, Christians of the earliest period neglected it not because they found it meaningless in its OG form but because they knew that its meaning (and form) were disputed and because they could find other scriptural texts to support ideas of Jesus' divine sonship (notably Ps 2.7; 2 Sam 7.14).

At vs 4 the OG phrase *kata tēn taxin* presents a clear interpretation of the more ambiguous Hebrew *'al-dibrâtî* as meaning "according to the succession or nature." [15]

Overall, the OG, like the MT, delineates a divinely exalted personage who governs and makes war irresistibly. Also, like the MT, the OG suggests that he is a human monarch in Jerusalem.

Testament of Job 33.3.—There is wide agreement today that this midrashic work is Jewish in origin and dates from the first century BCE or the first century CE.[16] It depicts Job not only as a model of

[12] S. Mowinckel, *He That Cometh*, ET G. W. Anderson (Nashville: Abingdon, 1956), 67.

[13] So A. Bentzen, *Introduction to the Old Testament* (Copenhagen: Gad, 1952), 100.

[14] *Psalmen* 2,764.

[15] See W. Bauer, W. F. Arndt, and F. W. Gingrich, *A Greek-English Lexicon of the New Testament and Other Early Christian Literature* (Chicago: Univ. Press, 1957), s.v. The Greek phrase would not suggest the meaning "because of" which the Hebrew would allow (a sense built upon by R. Ishmael—see below, p. 28).

[16] See K. Kohler, "The Testament of Job," *Semitic Studies in Memory of A. Kohut*, ed. G. A. Kohut (Berlin: Calvary, 1897), 272, 282, 286 f, 295; Kohler, JE 8,200-202; C. C. Torrey, *The Apocryphal Literature* (New Haven: Yale Univ. Press, 1945), 140-45; Pfeiffer, *History*, 70; M. Philonenko, *Le Testament de Job* (Semitica 18; Paris: Librairie d'Amerique et d'Orient Adrien-Maisonneuve, 1968), 21-24. There is no compelling reason to credit the work to a Christian author. Otherwise: M. R. James, *Apocrypha Anecdota 2* (Texts and Studies 5.1; Cambridge: Univ. Press, 1897), xciv (author is a Christian Jew). A careful recent investigation concludes that the work is entirely a specimen of pre-Christian hellenistic Jewish

charity and endurance but also as a king and visionary who can perceive his dead children glorified in heaven and angels who visit this world.[17] While Job sits on a dunghill, Elihu mournfully asks him eleven times, "Where now is the glory of your throne?" [18] To this Job responds:

> Be silent. Now I will point out to you my throne, its glory and its splendor. My throne is in the heavenly world and its glory and splendor are at the right hand of God (*ek dexiōn tou theou*).[19]

Job goes on to declare that, while this world will pass away, his throne is eternal. He concludes:

> My kingdom stands forever, and its splendor and glory rest on the chariots (*harmata*) of the Father.

At the end of T Job angels appear in divine chariots (*harmata*) to bear Job's soul to heaven. The document seems to reflect an early stage of Merkabah mysticism. The heavenly chariots and throne are tokens of the hero's vindication by God.[20] The allusion to Ps 110.1 in T Job 33.3 seems patent. Job's throne at God's right hand exists even while he himself is still alive on earth; he receives it after death as an imperishable reward. Here, then, the psalm—or a small portion of it—is interpreted of the divine exoneration of a pious individual.[21]

Apart from the materials just discussed, evidence for pre-Christian interpretations of Ps 110 is ambiguous. Yet significant possibilities must be explored. It is noteworthy that all these possibilities concern not pious individuals (as in the T Job) but rulers or judges who

---

mission literature (D. Rahnenführer, "Das Testament des Hiob und das Neue Testament," ZNW 62 [1971], 68-93).

[17] T Job 40.3-4 (cf 39.12) ; 52.9 (cf 33.2). Verse references and quotations of the text are based on S. P. Brock, *Testamentum Iobi* (Pseudepigrapha Veteris Testamenti Graece 2; Leiden: Brill, 1967), 1-59. Cf Philonenko, *Testament*, 17 f.

[18] T Job 32.2-12.

[19] The term *theou* is textually uncertain (see Brock, *Testamentum*, 8, 83). Some MSS read *patros* or *sōtēros*. Job's speech is presented in T Job 33.2-9; the clause about a throne at God's right appears in 33.3.

[20] Cf T Job 41.4-5. On the affinities with later Merkabah mysticism, see Kohler, "Testament," 282 and Philonenko, *Testament*, 17 f.

[21] Though Job is described as a king, his royal office and rule are not stressed. There is no clear allusion to any part of Ps 110 except vs 1b, and the heavenly kingdom of Job (33.9) is not explained. He is never described as a ruler or messiah of Israel.

determine the fate of many men. In some cases the rulers or judges are human, in other instances they are superhuman.

Application to Hasmonean Rulers.—While the Hasmoneans probably did not compose the psalm,[22] they probably did use it to defend their claims to priestly and royal prerogatives. It was suitable for that purpose, possibly more suitable than any other scriptural passage.

Positive evidence of Hasmonean usage is offered by several texts. 1 Macc 14.41 describes Simon's appointment to supreme office as one to be *archiereus eis ton aiōna* (cf Ps 110.4). A plain allusion to the Hasmoneans in As Mos 6.1 styles them kings who "shall call themselves priests of the Most High God." Another allusion, almost as certain, occurs in Jub 32.1, where Levi dreams that he has been declared "priest of the Most High God, him and his sons for ever." In T Levi 8.3, a passage probably related to the Hasmonean house, the phraseology of the psalm is recalled:

From henceforth become a priest of the Lord, you and your seed for ever. And the first man anointed me with holy oil, and gave to me the staff of judgment [Cf Ps 110.2].[23]

In vss 14-15 of the same chapter, it is said that some of Levi's descendants will receive a new name when a king arises and establishes a new priesthood as a "prophet of the Most High." R. H. Charles urges that this refers to John Hyrcanus, the "new name" being "priests of the Most High God" (cf Jub 36.16).[24] Elements of the hymn in

---

[22] Apart from the considerations already noted favoring a pre-exilic date for the psalm, several factors militate against the idea that it was composed for the Hasmonean rulers. The psalm ascribes priesthood to a king (vs 4), whereas the Hasmoneans were priests by birth and required legitimation of their kingly office. So the psalm, while fitting their propaganda needs, did not fit them exactly; it seems to have been written for other monarchs. Perhaps the fact that early Christian texts like Mk 12.35-37 par and Acts 2.34-36 unhesitatingly assume Davidic authorship argues against an origin in the Hasmonean period. For an argument based on the psalm's incorporation into the Pharisaic canon, see J. J. Petuchowski, "The Controversial Figure of Melchizedek," *Hebrew Union College Annual* 38 (1957), 135.

[23] The translation is adapted from R. H. Charles, *The Apocrypha and Pseudepigrapha of the Old Testament in English* 2 (Oxford: Clarendon Press, 1913), 308 f. On the connection with the Hasmoneans and the psalm: H. L. Jansen, "The Consecration in the Testamentum Levi," *The Sacral Kingship*, ed. G. Widengren et al. (Leiden: Brill, 1959), 356-65; G. Widengren, "Royal Ideology and the Testaments of the Twelve Patriarchs," *Promise and Fulfillment*, ed. F. F. Bruce (Edinburgh: Clark, 1963), 202-12; J. W. Bowker, "Psalm CX," VT 17 (1967), 31-41. Opposed to the Hasmonean interpretation: T. W. Manson, "Miscellanea Apocalyptica III: Test. XII Patr.: Lev viii," JTS 48 (1947), 59-61.

[24] *Apocrypha and Pseudepigrapha* 2,309 n.

T Levi 18 also suggest connections between the Hasmoneans and Ps 110:

Then shall the Lord raise up a new priest . . . and he shall *execute* a righteous *judgment* upon the earth for a multitude of days [cf Ps 110.6]. And his *star* shall arise in heaven as of a king [cf Ps 110.3].

. . .

And there shall none succeed him for all ages *for ever.*

. . .

And Beliar shall be bound by him
And he shall give power to His children to *tread upon* the evil spirits [cf Ps 110.1c].[25]

Finally there is the hint of a tie with Ps 110 in the official designation the Hasmoneans chose for themselves, "priests of the Most High God." [26] The term "Most High" as a name for God is relatively uncommon in ancient Jewish literature, although it enjoys some prominence in materials dating from the third to first centuries BCE.[27] The phrase "Most High God" is used three times in Gen 14.18-20 in connection with Melchizedek, and the Jewish scriptures do not connect it with any other priest. If the Hasmoneans deliberately selected a title recalling the precedent of Melchizedek, they probably also appropriated the one scriptural passage besides Gen 14 which mentions him— Ps 110.[28]

Probably the psalm entered the NT age trailing associations of the dusty glory of the Hasmoneans.[29] When early Christians employed it, at least some will have consciously compared their kingship with that of Jesus. Conceivably a wish to repudiate those old memories led

[25] Translation from Charles, *Apocrypha and Pseudepigrapha* 2,314 f.

[26] Josephus, *Ant,* 16.6.2§163; b. Rosh Hashanah 18b. Cf E. Bickermann, "The Historical Foundations," in *The Jews* 1, ed. L. Finkelstein (New York: Harper, 1955) , 97.

[27] Notably in Daniel, Sirach, and Jubilees.

[28] An appeal to the precedent of Melchizedek is not precluded by the fact that the Hasmoneans seem to have also claimed Phinehas as a progenitor (e.g., 1 Macc 2.26,54) . The latter's zealous violence and perpetual priesthood (Num 25.12-13) must have commended him as a model; but, unlike Melchizedek, Phinehas was not a king. Cf V. Aptowitzer, *Parteipolitik der Hasmonäerzeit im rabbinischen und pseudepigraphischen Schrifttum* (Vienna: Kohut Foundation, 1927) , 5-7, 11 f, 86 f, 95-98; W. R. Farmer, *Maccabees, Zealots and Josephus* (New York: Columbia Univ. Press, 1956) , 178.

[29] This possibility is neglected by Dodd (*Scriptures,* 120) and Lindars (*Apologetic,* 45 f) , who urge that Jews of the first century CE would inevitably suppose that Ps 110.1 described a heavenly monarch. Cf K. H. Rengstorf, "Old and New Testament Traces of a Formula of the Judaean Royal Ritual," NovT 5 (1962) , 229-44.

the primitive church to disregard the psalm's more militant passages, confining its quotations and allusions to vss 1 and 4. If Mk 12.35-37 is authentic, an anti-Hasmonean interpretation might even be ascribed to Jesus himself.

Daniel 7.9-14 and Rabbi Akiba.—In Dan 7.9 a vision of the heavenly court mentions the placing of thrones (plural), and God ("the Ancient of days") taking his seat. Subsequently "one like a son of man" appears before God and is given an eternal kingdom. It may be that he is understood to receive one of the heavenly thrones.[30] R. Akiba taught that the passage implies that one throne is for God and one for the Davidic messiah.[31] It seems distinctly possible that both Akiba and the writer of Dan 7 were thinking of Ps 110.1 (the only scriptural text which explicitly speaks of someone enthroned beside God).[32] If the author of Dan 7 did so, we then have an interpretation of the psalm dating from the first half of the second century BCE which connects it with the enthronement of a heavenly being. The locale of the enthronement is not clear in the case of Akiba's remark. But, if he was thinking of the psalm, he is an early (although not pre-Christian) witness of its application to the messiah.

Enoch Literature.—Several scholars have detected allusions to Ps 110.1 in statements in the "similitudes" of 1 Enoch.[33] There is no strong verbal parallelism, but the possibility of allusion is undeniable. Here the "son of man" or "elect one of God" is seated by God on his own throne of glory to pass judgment on nations and angels.[34] His word is described as "strong before the lord of spirits."[35] In

[30] By contrast, the son of man in 4 Ezra 13 does not appear in a heavenly court scene. The judgmental and saving events with which he is associated "do not happen immediately under the eyes of the Ancient of Days" (H. E. Tödt, *The Son of Man in the Synoptic Tradition,* ET D. M. Barton [Philadelphia: Westminster, 1965], 27).

[31] b. Sanhedrin 38*b.* It is noteworthy that other rabbis opposed the notion of persons elevated to a throne beside God's (see Str-B 1,978 f). Yet Akiba's opinion is certainly important. Cf G. F. Moore, *Judaism* 2 (Cambridge: Harvard Univ. Press, 1927), 337; Mowinckel, *He That Cometh,* 352.

[32] I owe this suggestion to Professor N. A. Dahl. A possible bridge between Dan 7.13 and Ps 110.1 is provided by Ps 80.18, "Let your hand be upon the man of your right hand, and the son of man whom you have made strong for yourself."

[33] E.g., J. Jeremias, "Otto Michel: Der Brief an die Hebräer" (Review), *Theologische Blätter* 16 (1937), 309; E. Schweizer, *Lordship and Discipleship* (SBT 28, 1960), 28 f.

[34] 1 Enoch 45.1,3; 51.3; 52.1-7; 55.4; 61.8; 69.27,29.

[35] 1 Enoch 69.29. Does this partly mean that the son of man is an effective *intercessor?*

3 Enoch we may have deliberate modification of these ideas about the son of man's exaltation. There the key figure, Metatron, is made God's representative, the intermediary between him and angels and the revealer of his secrets to men. But the throne given Metatron is merely *like* the glorious one of God; it is definitely not God's throne.[36] Again in 2 Enoch, we may have an echo of Ps 110.1*b* in God's words to the one who shall hear divine secrets: "Enoch, sit down on my *left* hand with Gabriel." [37]

The dating of all these Enochian documents is notoriously difficult, but they *may* attest pre-Christian interpretations of Ps 110 which applied it to heavenly enthronements.[38]

11Q Melchizedek.—In all the Qumran writings thus far published, including this one, no clear reference to Ps 110 is to be found.[39] Yet in this fragmentary text Melchizedek is the central figure, a heavenly eschatological warrior and savior.[40] The document never plainly alludes to either the psalm or Gen 14.18-20; and, while those texts represent him as a priest, 11Q Melch does not. Still, could any Jew acquainted with those scriptural passages fail to think of them when mentioning Melchizedek? If the author of this Qumran writing did have the psalm in mind, he must have applied at least its fourth verse to the heavenly Melchizedek; and he may have taken its first verse as testimony to Melchizedek's celestial enthronement.

Interpretations in Later Jewish Witnesses

Rabbinic writings and other Jewish literature produced after the beginning of Christianity contain numerous references to Ps 110. The

[36] 3 Enoch 10.1; 48C.5. See H. Odeberg, *Third Enoch* (Cambridge: Univ. Press, 1928), 79-90. Cf G. Scholem, *Major Trends in Jewish Mysticism*, 3rd ed. (New York: Schocken, 1954), 45,67-70.

[37] 2 Enoch 11 (24.1). The text is uncertain; see A. Vaillant, *Le Livre des secrets d'Hénoch* (Paris: Institut d'études slaves, 1952), 29.

[38] Cf G. Widengren, *Sakrales Königtum* (Stuttgart: Kohlhammer, 1955), 52 f. According to Scholem (*Mysticism*, 42-44), "the earliest Jewish mysticism is throne-mysticism," and "subterranean but effective" links join later Merkabah mysticism with the Jewish pseudepigraphical and apocalyptic literature produced between 100 BCE and 100 CE, esp. the Enoch literature. One must suppose that at least some early Christian thinking about God's throne (e.g., in Revelation!) and Jesus' position at God's right was influenced by this Jewish tradition. See further J. Maier, *Vom Kultus zur Gnosis* (Salzburg: Müller, 1964).

[39] Cf J. A. Sanders, *The Dead Sea Psalms Scroll* (Ithaca: Cornell Univ. Press, 1967), 143-49. F. F. Bruce suggests that the Qumran sectaries neglected Ps 110 out of hatred for the Hasmoneans, who had used it in their propaganda (*The Epistle to the Hebrews* [NICNT; Grand Rapids: Eerdmans, 1964], 96 f n. 35).

[40] See the discussion of this text below, pp. 137 f.

27

evidence suggests that Jews of the NT period applied the psalm to several different persons, among them the messiah, and in other respects also developed interpretations paralleled in early Christian exegesis.

Messianic interpretation of the psalm is not clearly attested in rabbinic sources before the second half of the third century CE, but thereafter it appears frequently. The earliest advocates of it are identified as R. Hama b. Hamina (*ca* 260), R. Eleazar b. Pedat (*ca* 270), R. Levi (*ca* 300), R. Abbahu (*ca* 300), and R. Huna b. Abbin Hakohen (*ca* 350).[41] The targum on the psalm, which *may* reflect quite ancient tradition,[42] applies it to David as a messianic figure ("prince of the world to come"). Likewise Seder Eliyahu Rabbah 18 (90) declares that in the eschatological time God will set David at the right hand of the shekinah as a reward for his good works.[43] Midrash Tehillim interprets Ps 110.1 messianically.[44]

Sometimes, however, the rabbis applied the psalm to David simply as an illustrious man of the past (though this line of exegesis is not attested before the fourth century).[45] In the middle of the second century Justin Martyr assails Jews who apply the psalm to Hezekiah. Extant rabbinic sources give no hint of this application.[46]

The earliest discussion of Ps 110 in rabbinic literature is credited to R. Ishmael, who died around 135 CE. He taught that God had intended to make Shem (i.e., Melchizedek) the progenitor of the priestly line, but transferred that honor to Abraham when Melchizedek erred by naming a man before God in the blessing of Gen 14.19. God then spoke the words of Ps 110.1 and 4 to Abraham.[47] The story appears to reflect special animosity toward Melchizedek (which I shall

---

[41] E.g., *Genesis Rabba* 85.9. See Str-B 4,457 f. On the possibility that Akiba (*ca* 125) applied the psalm to messiah, see above, p. 26.

[42] On the general question of dating the targum, see W. Bacher, JE 12,57-63; J. Bowker, *The Targums and Rabbinic Literature* (Cambridge: Univ. Press, 1969). R. Harris argued that the phrase "by his Word" in Odes Sol 29.9 depends on the first verse of the targum on Ps. 110 (R. Harris and A. Mingana, *The Odes and Psalms of Solomon*, 2 [New York: Longmans, Green & Co., 1920], 86 f, 365). This is impressive but hardly compelling evidence that the targum as we know it existed by the second century CE.

[43] Cited in Str-B 4,457.

[44] Midrash Tehillim on Ps. 18§29. The same view is found in *Yalḳuṭ Shim'oni* on Ps 110.1 §869.

[45] Str-B 4,458.

[46] Justin, *Dial.* 33 and 83. Tertullian also reports that Jews take this view (*Marcion* 5.9). See Str-B 4,456.

[47] b. Nedarim 32b=Leviticus Rabba 25.6.

discuss later), but the application to Abraham is attested in other passages where no polemical purpose is evident.[48] Perhaps this pattern of exegesis was molded by the synagogue lectionary. J. Mann maintains that seder 11 of the triennial cycle of readings ran from Gen 14.1 to 15.1 and is traceable before 70 CE. The haftarah associated with this seder was Isa 41.2-5, 8-13, and Mann thinks the prophetic passage was applied to Abraham and his victory over the kings in Gen 14. Now Mann further believes that in certain midrashim one can detect the selection of particular psalms to be recited on particular sabbaths, these psalms being linked with either the sedarim or their corresponding haftarot.[49] A priori one might suppose that rabbis would find Ps 110 unusually appropriate as a ketubim reading to be joined with Gen 14: both passages mention a divinely upheld conqueror of kings, and they are the only scriptural passages mentioning Melchizedek. Now there is evidence in the Mekilta to support this hypothesis. There Exod 15.7-8 is elucidated by cross-references to Gen 14.9,15; Isa 41.2-3; and Ps 110.1-5.[50] A similar coupling of Gen 14 and Isa 41 is found in the comments on Ps 110 in Midrash Tehillim.[51]

Having reviewed the evidence, Billerbeck concluded that messianic interpretation was the norm for rabbis of the first century. In part his argument is that the psalm's language is so exalted that Jews of that time would naturally think of the messiah. In part his argument hinges on NT evidence. Every early Christian writer who mentions the psalm interprets it messianically, a circumstance easily explained if that was the standard Jewish interpretation as well. Of particular importance is Mk 12.35-37 par; Billerbeck and many commentators urge that Jesus' argument reveals the ubiquity of the messianic exegesis in first-century Judaism.[52] R. Ishmael's application of the psalm to Abraham was devised, says Billerbeck, to undercut Christian interpretations. In effect Ishmael denied that the psalm concerned the messiah,

---

[48] See esp. Midrash Tehillim on Ps 110§4 b. Sanhedrin 108b.

[49] J. Mann, The Bible as Read and Preached in the Old Synagogue (Cincinnati: By the author, 1940), 15, 104-6.

[50] See J. Z. Lauterbach, Mekilta de-Rabbi Ishmael 2 (Philadelphia: Jewish Publication Society, 1935), 45 (Shirata 6.38-41).

[51] Midrash Tehillim on Ps 110§4; b. Sanhedrin 108b. See further A. Guilding, "Some Obscured Rubrics and Lectionary Allusions in the Psalter," JTS 3 (1952), 51-55. Cf L. Morris, The New Testament and the Jewish Lectionaries (London: Tyndale, 1964), 11-40.

[52] Str-B 4,452-60. Several scholars, including Billerbeck, think that the OG of Ps 110.3 implies a messianic interpretation. See W. D. Davies, Paul and Rabbinic Judaism, 2nd ed. (London: S.P.C.K., 1955), 161.

and he explicitly asserted that vs 4 implied God's condemnation of Melchizedek, whom Christians had come to venerate as a type of Christ. Billerbeck argues convincingly that R. Ishmael was an energetic foe of Christianity.[53]

How valid are Billerbeck's views? The contention that first-century Jews would not readily think of anyone in connection with Ps 110 except the messiah may presume too much about what Jews of two millennia ago would have thought "reasonable." Since evidence definitely links the psalm with Abraham, David, and even Hezekiah, it would seem that exegesis in terms of a future messiah was not, after all, inevitable. R. Ishmael's interpretation does seem polemical, but the orientation to Abraham may have been inspired by contemporary lectionary practice. The universal opinion of early Christians that the psalm is messianic is readily explained if Jews of that period commonly took that view. Likewise the argument of Jesus about David's son is most easily understood if a messianic interpretation prevailed. Messianic exegesis *could* have begun with Jesus or the early church, and the implications of Mk 12.35-37 par about Jewish interpretations *could* be pure Christian invention. Still, we have proof that within two centuries of Paul the rabbis were freely reading the psalm messianically, and the targum may attest messianic interpretation at a considerably earlier date. There is nothing in the psalm which, to our knowledge, Jews could not have predicated of the messiah. On balance, then, it seems fair to suppose that in the NT era a messianic interpretation of Ps 110 was current in Judaism, although we cannot know how widely it was accepted.

Leaving aside the identity of the person described, what did the rabbis think the psalm said about him?

The opening words about a SESSION at God's right hand were regularly taken to connote very high, if not the highest, honor.[54] Significantly, there is a pronounced tendency for this SESSION to be regarded as a symbol of passivity. Thus, when applied to David, it means he must *wait* till Saul dies before becoming king himself (the

[53] Str-B 4,458-60.

[54] E.g., b. Nedarim 32b Midrash Tehillim on Ps 18§29. In the relatively late Christian-Jew Dialogue Between Athanasius and Zacchaeus (§85), the Jew argues that Ps 110.1b, if applied to the messiah, entails that he is superior to God! Instead of "sit at my right hand," the translation of Symmachus has "wait for (*prosdokēson*) my right hand." Was this a Jewish-Christian or anti-Christian rendering aimed at denying that Jewish scripture ever represented someone seated beside God? (Some sources, e.g. Eus EH 6.17, say that Symmachus was an Ebionite.)

period of sitting at God's right precedes David's reign).[55] Or it means that God will fight the battles of the messiah or Abraham, while that person sits quietly, perhaps studying Torah,[56] or that the messiah is not to show himself while sitting beside God.[57] Ps 110.1 is often connected with battles, especially those of Abraham in Gen 14; but the rabbis tended to emphasize that God, not the person seated on his right, fought them.

Was the right-hand SESSION ever conceived by rabbis as an enthronement in heaven? Possibly this is the sense of certain messianic interpretations, but none to my knowledge plainly expresses such an idea.[58]

At least one late rabbinic text applies Ps 110.1 (along with Exod 4.22; Isa 42.1; 52.13, and Dan 7.13-14) to the whole nation of Israel (Midrash Tehillim on Ps 2§9). Possibly this was interwoven with ideas of the messiah, the son of man, or the Isaianic servant as representative figures. At all events, Jewish precedents may have been recalled when early Christians spoke of believers sharing the heavenly enthronement of Jesus.[59]

Since the psalm's fourth verse is the only other one incontestably cited by Christians of the earliest period, we may turn immediately to consider how the rabbis regarded it. Sometimes they applied it to Abraham to explain his priestly qualifications to offer the sacrifice of Isaac[60] or his investiture as priest in place of Melchizedek.[61]

The targum, which applies the whole psalm to David, transmutes the verse's message into "You are appointed prince of the world to come, for you have been a righteous king." [62] The thought of priesthood and the name "Melchizedek" have vanished, but the verse is regarded as messianic and eschatological. In Aboth R. Nathan 34.4 (30b) the verse is taken as proof that the messianic king is more

[55] Targum on Ps 110.1; Midrash Tehillim on Ps 110§5. The verb yāšab clearly connotes passivity in passages like Hos 3.3 and Jer 3.2 (in both passages Symmachus translates the term with forms of prosdokān).

[56] Midrash Tehillim on Ps 110§4.

[57] R. Obadiah ben Joseph Sforno, cited in J.-J. Brierre-Narbonne, Les prophéties messianiques de l'Ancien Testament dans la littérature juive en accord avec le Nouveau Testament (Paris: Librairie Orientaliste, 1933), 30.

[58] R. Isaac ben Moses Arama held that Ps 110.1 described the messiah seated at God's right hand before the creation of the sun (Brierre-Narbonne, Prophéties messianiques, 30).

[59] See below, pp. 94-101.

[60] Genesis Rabba 55.7; Deuteronomy Rabba 2.7.

[61] b. Nedarim 32b. Cf Genesis Rabba 46.5.

[62] Following the rendering in Str-B 4,457.

beloved than the righteous priest. Still another commentator said that the verse speaks of the king messiah who is also the righteous savior.[63]

The sheer diversity of these interpretations suggests that the rabbis were none too sure what to make of vs 4. The title "priest" here tends to be given honorific rather than functional meaning; especially the messianic interpretations fail to specify any priestly work performed. Only in R. Ishmael's comment is there stress on the difference between the priesthood of Melchizedek and that of Levi (descended through Abraham).[64]

We may turn, finally, to ask about the specifically messianic interpretations of the other portions of the psalm. In vs 2 rabbinic attention tended to focus on the "rod of power." A saying attributed to R. Huna b. Abbin Ha-kohen states that the staff Judah gave Tamar symbolized the messiah, as in the verse "The staff of your strength the Lord will send out of Zion" (Genesis Rabba 85.9). Again, in Numbers Rabba we find:

"And the staff of Aaron"—that same staff was held in the hand of every king until the Temple was destroyed, and then it was divinely hidden away. That same staff is destined to be held in the hand of the King Messiah . . . , as it says (Ps 110.2 is quoted).[65]

Strikingly enough, Ps 110.3 is sometimes understood as pertaining to the messiah's birth. R. Isaac ben Moses Arama (15th century) quotes the verse in his commentary on Gen 47, stressing the unique and marvelous character of this prophecy of the messiah's nativity.[66]

In general we have little that directly relates the messiah to vss 5-7.[67] The targum is vague about the identity of the person acting in vss 6-7, but probably we are to assume that it is the messiah crushing his foes. Pesikta Zutarta says that vs 6 describes the messiah's earthly victories.[68] Perhaps the absence of more evidence is merely accidental. The Targum of Pseudo-Jonathan on Gen 49.10-12 suggests how those verses in the psalm might have yielded messianic inspiration:

[63] Cited in J. J. Brierre-Narbonne, Exégèse midrašique des prophecies messianiques (Paris: Librairie Orientaliste, 1935), 162.

[64] Heb 7.7-10 also contrasts these two priesthoods. Was Ishmael acquainted with this particular Christian argument?

[65] Numbers Rabba 18.23, ET J. J. Slotski in Midrash Rabbah 6, ed. H. Freedman and M. Simon (London: Soncino Press, 1939), 744.

[66] Cited in Brierre-Narbonne, Prophéties messianiques de l'Ancien Testament, 30.

[67] Ibid.

[68] Brierre-Narbonne, Exégèse midrašique, 121.

How fair is King Messiah, who is hereafter to arise from the house of Judah! He girds up his loins, and goes forth to battle against his foes, smiting kings with their princes, reddening their rivers with the blood of the slain. . . .[69]

In sum, rabbinic exegetes often interpreted Ps 110 messianically, and that custom was probably established among Jews of Jesus' time. The rabbis were inclined to develop this line of exegesis with visions of a messiah whose work and victories were earthly; his SESSION at God's right hand was often regarded as connoting inactivity, and perhaps it was occasionally construed as a heavenly situation. The priestly ideas of vs 4 were applied to the messiah rarely and then, apparently, without enthusiasm. This may reflect general uncertainty whether the messiah would really be a priest at all. Perhaps in some cases it grew out of bitter recollections of Hasmoneans who claimed both royal and sacerdotal offices.[70]

Summary

Ps 110 probably came into being as an oracle legitimating a particular Israelite king of the pre-exilic period. The earliest definite interpretations are those of the OG translation and the Testament of Job; in the latter a pious individual is promised a throne at God's right as his heavenly reward. Possibly other Jewish interpreters of the pre-Christian era applied the psalm to human leaders (the Hasmoneans, the future Davidic messiah), or to supernatural figures (the son of man, Enoch, the heavenly Melchizedek). Later Jewish literature frequently applied it to the messiah, sometimes to Abraham or other men. In all these interpretations the psalm was construed as describing a person who enjoyed extraordinary favor with God. The right-hand SESSION was not, however, regularly associated with any single function or activity of that person. Sometimes it was understood to imply his inactivity.

---

[69] Adapted from R. Young, *Christology of the Targums* (Edinburgh: By the author, 1853), 3.

[70] A useful but biased survey of medieval Jewish exegesis is offered by R. A. Stewart, "Mediaeval Hebrew Interpretations of Psalm 110," *Glasgow University Oriental Society Transactions* 19 (1961-62), 63-73.

CHAPTER 2
Psalm 110 in Early Christian Interpretation

The history of early Christian use and interpretation of the psalm cannot be understood in isolation from the history of Jewish exegesis, but neither can the former be subsumed under the latter. Exegetes who applied the psalm to Jesus faced unique problems and opportunities. The idea of an enthronement beside God would have to be reconciled with the record that Jesus never possessed an earthly kingdom. Jewish traditions spoke of heavenly thrones given to men and to supernatural beings other than God; Christians would naturally think along such lines and interpret Ps 110.1 of Jesus' post-resurrection glory. On the debit side, the SESSION image might seem too physical for describing the ascended Christ, and the sitting posture in particular could suggest intolerable inactivity. Christians who believed that Jesus preferred non-violence to zealotism may have been troubled by the psalm's militaristic clauses. Insofar as they accepted them, they would tend to think of Christ's assault on demonic powers or his role in the final judgment of mankind. The words about a priest of Melchizedek's order could appeal to Christians anxious to distinguish their religion from the temple cult linked with Aaron's sons. Yet, since only one early Christian writing (Hebrews) ventures to explicate Ps 110.4, we may infer that many believers found these words more mysterious than illuminating. Their difficulties at this point are probably connected with the diversity of contemporary Jewish opinion concerning Melchizedek and the fact that the psalm verse appears in rabbinic literature as something of an enigma.

Textual Forms of Early Quotations and Allusions

Christian literature before Justin Martyr presents seven partial or complete quotations of Ps 110.1 (Mk 12.36 = Mt 22.44 = Lk 20.42-

43; Acts. 2.34-35; Heb 1.13; 1 Clem 36.5; Barn 12.10) and three quotations of Ps 110.4.[1] Most of these citations agree almost perfectly with the OG and prove that it, or a version almost identical with it, was widely known in the primitive church. Two minor divergences from the OG regularly appear. The best MSS for all the quotations of vs 1a of the psalm agree in reading *eipen kyrios* against *eipen ho kyrios* in the OG.[2] Likewise the best manuscript readings for the quotations of vs 4 in Hebrews consistently lack the *ei* found in the OG.[3] Thus, early Christians evidently used a Greek version which lacked these terms.

A further peculiarity is that, while all the quotations of vs 1b of the psalm agree with the OG in reading *ek dexiōn,* a large proportion of the *allusions* to it have constructions with *dexia* (*en dexia* Rom 8.34; Col 3.1; Eph 1.20; 1 Pet 3.22; Heb 1.3; 8.1; 10.12; 12.2; *tē dexia* Acts 2.33; 5.31; *epi dexia* Sib Or 2.243). These divergences might have arisen because (1) the authors of the allusions utilized Greek versions which differed at this point, (2) they used the MT and translated *en dexia,* (3) they depended not directly on the psalm but on early Christian liturgical materials which expressed the SESSION with *dexia.* The three explanations are not mutually exclusive. It *is* striking that the author of Hebrews quotes the psalm with *ek dexiōn* (1.13) but phrases all his allusions (1.3; 8.1; 10.12; 12.2) with *en dexia.*[4]

The quotations in Mk 12.36 and Mt 22.44 read *hypokatō* where the OG has *hypopodion.* The other quotations of Ps 110.1 read *hypopodion.* This deviation in Mark and Matthew may betoken the use of different Greek versions, but more probably it reflects conflation of Ps 110.1 and Ps 8.7 (which concludes *panta hypetaxas hypokatō tōn podōn autou*). The tandem appearance of the two psalm passages in 1 Cor 15.25-27; Eph 1.20-22, and Heb 1.13–2.8 shows that other Christian writers detected a connection between them. Yet Mark

---

[1] For this and other observations on the texts of quotations and allusions to Ps 110, see the Appendix.

[2] According to Rahlfs' edition, one MS of the OG (R) has anarthrous *kyrios;* all others read *ho kyrios.* For Barn 12.10, Codex S has anarthrous *kyrios;* other MSS have the article. Justin Martyr quotes Ps 110.1 five times, three times with the article (*Apol* 45.2; *Dial* 32.6; 56.14) and twice without it (*Dial* 83.2; 127.5).

[3] The OG MSS of Ps 110.4 do not present a solid front in favor of the verb; codex A omits it.

[4] Codex A reads *ek dexiōn* at Heb 10.12, but this is surely a scribal harmonization.

and Matthew do not offer clues as to how the two psalm texts are related—if that indeed is the basis of the *hypokatō* reading in question.

The allusions to the psalm differ widely among themselves in phrasing. Various terms and titles are employed to designate God and Jesus, and several different verbs denote his posture at the right hand. While most allusions to Ps 110.1*b* describe him as sitting, Acts 7.55-56 represents him as standing, and several other passages leave open the question of whether or not he is seated (Rom 8.34; Acts 2.33; 5.31; 1 Pet 3.22; Apcr Jas 14.30-31).[5]

The freedom with which early Christians paraphrased the psalm is nicely illustrated in the allusions to vs 1 in 1 Cor 15.25 and Heb 10.12-13. Both Paul and the author of Hebrews adjust the forms of "make" and "your enemies" in the psalm to fit their own literary contexts. More significant is Paul's introduction of his allusion with *dei auton basileuein;*[6] plainly he conceives of Christ as vigorously active until all the foes are overcome. By contrast, Heb 10.12-13 interposes *to loipon ekdechomenos* between allusions to vs 1*b* and vs 1*c* of the psalm; here the SESSION connotes inactive waiting. Again, where vs 1*c* of the psalm (OG) reads *heōs an,* Paul writes *achri hou* and the author of Hebrews *heōs.* All three expressions mean "until," pointing to a delay which (as will be seen later) has high importance for both NT authors. It seems probable, then, that both altered the psalm's wording precisely to call attention to the idea of a delay.

There are two further significant differences from Ps 110 OG in 1 Cor 15.25. First, Paul has *hypo tous podas autou* instead of *hypopodion tōn podōn sou.* Secondly, Paul writes "all (*pantas*) his enemies," whereas Ps 110 OG has only "his enemies." Conceivably the apostle used a version of the psalm otherwise unknown to us (differing from both OG and MT), but a simpler explanation is suggested by the citation of Ps 8.7 in 1 Cor 15.27. There Paul again writes *hypo tous podas autou* where OG has *hypokatō tōn podōn autou.* Paul (or some predecessor on whom he relies) seems to have deliberately changed both psalter texts to make them coincide at this point and so to emphasize that they are matching prophecies of Christ's reign. The

---

[5] Thus it is an error to suggest (as does, e.g., C. K. Barrett, "Stephen and the Son of Man" [*Apophoreta*, Festschrift E. Haenchen; Berlin: Töpelmann, 1964], 32 n. 2) that Acts 7.55-56 is the *only* early Christian passage alluding to Jesus' right-hand position which does not indicate that Jesus is seated.

[6] Rather than simply being an "introduction" to the allusion to vs 1*c*, this clause may be an allusion to, or paraphrase of, vs 1*b* of the psalm: "Sit at my right hand" is interpreted as a commission to reign.

word "all" (*panta*) occurs in Ps 8.7 OG and in 1 Cor 15.27, and the apostle's interpolation of it into his allusion to Ps 110.1 in 15.25 seems grounded on the supposition that the two psalm texts interpret one another. The word "all" has great significance in Paul's argument, occurring no fewer than eleven times in 15.20-28. Here, then, he freely modifies Ps 110.1, but evidently justifies his freedom on the basis of a second scriptural text.

Besides quoting Ps 110.4 three times, the author of Hebrews alludes to it eight times within the space of three chapters. Yet no two allusions are identical. For example, Jesus' installation into his priestly office (or his possession of it) is indicated by a different verb in almost every allusion. In three allusions he is styled "priest" (7:3,11,15), in three "high priest" (5.10; 6.20; 7.28). Confronted with an argumentative need to refer often to the psalm passage (Hebrews contains more references to Ps 110.4 than to any other scriptural text), the epistle's author exhibits his literary dexterity by usually repeating in each allusion no more of the verse's thought than he requires for the moment, and then by changing its wording so as to forestall boredom or sharpen the point to be made.

Several scholars have recently argued that NT writers sometimes employ a *pesher* method of scriptural citation.[7] A basic suggestion of this terminology is that the Christian writer alters the form of the scriptural passage *ad hoc* or selects one form from among several textual and targumic traditions so as to bring out his interpretation of the passage. Insofar as this is meant to imply further that the form of these NT citations closely resembles that of citations in the Qumran scrolls (especially the Habakkuk commentary), one may hesitate to find many examples of *midrash pesher* in early church writings.[8] In any case, early Christian quotations of Ps 110 do not seem to illustrate such interpretive reshaping.[9] On the other hand, one expects *allusions* to reflect the stylistic and substantive purposes of the writers who make them. All the allusions to Ps 110, but especially those to its

[7] Notably K. Stendahl (*The School of St. Matthew*, 2nd ed. [Philadelphia: Fortress, 1969], 183-202), Lindars (*Apologetic*, 15-17, 24-31, 259-86), E. E. Ellis (*Paul's Use of the OT* [Edinburgh: Oliver & Boyd, 1957], 139-47).

[8] See esp. B. Gärtner, "The Habakkuk Commentary (DSH) and the Gospel of Matthew," *Studia Theologica* 8 (1954), 1-24.

[9] Unless Mk 12.36=Mt 22.44 is an instance. But, as indicated above, the interpretation of the psalm in those passages does not have a connection with the deviation from the OG.

first verse in 1 Cor 15.25 and Heb 10.12-13, and those to its fourth verse in Heb 5–7, display such purposive rephrasing.

Indirect Sources of the Psalm Material

One of the most intriguing aspects of the use of Ps 110 in early Christian literature is that a large proportion of the quotations and allusions appear to be based not directly on the psalm but on *Vorlagen* in the form of testimony collections, confessions, or hymns.

At least three quotations of Ps 110.1 seem derived from collections of scriptural testimonies. The clearest instance is Barn 12.10-11. Here quotations of the psalm verse and of Isa 45.1 are juxtaposed, and the original juxtaposition must have been made on the assumption that both texts supported the use of the title *kyrios* for the messiah.[10] While the psalm citation agrees almost exactly with the OG, the Isaiah text has been drastically revamped to form a parallel to the former.[11] Yet the author of Barnabas can hardly have been the one who so modified the prophetic text, since that text (even in its altered form) contributes only an interruption to his argument. His train of thought would lose nothing and gain in clarity if 12.10 were followed at once by 12.11c; his purpose is not to establish that Jesus is "lord," but that he is the Son of God. From this one may conclude that he took his psalm quotation from a collection of scriptural testimonies.[12]

The quotation in Heb 1.13 falls within a passage (1.5-14) in which the author seems to set forth material he expects his readers to know and readily accept. Despite the questions introducing scriptural citations in 1.5,13, the author is not attempting a proof in any strict sense but merely summarizing the testimony of Jewish scriptures to support the assertions of 1.2-4. If there is any real argument, it is a

---

[10] The mention in both texts of the "right hand" and the defeat of enemies probably also helped bring them together.

[11] The chief alteration is the insertion of an iota, which transforms "Cyrus" into *kyrios* (some MSS of Barn read *Kyros/Cyrus*, probably as a correction). The Isaiah text is brought still closer to Ps 110.1 by a replacement of its *houtōs legei* with *eipen* and by the omission of its *ho theos*.

[12] The same psalm and Isaiah texts are linked by Irenaeus (*Proof* 48-49), Tertullian (*Praxeas* 11.7-8), and Lactantius (*Institutes* 4.12). Cyprian and Gregory of Nyssa also seem to know the combination. See R. Harris and V. Burch, *Testimonies* 1 (Cambridge: Univ. Press, 1916), 37; R. A. Kraft, "Barnabas' Isaiah Text and the 'Testimony Book' Hypothesis," JBL 79 (1960), 336-50 (esp. 341 f); R. A. Kraft, *Barnabas and the Didache* (The Apostolic Fathers 3; New York: Nelson, 1965), 122; P. Prigent, *L'Epître de Barnabé I-XVI et ses sources* (Paris: Lecoffre, 1961), 64, 126; Prigent-Kraft, *Epître de Barnabé* (Sources Chrétiennes 172; Paris: Cerf, 1971), 172-74.

mild polemic against overestimating angels (cf Heb 2.5,16); but the questions about angels sound more rhetorical than serious.[13] Further, much of the content in 1.5-14 is not closely related to the rest of the epistle. If the author was using a traditional collection of quotations, the length and partial irrelevance of the passage would be more comprehensible.[14]

The likelihood that Heb 1.5-14 derives from a scriptural florilegium is increased by the obvious similarities between that passage and 1 Clem 36. In the latter, Christ is styled "the high priest of our offerings, the defender and helper of our weakness" (cf Heb 2.17-18; 4.15-16). There follows a set of affirmations with close verbal resemblances to Heb 1.3-4 and then quotations of Pss 104.4 and 2.7-8 (the same texts are cited, in reverse order, in Heb 1.5,7). Finally Ps 110.1 is cited, and the paragraph ends with an interpretation of Christ's foes. The christological ideas and language of the two passages are so alike that some literary relationship must be posited. The majority of scholars suppose that Clement borrowed from Hebrews. Yet there are major dissimilarities in theology between the two documents, differences so great as to make that explanation problematic. The only alternative is to postulate a common source, probably one which existed in writing and was used in early church worship, a source containing or consisting in a catena or scriptural citations.[15] G. Schille plausibly argues that the language of 1 Clem 36 suggests baptism as the *Sitz im Leben* of this source.[16]

As for early Christian allusions to the psalm, a considerable number apparently derive not directly from the psalm but from primitive church confessions or hymns in which were embedded phrases or ideas ultimately drawn from Ps 110. What is the evidence for this? To begin with, we note the near identity of three allusions:

Rom 8.34 *hos estin en dexia tou theou*

1 Pet 3.22 *hos estin en dexia (tou) theou*

Col 3.1 *ho Christos estin en dexia tou theou kathēmenos*

---

[13] The questions of the form "To what angel did God ever say . . . ?" make graceful introductions to the quotations. Cf H. Windisch, *Der Hebräerbrief*, 2nd ed. (HNT; Tübingen: Mohr, 1931), 17; E. Käsemann, *Das wandernde Gottesvolk*, 4th ed. (FRLANT 55; Göttingen: Vandenhoeck & Ruprecht, 1961), 60.

[14] Cf H. Montefiore, *A Commentary on the Epistle to the Hebrews* (BNTC; London: Black, 1964), 43 f.

[15] See now G. Theissen, *Untersuchungen zum Hebräerbrief* (Studien zum NT 2; Gütersloh: Mohn, 1969), 34-37; Käsemann, *Gottesvolk*, 107 f. Cf O. Michel, *Der Brief an die Hebräer* (Meyer; Göttingen: Vandenhoeck & Ruprecht, 1966), 29.

[16] G. Schille, "Die Basis des Hebräerbriefes," ZNW 48 (1957), 274-76.

None of the three has a single word in common with the OG. Even if Paul wrote Colossians, it is hard to imagine him deliberately copying the clause from Romans, and there is no conclusive evidence that the author of 1 Peter knew Romans.

Another clue suggesting the existence of traditional formulas behind certain allusions is the sheer superfluity of some of those allusions. Col 3.1 [17] and Pol *Phil* 2.1 contain allusions which seem to add little or nothing to the sense of the passages in which they occur (perhaps the same is true of 1 Pet 3.22). The less essential to its context an allusion is, the more we must be ready to regard it as a stereotyped truism, quite possibly inserted by the writer without much thought just because it was so familiar to himself and his readers.

Most significant, however, is the fact that many of the allusions appear in settings indicative of creed-like origin. The arguments which have been advanced to show that these settings do depend on *Vorlagen* cannot be analyzed here; we must content ourselves with a listing of passages and references to pertinent secondary literature.[18]

It is widely agreed that the two relative clauses in Rom 8.34 (*hos estin en tou theou, hos kai entygchanei hyper hēmōn*) are pre-Pauline in origin, perhaps derived from an extended confession.[19]

Eph 1.20-23 has a balanced, rhythmical, two-couplet form suggestive of a hymnic background, and Eph 2.4-10 may also come from a hymn. The psalm allusion in 1.20 and its echo in 2.6 (cf Col 2.12-13) suggest a baptismal *Sitz im Leben* for the *Vorlage*.[20]

An early creed or hymn seems to underlie much of 1 Pet 3.18-22,

---

[17] E. Norden (*Agnostos Theos*, 4th ed. [Darmstadt: Wissenschaftliche Buchgesellschaft, 1956 (1913, 2nd ed.)], 273) emphasizes this point, following Seeberg.

[18] The methodological problems involved in identifying such *Vorlagen*, their precise limits and purposes, are well known. While it might be contested that all the passages listed here depend on *Vorlagen*, probably most of them in fact do so.

[19] See esp. E. Fuchs, *Die Freiheit des Glaubens* (BEvT 14, 1949), 117-21; J. N. D. Kelly, *Early Christian Creeds* (London: Longmans, Green, & Co., 1950), 17; R. Zorn, *Die Fürbitte im Spätjudentum und im Neuen Testament* (unpubl. Univ. of Göttingen diss., 1957), 147-52; G. Schille, "Die Liebe Gottes in Christus," ZNW 59 (1968), 234 f.

[20] E. Käsemann (RGG, 3rd ed., 2, col. 519) contends that hymnic fragments underlie 1.20 ff and 2.4-10. Similar views are expressed by M. Dibelius and H. Greeven (*An die Kolosser, Epheser, an Philemon* [HNT, 1953], 64 f) and by H. Conzelmann ("Der Brief an die Epheser," *Die kleineren Briefe des Apostels Paulus* [NTD, 1962], 63). Cf H. Schlier *Der Brief an die Epheser*, 3rd ed. (Düsseldorf: Patmos, 1962), 117 f, 123 n. 1.

including the allusions to Christ's right-hand exaltation. Especially in view of vss 20-21, a baptismal origin seems most probable.[21]

Structural features and substantive resemblances to other Christ hymns mark Heb 1.2*b*-3 as dependent on an early hymn or creed, perhaps one connected with baptism.[22] Since all the other allusions to Christ's SESSION in Hebrews agree with that in 1.3 in using *en dexia* against the *ek dexion* of the direct quotation of Ps 110.1 in Heb 1.13, it seems likely that those allusions are based on this confession rather than the psalm text.[23]

In Pol *Phil* 2.1 we seem to reach an advanced stage in the liturgical stereotyping of allusions to the psalm. Though not itself in a relative construction, the reference to the SESSION is surrounded by relative clauses and probably comes from a baptismal confession.[24]

Several scholars have regarded the psalm allusion in Mk 14.62 as taken from an early Christian confession.[25] That it came to be regarded as a kind of model declaration of faith is shown by the close parallels in Acts 7.56 and Heg (EH 2.23.13).[26]

The recital of post-resurrection events in "Mk" 16.9-20 has the appearance of being dependent on liturgical or catechetical tradition.[27]

---

[21] See esp. R. Bultmann, "Bekenntnis- und Liedfragmente im ersten Petrusbrief," *Coniectanea Neotestamentica* 11 (1947) 1-14; M.-E. Boismard, *Quatre hymnes baptismales dans la première épître de Pierre* (Paris: Cerf, 1961), 57-109; W. J. Dalton, *Christ's Proclamation to the Spirits* (Rome: Pontifical Institute, 1965), 87-102; G. Schille, *Frühchristliche Hymnen* (Berlin: Evangelische Verlagsanstalt, 1965), 38 f.

[22] See G. Bornkamm, "Das Bekenntnis im Hebräerbrief," *Studien zu Antike und Urchristentum* (Munich: Kaiser, 1959), 197-99; Schille, *Hymnen*, 42; R. H. Fuller, *The Foundations of NT Christology* (New York: Scribners, 1965), 220 f; G. Friedrich, "Das Lied vom Hohenpriester im Zuzammenhang von Hebr. 4,14–5,10," *Theologische Zeitschrift* 18 (1962), 101 f.

[23] Cf Michel, *Hebräer*, 104 f.

[24] See O. Cullmann, *Les premières confessions de foi chrétiennes* (Paris: Presses Universitaires de France, 1948), 49; Bultmann, "Liedfragmente," 8; Bultmann, *Theology of the NT* 2, ET K. Grobel (New York: Scribners, 1955), 153.

[25] See, e.g., Norden, *Agnostos Theos*, 194 f, 272; A. E. J. Rawlinson, *St. Mark* (London: Methuen, 1925), 222. On the general historical difficulties posed by Mark's trial narrative, see esp. T. A. Burkill, *Mysterious Revelation: an Examination of the Philosophy in St. Mark's Gospel* (Ithaca: Cornell Univ. Press, 1963), 280-94; P. Winter, "Markus 14.53*b*, 55-64 ein Gebilde des Evangelisten," ZNW 53 (1962), 259-63. Recent defenders of the essential authenticity of Mk 14.62 include M. D. Hooker, *The Son of Man in Mark* (Montreal: McGill Univ. Press, 1967) and F. H. Borsch, *The Son of Man in Myth and History* (Philadelphia: Westminster, 1967), 391-94.

[26] Cf O. Michel, TWNT 5, 211 (=TDNT 5, 210 f).

[27] Cf B. H. Streeter, *The Four Gospels* (London: Macmillan, 1924), 350; G. Delling, TWNT 4, 8 f (=TDNT 4, 8).

Chart 1: Intermediate Sources Incorporating Citations of, or Allusions to, Psalm 110

Nature of Source and Approximate Content	*Passages Using Source* (texts grouped together with commas *may* all depend on a single intermediate source)
Confession: Jesus Christ, who is at the right hand of God	Rom 8.34, Col 3.1, 1 Pet 3.22
Confession: the son of man seated at the right hand of God	Mt 26.64=Mk 14.62=Lk 22. 69, Acts 7.55-56 (?), Heg (EH 2.23.13) (?)
Multi-clause Confession or Hymn: Jesus Christ sat down at the right hand of God (within a series of affirmations about Christ's exaltation)	Eph 1.20, Heb 1.3, "Mk" 16.19, Pol *Phil* 2.1
Collection of Scriptural "Testimonies": Ps 110.1 (together with other scriptural texts)	Heb 1.13, 1 Clem 36.5, Barn 12.10
Multi-clause Confession or Hymn: Clauses affirming Christ's status as priest (with an allusion to Ps 110.4)	Heb 5.10 7.3 7.28

Chart 2: Scriptural Passages Significantly Associated with Early Christian References to Psalm 110

(References are to Ps 110.1 unless Ps 110.4 is specified in parentheses.)

Text	*Early Christian Reference*
Gen 14.18-20	Heb 7 (Ps 110.4)
Ps 2.7-8	Heb 1.3-5
	1 Clem 36.4-6
	Heb 5.5-6 (Ps 110.4)
Ps 8.7	Mk 12.36=Mt 22.44 (?)
	1 Cor 15.25-27
	Eph 1.20-22
	Heb 1.13–2.8
	1 Pet 3.21-22 (?)
	Acts 7.55-56 (?)
Isa 45.1	Barn 12.10-11
Dan 7.13	Mk 14.62=Mt 26.64
	Acts 7.55-56 (?)
	Heg (EH 2.23.13)

The whole passage, apart from Jesus' words to the disciples, has a compendious style recalling creedal formulations. This is particularly true of vs 19, which mentions the SESSION.[28]

Thus far this discussion of intermediate sources has been focused on Ps 110.1. There are also grounds to support that vs 4 of the psalm was alluded to in some kind of liturgical source known to the author of Hebrews. Heb 5.7-10 and 7.26-28, which mention Christ's priesthood in relation to Melchizedek's, offer highly compressed declarations in rhythmic prose suggestive of a hymnic background.[29]

The results of this analysis of intermediate sources are presented in Chart 1. It would seem that a large number of allusions to Ps 110 in early Christian writings were taken from creeds or hymns. Oddly, it would be difficult to show that even two of the passages depend on the same liturgical ancestor (apart from the catenae of quotations in Heb 1 and 1 Clem 36). Perhaps, however, we should be wary of assuming that early Christian hymns and confessions were as fixed in their wording as church creeds of later times.[30]

What conclusions follow from the fact that many quotations and allusions to the psalm seemingly depend on intermediate sources? One consequence is that many passages which we have identified as allusions to the psalm may actually have been composed by persons aware only of citing or echoing a church confession or hymn. In the case of other allusions, their authors indicate that they knew of the connection with the psalm text.[31] Yet even they may have taken their allusions from Christian *Vorlagen* without consulting the original psalm. In general, as we shall see, early Christian references to Jesus'

---

[28] Cf Norden, *Agnostos Theos*, 273 n. 1; H. B. Swete, *The Gospel According to St. Mark* (London: Macmillan, 1905), 407; E. Lohmeyer, *Das Evangelium des Markus* (Meyer, 1937), 363.

[29] On the general question of a primitive Christian tradition employing Ps 110.4, see W. Manson, *The Epistle to the Hebrews* (London: Hodder & Stoughton, 1951), 54, 108. On Heb. 5, see G. Schille, "Erwägungen zur Hohepriesterlehre des Hebräerbriefes," ZNW 46 (1955), 97 f; G. Friedrich, "Lied vom Hohenpriester," 102-11; E. Brandenburger, "Text und Vorlagen von Hebr. V.7-10," NovT 11 (1969), 190-224. On Heb 7.26-28, see Windisch, *Hebräerbrief*, 2nd ed., 67; Michel, *Hebräer*, 278. Cf Theissen, *Untersuchungen*, 20-28.

[30] N. A. Dahl emphasized this point in an unpublished paper presented to the Paul Seminar at the 1970 annual meeting of the Society of Biblical Literature ("The Pauline Letters: Proposal for a Study Project," 12 f).

[31] These are authors who quote from the psalm directly besides alluding to it. Since, e.g., Paul quotes the psalm in 1 Cor 15.25, he probably is conscious of alluding to it in Rom 8.34. Other early Christian authors in this category are the synoptic evangelists and the writer of Hebrews.

SESSION or to other ideas in Ps 110.1 do not obviously reflect knowledge of other elements in the psalm. Yet the considerable number of verbatim quotations of Ps 110 from the NT period shows that its connection with these ideas was not widely forgotten. Possibly it would be most accurate to label passages like Col 3.1 as "references to Jesus' SESSION, references whose authors may or may not have been conscious of a relation to Ps 110." [32] Still, conscious and unconscious allusions alike inform us about the significance of the psalm for the early church.

In the case of direct quotations, contextual data uniformly indicate that the authors know they are citing a Jewish scriptural passage. Yet if Barnabas, Clement, and the author of Hebrews took their citations of Ps 110 from testimony collections, they may have ignored, or been ignorant of, the parts of the psalm which they did not quote. Since the author of Hebrews connects so much of his doctrinal argument with vss 1 and 4 of the psalm, however, it is likely that he, at least, studied the psalm text directly.[33]

The second major consequence of the derivation of allusions and quotations from *Vorlagen* is that early Christians must have been conditioned in their interpretation of Ps 110 by those *Vorlagen*. Christians who knew of Christ's SESSION from a church confession or hymn must have immediately understood that it described his post-resurrection exaltation. We have seen that a number of the intermediary sources may have been created in association with baptism. Christians familiar with such sources would easily connect the image of a position at God's right not only with Jesus' exaltation but also with their own. Those who learned to quote the psalm from testimony collections would be inclined to link it exegetically with the other scriptural passages in those florilegia. Yet it is noteworthy that no single scriptural passage is regularly cited by early Christians alongside Ps 110.1 (cf Chart 2). The passage most often linked with it,

---

[32] Passages in this class are "Mk" 16.19; Eph 1.20; 2.6; Col 3.1; 1 Pet 3.22; Rev 3.21; Pol *Phil* 2.1; Apoc Pet 6; Sib Or 2.243; Apcr Jas 14.30-31; Heg (EH 2.23.13). For the sake of convenience, these passages will often be cited in this study as references or allusions to Ps 110, but it must be understood that the reference may be unconscious.

[33] F. C. Synge, however, argues that the writer of Hebrews worked exclusively from a testimony collection (*Hebrews and the Scriptures* [London: S.P.C.K., 1959], 53 f). One might reply that, e.g., the contiguity of Heb 7.28 and 8.1 suggests an awareness that those texts allude to different passages in the same psalm. But this impression is not susceptible of proof.

Ps 8.7, might have been connected with it independently by various Christians simply because of the similarity of the two psalm texts.

Overview of Early Christian Interpretations to Justin Martyr

The charts on pages 45-47 give an overview of the main directions taken by early Christian interpretation. The functions which the psalm took on in this period are complex and will be analyzed in detail in Part 2 of this study. Some summary observations, however, will be useful here.

Plainly the element in the psalm which attracted Christians most was the idea of someone seated at God's right hand. No early Christian writer who refers to any part of the psalm fails to allude to this image or to quote vs 1*b*. The image was regularly related to Jesus' post-resurrection glory. Most citations or allusions imply that this exaltation began directly after his resurrection (or ascension), but some represent it as commencing only with the last judgment (Apoc Pet 6; Sib Or 2.243; Mk 14.62 [?]). Sometimes the documents imply that believers share this exaltation, either in the present life by virtue of baptism (Eph 2.6; Col 3.1) or as a reward after death (Rev 3.21).

Chart 3: Early Christian Interpretations of Psalm 110.1

(Numbers and small letters indicate portion of Ps 110.1 to which reference is made. An asterisk indicates direct quotation.)
(The following functions are identified by number: (1) vindication or glory of Jesus, (1*a*) glory or empowerment of Christians, (2) support for christological titles, (3) subjection of powers to Jesus, (4) intercession or priesthood of Jesus. Terms in brackets indicate christological titles in context of citation. A question mark indicates a doubtful function.)

Text	Reference	Primary Function of Quotation or Allusion	Secondary Function
Mt 22.41-46	1*a-c**	(2) argue about applicability of "son of David" to messiah	1
Mt 26.64	1*b*	(1) predict future vindication of Jesus	2 [son of man], 3 (?)
Mk 12.35-37	1*a-c**	(2) argue about applicability of "son of David" to messiah	1
Mk 14.62	1*b*	(1) predict future vindication of Jesus	2 [son of man], 3 (?)
"Mk" 16.19	1*b*	(1) describe Jesus' heavenly enthronement	2 [lord], 3 (?)
Lk 20.41-44	1*a-c**	(2) argue about applicability of "son of David" to messiah	1

45

Text	Reference	Primary Function of Quotation or Allusion	Secondary Function
Lk 22.69	1b	(1) affirm future vindication of Jesus	2 [son of man]
Acts 2.33-36	1a-c*	(1) affirm Jesus' heavenly enthronement	1a, 2 ["lord," "Christ"]
Acts 5.31	1b	(1) affirm Jesus' vindication as savior	
Acts 7.55-56	1b	(1) affirm Jesus' vindication and glory	1a, 2 [son of man], 3 (?), 4 (?)
Rom 8.34	1b	(4) affirm Jesus' heavenly intercession	1, 3 (?)
1 Cor 15.25	1c	(3) argue about resurrection of believers	1
Eph 1.20	1b	(1) affirm glory and power of Christ	1a
Eph 2.6	1b	(1a) affirm exaltation of believers	
Col 3.1	1b	(1) exhort believers to set minds on heaven where Jesus is	1a
Heb 1.3	1b	(1) affirm Jesus' heavenly glory	2 [Son of God]
Heb 1.13	1b-c*	(1) affirm Jesus' heavenly glory	
Heb 8.1	1b	(4) argue that Jesus is a heavenly priest	1, 2 [high priest]
Heb 10.12-13	1b-c	(4) argue that Jesus' sacrifice is perfect	3
Heb 12.2	1b	(1a) exhort believers to persevere	1
1 Pet 3.22	1b	(1) affirm Jesus' heavenly glory	3, 4 (?)
Rev 3.21	1b	(1a) exhort believers to faithfulness	1
1 Clem 36.5-6	1b-c*	(1) affirm Jesus' heavenly glory	2 [Son of God], 3
Pol *Phil* 2.1	1b	(1) affirm Jesus' heavenly glory and rule	1a (?), 3
Barn 12.10-11	1a-c*	(2) argue that Jesus is not "son of David" but is "lord"	1
Apoc Pet 6	1b	(3) describe last judgment	1
Sib Or 2.243	1b	(3) describe last judgment	1
Apcr Jas 14.30-31	1b	(1) affirm Jesus' future heavenly glory	
Heg (EH 2.23.13)	1b	(1) affirm Jesus' heavenly glory	2 [son of man], 3

Chart 4: Early Christian Interpretations of Psalm 110.4

(Numbers and small letters indicate portion of Ps 110.4 to which reference is made. An asterisk indicates direct quotation.)

Text	Reference	Primary Function of Quotation or Allusion	Secondary Function
Heb 5.6	4b-c*	argue Jesus' humility in waiting for appointment as high priest	introduce Ps. 110.4 into argument
5.10	4b-c	reaffirm God's appointment of Jesus as high priest	connect Jesus' priesthood with his saving work
6.20	4b-c	affirm that Jesus is priest in heaven	reintroduce theme of Jesus' Melchizedekian priesthood
7.3	4b	explain Jesus' relation to Melchizedek	
7.8	4b	argue superiority of Melchizedek to levitical priests	imply superiority of Jesus to levitical priests
7.11	4b-c	argue inadequacy of levitical priests	

46

Text	Reference	Primary Function of Quotation or Allusion	Secondary Function
7.15-17	4b-c*	affirm that Jesus is a priest	explain basis of Jesus' priesthood (life)
7.21	4a-b*	argue Jesus' superiority to levitical priests (oath)	
7.24-25	4b	argue Jesus' superiority to levitical priests (permanence)	affirm Jesus' eternal intercession for believers
7.28	4a-b	affirm Jesus' superiority to levitical priests (perfection)	sum up significance of Ps. 110.4

Only one passage (Acts 2.33-36) employs the psalm in a plainly apologetic setting to argue that Jesus is the Christ. It would appear that the psalm was chiefly employed to supply symbolic language and arguments for intrachurch communication. Ps 110.1a is cited to argue for the appropriateness (or inappropriateness) of certain titles for the messiah (Mk 12.35-37=Mt 22.41-46=Lk 20.41-44; Barn 12.10-11); Although these arguments could be meaningful to outsiders, they were probably used mainly for discussions within the church.

Many passages associate Ps 110.1b with the subjection of powers to Christ, and three (1 Cor 15.25; Heb 10.12-13; 1 Clem 36.5-6) argue about that theme directly from vs 1c of the psalm. The conceptions of the subjection process vary widely.

Among Christian writers of this period, only the author of Hebrews refers to Ps 110.4. Largely on the basis of vss 1 and 4 of the psalm, he erects a complex argumentative scaffolding to prove Jesus a heavenly priest. He assumes that his readers will accept the application of both verses to Jesus, and his argument also suggests dependence on a tradition that Jesus' SESSION implies intercession (Rom 8.34; Acts 7.55-56; 1 Pet 3.21-22).

Interpretations from Justin Martyr to the Council of Nicea

In approaching the use of Ps 110 in the period before Justin, we cannot ignore its employment by the church of later times. What was not written down in an extant document till the middle of the second century or later may yet have been known to Christians of the earlier period. In what ways did the later church of the pre-Nicene era agree with, or diverge from, interpretations of the psalm attested from the NT period?

One conspicuous feature of the use of the psalm in NT times is that only vss 1 and 4 are ever distinctly employed. Justin Martyr heralds a new approach by quoting the entire psalm as a testimony about Jesus (*Dial* 32.6). Justin's main concern in citing the psalm is to establish Jesus' glory as the Christ. In the same vein Cyprian includes Ps 110.1-2 in a collection of testimony texts from the OT and NT under the heading "That after he had risen again he should receive from his father all power, and that his power should be everlasting" (*Testimonies* 2.26). Hippolytus cites Ps 110.1 as proof that Christ is a heavenly rather than earthly monarch (*Antichrist* 61). Lactantius takes the verse as a prophecy of Christ's ascension, which he distinguishes chronologically from the resurrection (*Institutes* 4.12; *Epitome* 47). Tertullian (*Praxeas* 30; *Marcion* 4.41; 5.17) and Novatian (*Trinity* 9) interpret it in the same fashion.[34] Irenaeus takes it to refer to both ascension and SESSION.[35]

A quite unusual appropriation of Ps 110.1*b*, which yet has ties with more customary Christian uses, is found in the *Book of Baruch* by Justin the gnostic. Here the speaker is "the Good" (the cosmic Priapus) and the addressee is not Jesus but Elohim. The latter ascends into "the highest parts of heaven" to discover if the universe he has created lacks anything. The Good tells him, "Sit down at my right hand," meaning that Elohim should remain in this celestial realm and not return to his universe (Hippolytus, *Ref* 5.26.16-18). In the Excerpts from Theodotus (62.1-3; cf 38), Christ's right-hand SESSION is a psychic sojourn with the demiurge in an intermediate region between the hebdomad and the ogdoad.

Ps 110.1 was often used in more orthodox circles to argue the divine nature of Christ. Justin Martyr cites the verse alongside Gen 19.24 to show that the Holy Spirit accords the title "lord" to someone other than God the Father (*Dial* 56.14; 127.5). Tertullian cites Ps 110.1 to argue that the monarchy of the godhead is not disturbed by the distinction between Father and Son (*Praxeas* 4;11); he, too, stresses that scripture give both the title "lord" (*Praxeas* 13). Consistent with his view that God and Christ are identical, Praxeas is said to have held that God sits at his own right hand (ps-Tertullian, *Heresies* 8; cf Tertullian, *Praxeas* 30). Novatian cites the psalm text as proof that the Son must be differentiated from the Father (*Trinity*

---

[34] So also Apost Constitutions 6.30.9; Dialogue of Timothy and Aquila fol. 88ʳ (cited according to F. C. Conybeare, *Anecdota Oxoniensia: The Dialogue of Athanasius and Zacchaeus and of Timothy and Aquila* [Oxford: Clarendon Press, 1898]).

[35] *Heresies* 3.10.6 (3.11.6). References to this work are given first according to PG; if the chapter and verse division are different in the edition of W. W. Harvey (*Sancti Irenaei: Libros quinque adversus haereses* [Cambridge: Univ. Press, 1857]), this is indicated in parentheses. Cf Irenaeus, *Proof* 48, 85.

26). The Christian in the Dialogue Between Timothy and Aquila (fol 81ᵛ) cites it (with Gen 19.24) to show that Christ is the "counselor" of God.

References are sometimes offered to the synoptic debate story (Mk 12.35-37 par) in which Ps 110.1 figures prominently. The incident is recounted directly in the setting of Lk 2.41 ff in the Arabic Gospel of the Infancy of the Savior (50). Likewise Lactantius seems to allude to it when he asks whom David could call his lord except the Christ (*Institutes* 4.12). Irenaeus echoes the pericope when he remarks that David confessed Christ as lord at God's right hand (*Heresies* 3.16.3; 3.17.3; cf 3.6.1; 4.33.4; 4.52.1).

Ps 110.1c is frequently cited, but (as in writings from the NT period) the identifications of Christ's foes vary. According to Justin Martyr, they are the demons (*Apol* 45.1; cf *Dial* 83). Origen interprets this part of the psalm as a reference to Christ's victory over sin and death and also to the obedient subjection to Christ which believers should seek.[36] Tertullian identifies the foes as "the workers of evil" and emphasizes (following 1 Cor 15.25 or Heb 10.12-13?) that their subjugation is not yet completed (*Hermogenes* 11; *Praxeas* 30; *Resurrection* 22; *Marcion* 5.9).

Justin Martyr applies vs 2 of the psalm to Christian preaching:

Although our Jesus has not yet returned in glory, he has sent out into Jerusalem the scepter of power, namely the call to repentance to all nations over which the demons formerly ruled . . . (*Dial* 83.4; cf *Apol* 45.5).

A similar equation of "scepter" and kerygma seems assumed by Clement of Alexandria when he uses the verse to affirm that Christ's "rod" is chastising but saving (*Instructor* 61.3).

One of the most remarkable features of Christian use of Ps 110 in the NT period is that its third verse is never explicitly cited. From Justin onward, however, it is often appealed to as testimony to Christ's divinity. Justin uses it to speak both of Christ's pre-existence and his human birth (*Dial* 63.3; 76.7). Clement of Alexandria relates the verse to Christ's eternal being, citing it as a parallel to Jn 1.1 (*Exhortation* 6.3; 84.2).[37] Hippolytus seems to expound the verse in the same way (*Ref* 10.33.11). By contrast, Tertullian takes "before the

---

[36] *Prayer* 25.3; *Principles* 1.6.1; *Comm Jn* 6.295-96 (C. Blanc, *Origène, Commentaire sur Saint Jean* 2 [Sources chrétiennes; Paris: Cerf, 1970], 355).

[37] A similar view is taken in Exc Theodotus 20 and Origen, *Comm Jn* 6.18 (Blanc, *Origène* 2, 145).

morning star" to prophesy Christ's birth from Mary (*Marcion* 5.9; cf *Praxeas* 11). Opponents of modalism and Arianism interpret the verse polemically to show that Christ was begotten by the Father, not created.[38]

Ps 110.4, neglected in the NT era by all writers except the author of Hebrews, is often cited by church writers of the later period. Justin Martyr, for example, regards it as proof of Jesus' eternal priesthood and disproof of the Jewish claim that the psalm as a whole refers to Hezekiah (*Dial* 33; 118.1-2). Cyprian (*Testimonies* 1.17; *Epistle* 62 [63].4) and Lactantius (*Institutes* 4.14) also cite it as evidence of Jesus' status as everlasting priest. In the late Acts of Peter and Paul (30), it is regarded as a prophecy of Christ's sacrificial death. The thought of Heb 5.4ff is restated in Apostolic Constitutions 2.27.4: Jesus did not thrust himself into priestly office but waited for the summons of his Father expressed in Ps 110.4. By contrast, Justin the gnostic understood the oath in the psalm verse to refer to that sworn by Elohim when he promised not to reveal the mysteries connected with his vision of the Good (Hippolytus, *Ref* 5.24.1; 5.27.1-2). Hippolytus also reports that a certain Theodotus affirmed that Melchizedek is superior to Jesus. Part of his argument evidently rested on the phrasing of Ps 110.4, which he took to mean that Christ was modeled after the pattern of Melchizedek (the copy being inferior to the original).[39]

From Justin Martyr's hand we may cite a solitary interpretation of one of the psalm's concluding verses. The seventh, he says, shows that the messianic priest was first to be humble as a man and afterwards exalted (*Dial* 33.3). Thus he discerns both kenosis and glorification in the psalm. Christians of the NT period ordinarily dwelt only on the latter.

Summary

Early Christian interpreters of Ps 110 generally extended the messianic and transcendental lines of exegesis which Judaism had apparently already established as viable options. They depended primarily or exclusively on a form of the psalm text very close to OG, but paraphrased it freely in accord with their theological purposes. Evi-

---

[38] Hippolytus, *Noëtus* 16 (PG 10.825); Alexander of Alexandria, *Epistle to Alexander of Constantinople* 8 (PG 18.560), and *Catholic Epistle* 4 (PG 18.576).
[39] Hippolytus, *Ref* 7.36.1. See further ps-Tertullian, *Heresies* 8.

dently many of the quotations and allusions from the NT period are based not directly on the psalm itself but on intermediary sources, sources which presumably colored interpretations of the psalm to a large degree. Early Christians regularly used the psalm to affirm the glory of Christ, but did so in a wide variety of ways. From Justin Martyr to the Council of Nicea, Christians generally built up their interpretations in accord with patterns established in the earlier period. They went beyond writings of the NT age principally in two respects: in applying the entire psalm to Jesus, and in arguing explicitly for his divinity on the basis of its first and third verses.[40]

[40] Cf the important article (in three parts) by M.-J. Rondeau, "Le 'Commentaire des psaumes' de Diodore de Tarse et l'exégèse antique du psaume 109/110," *Revue de l'histoire des religions* 176 (1969), 5-33, 153-88; 177 (1970), 5-33. Rondeau is mainly concerned with fourth-century exegesis, but the first installment of his article emphasizes the role of the psalm in the development of pre-Nicean christological thought.

Part 2

A Functional Analysis of Early Christian References to Psalm 110

CHAPTER 3

The Use of Psalm 110 in Expressions of Exaltation to the Right Hand of God

The Background: Pagan, Jewish, and Christian

The very frequent use of Ps 110.1 in early Christian literature to affirm Jesus' elevation beside God becomes more understandable when set in the context of the general symbolic evaluation of the right side in antiquity.

Ideas About the Right Hand and About a SESSION at the Right Hand in Paganism.—In the ancient world, the right side was often identified with greatness, strength, divinity, goodness; the left side with that which was limited, weak, demonic, evil, or of little value. This pattern of valuation was probably rooted in human physiology (right-handedness, etc.), and it seems to have been almost universal in Mediterranean cultures.[1]

Close parallels in pagan literature to the specific notion of a SESSION at the right side of a deity, as in Ps 110.1, are not abundant, but some do exist. Certain Egyptian pictures represent a pharaoh sitting on a divine throne to the right of a god. In others he stands or is enthroned in the midst of a company of gods.[2] In a Ugaritic text a god is honored at a banquet by being "seated at the right

---

[1] See A. Gornatowski, *Rechts und Links im antiken Aberglauben* (Breslau: Nischkowsky, 1936); T. H. Gaster, *Myth, Legend, and Custom in the Old Testament* (New York: Harper & Row, 1969), 775 f; O. Nussbaum, "Die Bewertung von Rechts und Links in der römischen Liturgie," *Jahrbuch für Antike und Christentum* 5 (1962), 158.

[2] H. Gunkel, *Die Psalmen* (HKAT; Göttingen: Vandenhoeck & Ruprecht, 1926), 481 f; H. Schmidt, *Die Psalmen* (HAT; Tübingen: Mohr, 1934), 203; S. Mowinckel, "General Oriental and Specific Israelite Elements in the Israelite Conception of the Sacral Kingdom," *The Sacral Kingship*, ed. G. Widengren *et al.* (Leiden: Brill, 1959), 287.

hand of the victor Baal." [3] According to H. Schmidt, the Babylonian New Year festival included a ritual in which the king was given a place at the right of the godhead.[4] Related symbolism is discernible in the pre-Islamic Arabian custom of seating the viceroy of a king at the latter's right (the viceroy took precedence over everyone but the king himself).[5] The Greek tradition offers comparable ideas in connection with certain deities. Poets often describe their gods as associated with Zeus (or another high deity) as *paredroi, sunedroi, sunthronoi*.[6] Pindar portrays Athena "sitting at the right hand of the father Zeus." [7] Callimachus declares that Apollo is able to grant honor and rewards to men "since he sits at the right hand of Zeus." [8]

The evidence suggests that in the ancient Mediterranean world the literary or graphic representation of someone seated to the right of a god was fairly common and that it signified divine honor and sometimes worldly authority and power. In Greece and Egypt it seems to have implied participation in divinity, although the ancients may have understood that the one at the right hand of a god was at best a subordinate deity.

One other important symbolic pattern must be noted. Long before Christianity's birth, there was a pagan tradition that after death the souls of the righteous take a right-hand path up to heaven, while those of the wicked go to the left down to the underworld.[9]

Ideas About the Right Hand and About a SESSION at the Right Hand in the Hebrew Scriptures and Ancient Judaism.—In many ancient Jewish writings, "right-hand" has a symbolic association with superiority or favor. A man who is expected to be divinely helped may be said to be at God's right or to be the ring on his

---

[3] Baal 2.5.46-48 (G. R. Driver, *Canaanite Myths and Legends* [Edinburgh: Clark, 1956], 99).

[4] Schmidt, *Psalmen*, 203.

[5] M. Buttenwieser, *The Psalms* (Chicago: Univ. Press, 1938), 796. Cf H. Cremer and J. Kögel, *Biblisch-theologisches Wörterbuch des neutestamentlichen Griechisch*, 11th ed. (Stuttgart: Perthes, 1923), 275.

[6] H. Hupfeld, *Die Psalmen*, 2nd ed., 4 (Gotha: Perthes, 1871), 195. Cf Th. Thalheim, *Pauly's Real-Encyclopädie der klassischen Altertumswissenschaft*, ed. G. Wissowa, 9.1 (Stuttgart, 1903), col. 575.

[7] Fragment 133 (C. Bowra [ed.], *Pindari Carmina*, 2nd ed. [Oxford: Clarendon Press, 1947]).

[8] *Hymn 2, to Apollo*, line 29 (A. W. and G. R. Mair, *Callimachus, Lycophron, Aratus* [LCL, 1921], 50-51).

[9] Plato, *Republic* 10.614C; cf. *Gorgias* 524A; Virgil, *Aeneid* 6.540 ff. See Gornatowski, *Rechts*, 48.

right hand (Ps 80.18; Jer 22.24). When God is said to stand at a man's right or to grasp that man's right hand, this means that the man receives divine protection, encouragement, and strength.[10] To speak of God's right hand is to speak of his power, especially of his power to save and sustain.[11]

From Ps 109.6,31 and Zech 3.1, we can infer that it was usual in ancient Israelite trials for both accuser and advocate to stand at the right hand of the person being judged.[12] That this meaning of "standing at the right" was not forgotten in later times is shown by a passage in the Pistis Sophia.[13] An association not only with judgment but also with acquittal is apparent in Midrash on Song of Songs 1.9: a court scene is depicted in which angels on the right cry "Not guilty!" and angels on the left cry "Guilty!" A vision in the Apocalypse of Abraham (22.5-7) represents humanity divided into two groups, those on the right destined for salvation, those on the left doomed to destruction.

A special association of the right side with revelation is occasionally attested. Moses is said to have received Torah from God's right hand.[14] One rabbinic passage says that Torah itself is at God's right hand, citing Deut 33.2 as proof.[15]

There is no parallel in the rest of Jewish scriptures to the injunction of Ps 110.1 that someone be seated at God's right hand. Several passages, however, describe persons set at the right hand of kings. When Bathsheba appears before Solomon to intercede on Adonijah's behalf, the king orders a seat placed for her to the right of his throne

[10] Isa 41.13; 45.1; 63.12; Pss 16.8; 110.5. The meaning of the reference to Yahweh at the king's right hand in Ps 110.5 seems about the same as that of the oracle for the king's session at Yahweh's right: God supports and guides the monarch, who is his earthly representative. Cf Weiser, *Psalms*, 696. For later Jewish passages of similar force, see 4 Ezra 10:30; 1 QS 11.4.

[11] Ex 15.6; Pss 74.11; 118.15-16; Lam 2.3; Wis 5.16; 2 Enoch 13 (39.5); Pss Sol 13.1; 1 QH 18.7; 1 QM 4.7; Sir 33.6; Aristobulus 2.41 ff. Cf 3 Enoch 48A.1-10.

[12] Cf de Vaux, *Ancient Israel*, 156; Gunkel, *Psalmen*, 479 f; Kraus, *Psalmen* 2,748, 750.

[13] 105, 108. See C. Schmidt and W. Till, *Koptisch-Gnostische Schriften 1. Die Pistis Sophia, die beiden Bücher des Jeû, unbekanntes altgnostisches Werk*, 2nd ed. (GCS 45, 1954), 67, 69. Ps 109.6 is interpreted to mean that "the Ruler of the outmost Darkness" shall remain at the right hand of the wicked man who is condemned in God's judgment.

[14] b. Shabbat 63ᵃ. See L. Ginzberg, *The Legends of the Jews*, ET H. Szold (Philadelphia: Jewish Publication Society, 1909-28), 3,469.

[15] *Numbers Rabba* 22.9. See further b. Shabbat 88*b*; 1 Q 34 2.7 (in A. Dupont-Sommer, *The Essene Writings from Qumran*, ET G. Vermes [Cleveland: World, 1961], 336).

(1 Kgs 2.19). From Ps 45.10 one might conclude that the queen (or queen mother) regularly *stood* at the king's right.[16] At Zech 6.13 the OG describes a priest at the right hand of a king, but the MT merely says he is situated beside the king's throne. In all these cases, the place at the right hand clearly symbolizes unique honor; in 1 Kgs 2.19 there may be a suggestion that a person so placed can intercede effectively with the monarch (even before Bathsheba voices her petition, Solomon presumably recognizes that she has come to make one).

Later Jewish writings also speak of persons seated to the right of kings. In 1 Esdr 4.29-30 the favorite concubine of a ruler sits on his right, playing with his crown. To the story of 1 Sam 20.24-33, Josephus adds the detail that Jonathan sat on Saul's right (*Ant* 6.[11.9]235). That ordinary citizens commonly seated honored friends on this side is shown in Sir 12.12: "Do not seat him [your foe] on your right hand."

We have already seen that the Testament of Job borrows the language of Ps 110 to describe a throne at the right hand of God appointed for the heavenly afterlife of its pious hero. A similar idea is expressed, without obvious reliance on the psalm, in the relatively late Apocalypse of Elijah, which declares of righteous martyrs that God will give them heavenly crowns and thrones at his right hand.[17] In T Benj 10.6 a day of eschatological triumph is described in which the great patriarchs Enoch, Noah, Shem, Abraham, Isaac, and Jacob shall be seen "rising on the right hand [of God?] in gladness." A rabbinic passage interprets Ps 16.11 and Deut 33.2 to mean that true teachers of torah will gain seats at God's right hand.[18] Certain other Jewish texts speak of righteous individuals receiving thrones or elevation near God after death without specifying a right-hand location (e.g., 4 Macc 17.5; 1 Enoch 108.12; T Isaac 1.5-6).

Since Christians so often spoke of the enthronement of Jesus in heaven, it is particularly interesting to see how post-biblical Judaism spoke of the divine enthronement of messiahs or other persons of preeminent importance for Israel or mankind. The Qumran sectarians believed that the "Branch of David" would sit on "a throne of glory" or "the throne of Zion" in the last days (4QpIsa, fragments C and D; 4QFlor 1.10-11). According to 2 Bar 72.1–73.1, the messiah will

---

[16] Cf Gunkel, *Psalmen*, 481 f.

[17] 37.3-4 (in P. Riessler, *Altjüdisches Schrifttum ausserhalb der Bibel* [Augsburg: Filfer, 1928], 122). Cf Aboth R. Nathan 12.4.

[18] Pesikta Rabbati 179[b]. See Str-B 1,210 f.

sit on "the throne of his kingdom" only after he has ruled and punished the nations. The dramatic poet Ezekiel represented Moses reporting a vision in which God gave his own throne to Moses.[19] Several documents promise that Adam will finally regain the throne of glory which he lost through the machinations of the devil.[20]

Finally we may note two striking expressions in the Wisdom of Solomon. The Wisdom of God is described as sitting beside God's throne (9.4), and the Logos of God which attacks Egypt is said to leap down "from heaven, from the royal throne" (18.15).

Ideas About the Right Hand and a SESSION at the Right Hand in Early Christianity and Christian Gnosticism.—Many early Christian writings including gnostic documents attest a general positive symbolic interpretation of the right side.[21] Thus the right hand of God or Christ is understood to connote divine power, often linked with creation and rule of the world, and almost always with salvation.[22] The Gospel of Philip correlates the polarity of good and evil with that of right and left.[23]

In the next section of this chapter we shall examine references to Jesus' SESSION in Christian literature of the NT age. Christian writings in subsequent periods frequently mentioned the SESSION, usually representing it as a position of glory in heaven which Christ assumed after his resurrection.[24] A somewhat different time perspective is expressed in the Gospel of Bartholomew 1.32 where Jesus tells a disciple:

[19] Eusebius, *Preparation* 9.29.4-5 (GCS 43.1.529). See the comments of E. R. Goodenough, *By Light, Light* (New Haven: Yale Univ. Press, 1935), 290. W. A. Meeks sets the statements of Ezekiel and Philo about Moses' exaltation in a broad stream of Jewish and Samaritan traditions dealing with this subject (many of the sources he cites, however, are of relatively late date). Meeks emphasizes that Moses' heavenly ascension was often conceived as a guarantee of certain revelations which he received; but this idea does not appear in Ezekiel's drama. See Meeks, "Moses as God and King," in J. Neusner (ed.), *Religions in Antiquity* (Festschrift E. R. Goodenough; Suppl. Numen; Leiden: Brill, 1968), 354-71.

[20] Life of Adam and Eve 48.1-3; Apocalypse of Moses 39. 2 ff; Cave of Treasures 2.17 ff.

[21] Nussbaum, "Bewertung," 162, 171. Cf F. J. Dölger, *Antike und Christentum* 1 (Münster: Aschendorff, 1929), 236-40.

[22] E.g., Rev 1.16,20; 5.1,7; Odes Sol 8.5-6; 14.4; 18.7; 22.7; 25.2-3; 28.15; 38.19-20.

[23] J. Leipoldt and H.-M. Schenke, *Koptisch-gnostische Schriften aus den Papyrus-Codices von Nag Hammadi* (Hamburg: Reich, 1960), 45 (log. 40). Cf K. Grobel, *The Gospel of Truth* (Nashville: Abingdon, 1960), 128, 130 f (and, in the Gospel's text, 32.5,9-14).

[24] Thus many ancient creeds of the eastern and western churches mention the SESSION between references to Jesus' resurrection and parousia.

even when I taught among you, I sat at the right hand of the Father and received the sacrifices in paradise.[25]

Melito of Sardis expresses a similar view.[26] In the ps-Clementine *Homilies* and the late Book of John the Evangelist, Christ's SESSION is projected back into the period before the incarnation.[27] In the Ascension of Isaiah, Christ sits down at the right hand of "the great glory" while "the angel of the Holy Spirit" sits on the left, evidently an inferior position (11.32-33; cf 7.14.15, 34-35).

Certain Gnostic writings say that Christ sits to the right of someone other than God (or the highest God). Justin's *Baruch* contains an angelic invitation to the boy Jesus to ascend and sit with Elohim; Elohim, in turn, is invited to sit at the right hand of the supreme deity, Priapus (Hipp *Ref* 5.25.16 and 30). The Sethian-Ophites held that after his ascension Jesus sits at the right of the Father Ialdabaoth. But, far from being the supreme god, Ialdabaoth is an evil and ignorant one whom Christ gradually deprives of power by receiving to himself the souls of men who have known him (Iren *Her* 1.30.14 [1.28.7]). According to Basilides, the saving gospel is given by the son of the Great Archon, who sits at the Archon's right hand. Yet the Archon, though creator of the universe, is inferior to the son in both goodness and wisdom and there is a still higher deity, "the cause of all" (Hipp *Ref* 7.23.5-6; 7.27.7). By varying the identity of the one by whom Christ (or the Son) sits, these systems obviously vary Christ's own rank and significance.

Some gnostics, evidently building on the SESSION tradition, went so far as to identify Christ with the Right. The Sethian-Ophites, for example, described him summarily as "the Right side and the Ascension." [28]

The notion that true believers will be rewarded after death with heavenly seats at the right hand is expressed quite frequently in early Christian (including gnostic) writings. In Pistis Sophia 78, Mary says to Jesus:

[25] H-S 1,491. Cf Epistle of the Apostles 17.

[26] See J. C. Th. Otto, *Corpus Apologetarum Christianorum Saeculi Secundi* 9 (Jena: Dufft, 1872), 420 f. Cf the reading *ho on en tō ouranō* at Jn 3.13.

[27] Hom. 7.3. See M. R. James, *The Apocryphal New Testament* (Oxford: Clarendon Press, 1953), 188.

[28] Irenaeus, *Her* 1.30.2 (1.28.1). Cf Acts of Thomas 48 (H-S 2,469) and Epistle of the Apostles 19.

In the dissolving of all the Confusion you will sit upon a power of light, and your disciples, namely we, will sit on your right and you will judge the tyrant gods. . . .[29]

According to the Odes of Solomon, the elect are set at *God's* right hand (8.21; cf 19.4-5). A beatitude in the Acts of Paul promises that those who have rightly loved God shall judge angels and receive blessing at the Father's right hand.[30] The Marcionites are said to have believed that the apostle Paul sits on the right hand of Christ in heaven just as Christ sits on God's right.[31] In the Shepherd of Hermas, the narrator is told by the ancient lady (who symbolizes the church) to sit down on the left and not *eis ta dexia merē*. To sit at the right is a privilege reserved for those who have pleased God and suffered for the Name (9.9–10.2 = *Vis.* 3.1.9–3.2.2). Clement of Alexandria and Hippolytus speak of a right side which is the place of the just and redeemed in contrast to a left-hand location for those who are wicked and damned.[32] Certain gnostic works mention a "place at the right" as a region of exaltation for persons (ordinary Christians) who do not attain the highest condition of bliss.[33]

Summary and Conclusions.—In ancient paganism and Judaism generally the right side symbolized potency and honor. Long before the Christian era pagans spoke of kings and gods exalted to thrones at the right of other gods, and they sometimes described bliss after death in terms of a right-hand location. The Hebrew scriptures and later Jewish writings spoke of men and supernatural beings gaining right-hand or heavenly thrones, often without implying that any particular function was linked with such elevation. The notions of Jesus sitting at the right hand of God and of his followers gaining similar honor seem to have widely fired the imaginations of early Christians. This development may be attributed in part to the use of Ps 110.1, but it must have been encouraged by the fact that wholly apart from the psalm such notions would be richly meaningful to contemporary pagans and Jews.

[29] Schmidt and Till, *Schriften,* 49. Cf Clement of Alexandria, *Misc* 4.15.6; Acts of Thomas 80 (H-S 2,486).

[30] Acts of Paul 2.6 (James, *Apocryphal NT,* 273).

[31] Origen, *Homily on Luke* 25 (GCS 49,150-51). There is an allusion to Mt 20.21.

[32] Hippolytus, *Against the Greeks* 1 (PG 10,797); Clement of Alexandria, *Of Punishments* (Fragment; GCS 17,229).

[33] Irenaeus, *Her* 1.5.1-2 (1.1.9); 1.6.1-2 (1.1.11); Exc Theodotus 23.3; 28; 34; 37; 40; 71.2; 72.1.

Jesus at the Right Hand

Phrases derived from Ps 110.1 are frequently used in hymnic or confessional materials from the NT age to express Jesus' glorification after death. Indeed, though early Christians used a variety of means to communicate their faith in his exaltation,[34] the single most popular symbol was that of the PLACE or SESSION.[35] All their references to Ps 110.1b bear more or less directly on that exaltation, though they express varied christological points of view. Several questions may be profitably kept in mind as we examine the quotations and allusions. To what particular moment or period in Christ's career does the PLACE or SESSION apply? What does it indicate about his relation to God the Father? Does the PLACE or SESSION imply that the heavenly Christ is active?

Pauline Passages.—Rom 8.34 presents Jesus' right-hand position as present fact in contrast to his past death and resurrection. The verbs in the relative clauses (*estin, entygchanei*) would by themselves indicate that Christ is there and intercedes now, i.e. during the whole career of the church; and this may well have been the sense of the *Vorlage* Paul used. Yet Rom 8.31-39 is primarily concerned with the future. The whole passage is an assurance to Christians that God's saving love and protection of believers may be counted on without reserve. This guarantee is fortified by the courtroom language of 8.33-34; the trial is that of the last judgment, and Christians are promised that the accusations of Satan will come to nothing.[36] Hence,

---

[34] E.g., the formulations in Phil 2.11; 1 Tim 3.16; Lk 24.26. Among the recent discussions of the general early Christian conception of Jesus' exaltation, see esp. V. Larrañaga, *L'ascension de Notre Seigneur dans le Nouveau Testament* (Rome: Pontifical Institute, 1938); P. Benoit, "L'ascension," RB 56 (1949), 161-203; J. G. Davies, *He Ascended into Heaven* (London: Lutterworth, 1958); G. Bertram, "Erhöhung," *Reallexikon für Antike und Christentum* 4 (1964), 22-43; W. Thüsing, "Erhöhungsvorstellung und Parusieerwartung in der ältesten nachösterlichen Christologie," *Biblische Zeitschrift* 11 (1967), 95-108, 205-22; 12 (1968), 54-80, 222-40. The following older treatments have special relevance: H. B. Swete, *The Ascended Christ* (London: Macmillan, 1910); A. J. Tait, *The Heavenly Session of Our Lord* (London: Scott, 1912); G. Bertram, "Die Himmelfahrt Jesu vom Kreuz aus und der Glaube an seine Auferstehung," *Festgabe für Adolf Deissmann* (Tübingen: Mohr, 1927), 187-217.

[35] The abbreviations PLACE (=position at the right hand of God) and SESSION (=session at the right hand of God) are used throughout this study. SESSION implies that a particular quotation or allusion specifies a sitting posture; PLACE implies that the passage in view does not specify sitting, or specifies standing (as in Acts 7.55-56). See above, p. 36.

[36] On the implication that the accuser is Satan, see F.-J. Leenhardt, *L'Epître de*

while 8.34 says nothing to deny that Christ is now at God's right hand, its driving concern is with the future eschatological acquittal of believers and with his intercessory action at that time.

The coupling of the relative clauses implies a connection of some sort between Jesus' position and his intercession. I shall analyze the significance of this intercession in a later chapter, but may note here the question of why the right-hand place should be particularly linked with that action. *One* reason may be that that position implies highest honor and therefore the success of a petitioner who occupied it.[37] Christ's honor with God guarantees the hope of his followers. The real question of our future is that of our future relation to God. The ideas and imagery in Rom 8.31-39 circle around the relation between God and Christ. Jesus died by God's sacrificial deliverance (8.32), he was raised (by God), is at God's right, intercedes (with God, the judge), and loves us with a love superior to every disaster because it is the love of God (8.35-39). All this emphasizes not only the uniqueness of Christ's glory but also its dependence on God.

1 Cor 15.25, alluding only to Ps 110.1c, does not mention a place at God's right hand. It may nonetheless be included in this discussion since Paul may well have had vs 1b of the psalm in mind here, and in any case was certainly referring to Ps 110 in connection with Jesus' glory. Yet, as in Rom 8.34, the context of the reference is not chiefly concerned with christology per se but with an assurance given believers for the future, particularly as that future is threatened by death. To them the promise of the psalm applies: Christ shall rule till all his enemies, including death, are defeated. Their security hinges on his supremacy.

Given the parallelism of the psalm citations in 15.25 and 27,[38] one cannot overlook the fact that behind 15.20-28 as a whole (as behind much of 15.42-50) there must lie a congeries of Adamic speculation of a quasi-gnostic type. The immediate application, without explanation, of Ps 8 to Christ implies that he is the Last Adam in such a way that scripture usually interpreted of the first man really pertains to him.[39] Paul stresses the difference between the bringer of death and the bringer of life (15.22), but perhaps he saw a positive correlation

---

Saint Paul aux Romains (CNT, 1957), 135; C. K. Barrett, *The Epistle to the Romans* (BNTC, 1957), 173.

[37] Cf above, p. 36.

[38] See above, pp. 36-37.

[39] Cf Borsch, *Son of Man,* 244; Str-B 3,681.

between the universal lordship promised Adam (cf Gen 1.26 ff) and that fulfilled (or to be fulfilled) in Christ.[40] In this passage, Paul manifests special concern for defining the relation of Jesus' glory not only to Adam's but also to God's. 1 Cor 15.27-28 states emphatically that God is the source of all the subjection of creation beneath the Son. Even if *thē* in vs 25 has Christ for its implied subject, Ps 110.1c is plainly meant here to point to the work of the Father.[41] Although the Son genuinely reigns, the climax of his rule is a yielding up of the kingdom to the Father; the end consists not in Christ's second coming, nor in a joint reign of Father and Son (cf Rev 22), but in the sole dominion of the Father. Although in 15.25 Paul probably thought of the rule as carried out "at God's right hand," his language does not suggest simply a sharing of government by two monarchs enthroned side by side. Rather Christ's government seems to be distinguished from God's in such a way that one might call him a divine plenipotentiary holding absolute sway for a limited period.[42]

When does that period of Christ's rule commence? There is no explicit answer to the question in this passage in 1 Corinthians, but some indirect evidence suggests that the reign is conceived as primarily or exclusively future. The ruling activity mentioned in 15.25-27 pertains above all to the subjugation of supernatural foes, and it is not clear that Paul supposed any of these to be fully overcome during the present age of the church. Contemporary Jews sometimes posited a future messianic interim reign,[43] and Rev 19-20 seemingly represents Christ's reign as beginning with his second coming. 1 Cor 15.23 appears to refer to a period between the parousia, when the limited number of "those who belong to Christ" will be raised (cf Rev 20.4-5) and the "end," when Christ shall have conquered every foe (cf Rev 20.14-15) —an end which evidently means the resurrection

[40] On the Adamic and son of man speculation behind 1 Cor 15, see Mowinckel, *He That Cometh*, 346-450; Cullmann, *Christology*, 137-92; R. Scroggs, *The Last Adam* (Oxford: Blackwell, 1966) ; E. Brandenburger, *Adam und Christus* (WMANT 7, 1962) .

[41] See F. Maier, "Ps 110.1 im Zusammenhang von I Kor. 15, 24-26," *Biblische Zeitschrift* 20 (1932) , 156. Among those who take Christ as the subject of *thē* are J. Weiss, *Der erste Korintherbrief* (Meyer, 1910) , 359; A. Robertson and A. Plummer, *First Epistle of St. Paul to the Corinthians* (ICC, 1914) , 356.

[42] Cf Hahn, *Titles*, 132. On Paul's concern here to oppose an identification of God and Christ as well as a doctrine of two gods, see E. Schweizer, TWNT 8,372 f.

[43] Cf W. Bousset and H. Gressmann, *Die Religion des Judentums im späthellenistischen Zeitalter*, 3rd ed. (HNT, 1926) , 286-89; Mowinckel, *He That Cometh*, 277, 321 ff, 367 f, 403 ff.

of the rest of humanity. Does Paul then apply Ps 110.1c only to this interval? One more fact must be borne in mind: the apostle recognizes and evidently approves the doctrine that the saints shall rule with Christ, but he rejects the notion that they already do so.[44] Does he also reject the idea that Christ already reigns? Nothing in the apostle's wording excludes such an interpretation.[45] At all events, the most important point to be emphasized with regard to time is that in 1 Cor 15.25, as in Rom 8.34, Paul's concern is focused not on the present but on the eschatological hour of deliverance. For him Ps 110.1 is mainly a text about the future.

In *Col 3.1* the thought of Christ's right-hand position as a definite location acquires primary importance. The stress is not on what he does, but on where he is. The setting of this allusion is a bridge paragraph joining the doctrinal exposition and argument of the opening chapters with the ethical teaching of chaps. 3 and 4.[46] In 3.1-4 the writer[47] gives classic expression to the idea "Be what you are." Since Christians have their true life mysteriously united with Christ, they should direct their minds to *ta anō*, "where Christ is seated at the right hand of God." The writer's hortatory purpose obviously conditions what he does and does not say about the exalted Christ here. It remains surprising that, in contrast to the allusions to our psalm verse in Rom 8 and 1 Cor 15, this one is not joined to any statements about the power or activity of the one at God's right hand. Here the SESSION suggests the invisible, non-worldly character of Christian life and security. The author here seems particularly inclined to define Jesus' post-resurrection situation and status in relation to God: to sit at God's right is to be "in God." But this is a

[44] 1 Cor 4.8. For a different interpretation, see C. K. Barrett, *From First Adam to Last* (London: Black, 1962), 100.

[45] Among those who think Christ's reign according to 1 Cor 15 begins with the parousia are H. Lietzmann, *An die Korinther I, II*, 4th ed. (HNT, 1949), 81; Maier, "Ps 110.1," 150. Those who take it to begin with Christ's resurrection include J. Weiss, *Korintherbrief*, 358; Bultmann, *Theology* 1, 346; Barrett, *Adam*, 94, 99 ff; H. A. Wilcke, *Das Problem eines messianischen Zwischenreichs bei Paulus* (ATANT 51, 1967), 98-101. A commendable agnosticism on the point is expressed by W. G. Kümmel in Lietzmann, *Korinther*, 4th ed., 193. O. Cullmann (*The Early Church*, ET A. J. B. Higgins and S. Godman [Philadelphia: Westminster, 1966], 112) presents a neat picture of the *Regnum Christi* beginning with the ascension and, after the parousia, "overlapping" into the future age. But is such a picture possible without a questionable harmonizing of texts?

[46] So, e.g., E. F. Scott, *The Epistles of Paul to the Colossians, to Philemon and to the Ephesians* (MNTC, 1930), 62; M. Dibelius and H. Greeven, *An die Kolosser, Epheser, an Philemon* (HNT, 1953), 40.

[47] Probably not Paul.

glory possessed in hiddenness, to be manifested only at the end (3.3-4).[48]

No doubt the lordship of Christ over both church and cosmos receives unusual attention elsewhere in the epistle.[49] The author can write unreservedly about the absolute power and authority of Christ (1.15-20), the completeness of his victory over the inimical powers (2.15), and the fullness to which Christians have come as members of his body (2.10). At the same time he insists that salvation is held only in hope (1.5), that the present time is a period for Christ's strength to be used in patient endurance (1.11), and that believers must still struggle to put off the works of the flesh (3.5-11). The mystery of Christ has as yet been revealed only to the church (1.25-27), and the riches of wisdom and knowledge in him are still concealed. The author has chosen to use the image of the SESSION—one so often employed to assert the manifest power and glory of Christ—precisely to express the hiddenness and eschatological reserve which he believes is characteristic of Christian experience of their savior's exaltation.

In their employment of Ps 110, as at so many other points, Ephesians and Colossians display an enigmatic combination of likeness and contrast. Both refer to the SESSION in passages of high prominence and allude to, rather than quote, the psalm text. Both link it, by implication, with baptism and use it primarily to interpret the present period of the church's career. The reference in *Eph 1.20*, however, stands not in a transition to parenesis but in the center of dogmatic exposition. Above all the author of Ephesians uses it to emphasize not the invisible mystery of Christ but rather the present manifestation of his power and majesty. More than with any other NT book, futuristic eschatology seems absent from Ephesians.[50] The chief meaning which this setting gives to Ps 110.1b is power. Immediately after mentioning the heavenly enthronement, the writer

[48] Cf Bertram, "Himmelfahrt," 209 n. 2; E. Sjöberg, *Der verborgene Menschensohn in den Evangelien* (Lund: Gleerup, 1955), 16-18, 26. On the general Jewish background of the idea of a hidden messiah, see Sjöberg, 41-98; T. F. Glasson, *The Second Advent*, 3rd ed. (London: Epworth, 1963), 231-37. Cf the tendency among the rabbis to stress the passivity or hidden waiting condition of the one addressed in Ps 110 (see above, pp. 30-31).

[49] Cf E. Lohse, "Christusherrschaft und Kirche im Kolosserbrief," NTS 11 (1964-65), 203-16; A. Grabner-Haider, *Paraklese und Eschatologie bei Paulus* (NTAbh 4; Münster: Aschendorff, 1968), 99-102.

[50] Cf Scott, *Epistles*, 165; E. Käsemann, *Leib und Leib Christi* (BHT, 1933), 143; H. Conzelmann, "Brief an die Epheser," 63.

presses on, partly by the use of Ps 8.7, to speak of Christ's absolute dominion over all things, including supernatural spirits (1.21-22). The main concern in 1.20–2.10 seems ecclesiology rather than christology, but Christ's supreme honor and puissance here find celebration that could hardly be surpassed. He is head over all things for the good of the church (1.23), but the church is subjected to him just as certainly as are the demonic powers (cf 5.24).[51] If in Col 3.1 the lordship connotations of the SESSION fade to the point of vanishing, here they are predominant. As in Colossians, however, there is also evident special reflection on the location of the exalted Christ. Being at God's right hand means that he is in "the heavenly places," though far above the angelic powers who also inhabit those regions.[52]

The reign of Christ thus designated with the psalm allusion is apparently conceived as inaugurated with, or immediately following, his resurrection, and nothing indicates that the future will bring any increment or termination to his rule. Ephesians agrees with 1 Cor 15.20 ff, however, that behind Christ's supremacy stands that of God the Father, whose sovereignty and predestination are the source of all the saving events recounted in Eph 1.3–2.10.

Passages Emphasizing Vindication or Judgment.—We turn now to consider references to Ps 110.1*b* representing a variety of traditions within the early church, references which nevertheless share a common concern to link Jesus' heavenly exaltation with his vindication by God or with his judgment of men (vindicating his followers or condemning his enemies).

While the saying in *Mk 14.62* (=Mt 26.64=Lk 22.69) is probably inauthentic,[53] it has extraordinary importance dramatically and theologically within Mark's gospel. Here for the first and only time the three decisive titles of Marcan christology are openly claimed by Jesus. Apart from Jesus' resolute confession and conduct, Mk 14 mainly depicts human weakness and sin: the malignant stealth of the priests and scribes (14.1-2) the treachery of Judas (10-11), Jesus' awareness of impending betrayal and desertion (17-21, 26-31), the failure of the disciples in the garden (32-42), the climactic betrayal and abandonment (43-50), the vicious trial proceedings (55-57, 65), and Peter's

---

[51] Cf H. Bietenhard, *Das tausendjährige Reich* (Bern: Zwingli-Verlag, 1955), 82.
[52] On the cosmology implied, see esp. H. Odeberg, *The View of the Universe in Ephesians* (Lund: Gleerup, 1934); Schlier, *Epheser*, 3rd ed., 45-48, 86 f.
[53] See above, p. 41 n. 25.

collapse (66-72). The contrast with Jesus' forthright declaration could hardly be sharper.

His confession has two main parts: in the first he responds that he is indeed Christ and Son of God, in the second he promises his judges that they will see the son of man enthroned and coming with the clouds. The second part plainly supplies further information—more than the high priest asked—but it also implies that the appearance of the son of man will confirm the truth of Jesus' claims (cf 8.38). For Mark, Jesus himself is the son of man, and when the judges behold his divine glory and power they will also "see" that he is messiah and God's Son, though they are now on the brink of condemnation and mockery. Thus Jesus' words about the future in 14.62, including his allusion to Ps 110.1, chiefly function as an announcement of his imminent vindication.[54]

Exactly how imminent 14.62 intends to suggest that vindication to be is warmly debated by scholars. It is quite generally agreed, however, that the final redactor of the gospel will have interpreted the words about coming on the clouds as a description of the parousia (cf 13.26). Some scholars urge—and their opinion cannot be disproven—that Mk 14.62 predicts two distinct events, the heavenly SESSION conceived as beginning with Jesus' resurrection, and his second coming.[55] Yet the *opsesthe* is so placed in the sentence that Jesus promises his judges that they will see both his sitting and his coming. Further, the text gives no hint of a time lapse between the two, and the parallelism of the participles suggests that there will be none. When will the sanhedrin members "see" Jesus seated beside God? Some scholars think this could refer to spiritual experiences or outsiders' observations of unusual phenomena within the early Christian communities.[56] Yet the promise is given to unbelievers (who,

[54] That Mk 14.62 is a classical vindication text is emphasized by Hooker, *Son of Man*, 169, 171; J. A. T. Robinson, *Jesus and His Coming* (Nashville: Abingdon, 1957), 44 f; Tödt, *Son of Man*, 40.

[55] Cf E. Grässer, *Das Problem der Parusieverzögerung in den synoptischen Evangelien und in der Apostelgeschichte* (Berlin: Töpelmann, 1957), 174; Lohmeyer, *Markus*, 329. The order of verbs ("sitting," "coming") implies that both refer to the *parousia*. J. A. T. Robinson (*Jesus*, 45 n. 2) significantly speculates that the order was different in the pre-Marcan tradition. See further (on the parousia orientation) H. K. McArthur, "Mark XIV.62," NTS 4 (1957-58), 158; Tödt, *Son of Man*, 38 f. Hooker (*Son of Man*, 170 f) urges that the order is unimportant since the citations of Ps 110 and Dan 7 are metaphorical and parallel "though not necessarily identical in meaning."

[56] E.g., V. Taylor, *The Gospel According to St. Mark* (London: Macmillan, 1952), 568. For criticism, see W. G. Kümmel, *Promise and Fulfillment*, ET D. M.

so far as we know, always remained such); and the term *dynamis* (like the image of arriving on clouds) suggests public and irrefutable revelation such as could be imagined only in connection with the parousia.[57] The text itself says nothing about an interim between trial and parousia, and Hahn has conjectured that this verse (unlike any other in the NT) represents the SESSION as beginning only at the end of the world.[58] This view is most unlikely, first just because so many other early Christians attest a general conviction that the SESSION began with Jesus' resurrection, secondly because 14.62 describes not the enthronement of the son of man but the revelation of him as enthroned.[59] The *kathēmenon* indicates not the beginning of a SESSION but its continuance. When Jesus comes on the clouds he will have the authority and might of the one sitting at God's right hand.[60] Probably, then, Mark concurred in the general opinion that Jesus sat down beside God with, or directly after, his resurrection.[61] The evangelist's interest, however, was concentrated on the parousia revelation, when Jesus' claims will be proven true.[62]

Barton (SBT 23, 1961), 50 f n. 102; A. L. Moore, *The Parousia in the New Testament* (Leiden: Brill, 1966), 105 f.

[57] A. M. Goldberg ("Sitzend zur Rechten der Kraft," *Biblische Zeitschrift* 8 [1964], 284-93) provides evidence from Jewish sources that *dynamis* in Mk 14.62 is no mere circumlocution but rather a term implying an eschatological revelation of divine judgment.

[58] Hahn, *Titles*, 130.

[59] Cf Tödt's distinction between exaltation and enthronement with power (*Son of Man*, 285 n. 2).

[60] So Vielhauer, *Aufsätze*, 172 f, 205. T. F. Glasson ("The Reply to Caiaphas (Mark xiv.62)," NTS 7 [1960-61], 88-93) and others have urged the dissonance of the images of an apocalyptic movement on the clouds and a quiet sitting beside God's throne. Such arguments may overstress the degree to which the words are meant to evoke visual images. Cf Lohmeyer, *Markus*, 329. Perhaps a better parallel than the vision of Ezek 1 is the reference in Jer 22.4 to kings who "sit on the throne of David" (i.e., reign) and come riding in chariots.

[61] It may be that Mk 12.35-37 (along with 1.38 and 10.45) implies the pre-existence of Christ. If so, perhaps the evangelist supposed he sat at God's right hand before the incarnation. Cf J. Knox, *Jesus, Lord and Christ* (New York: Harper, 1958), 153; Synge, *Hebrews*, 10.

[62] Cf Burkill, *Revelation*, 242 f. R. Bultmann (*The History of the Synoptic Tradition*, ET J. Marsh [New York: Harper, 1963], 270 f) rightly contends that the whole point of the sanhedrin trial in Mark is to show that Jesus died for confessing himself to be the messiah. This being so, we need not assume that Mark tried to represent the condemnation for blasphemy as historically credible. O. Linton ("The Trial of Jesus and the Interpretation of Psalm CX," NTS 7 [1960-61], 258-62) has recently argued that the condemnation resulted from the use of Ps 110, which—as interpreted by Christians—was meant "literally," so that Jesus thereby claimed divine prerogatives. Apart from the question of why Jesus'

In line with this concern, Mark does not specify what Jesus will *do* at God's right hand, although it seems plain that the position symbolizes his divine power. Given the widespread traditions attested elsewhere of the son of man as witness or judge at the last assize (e.g. Mk 8.38),[63] one may reasonably suppose that similar ideas lie in the background here. The elect will be saved and the false judges condemned.[64] Yet the driving interest of this allusion to Ps 110 is not the subjugation of Jesus' foes but the vindication of his messiahship. One may detect an undercurrent of concern in the passage to relate the glory of Jesus to that of God. Mark and his readers must have found strong irony in a verdict of blasphemy brought against the Son of God by a tribunal claiming to act in God's name.

The pre-Marcan history of this logion—or of the separate traditions behind it, if Mark composed it himself—is a matter of unsettled controversy.[65] Apart from Dan 7.13, it is uncertain whether other scriptural passages,[66] or son of man traditions[67] underlie it. Nor can the date of this formulation be set within narrow limits. While the conflation of two or more Jewish scriptural passages indicates some period of reflection and scriptural study, the period may not have been long.[68] The more one is disposed to see Mk 14.62 as a unitary proph-

---

enemies should be represented as knowing the Christian interpretation of Ps 110.1, I think that Linton assumes too much about how contemporary Jews ordinarily understood that text.

[63] Cf Tödt, *Son of Man*, 40-46; Hooker, *Son of Man*, 119; A. J. B. Higgins, *Jesus and the Son of Man* (London: Lutterworth, 1964), 74, 186.

[64] So, e.g., Higgins, *Jesus*, 74; Vielhauer, *Aufsätze*, 204 f.

[65] Cf A. Suhl, *Die Funktion der alttestamentlichen Zitate und Anspielungen im Markusevangelium* (Gütersloh: Mohn, 1965), 55.

[66] C. H. Dodd (*Scriptures*, 101 f) argues that Ps 80.18 explains the fusion of Ps 110.1 and Dan 7.13. J. W. Doeve (*Jewish Hermeneutics in the Synoptic Gospels and Acts* [Assen: van Gorcum, 1954], 152-54) thinks the fusion derived from a current midrash on Ps 110.3 (midrash reflected in the OG rendering of that verse). Such "explanations" cannot be ruled impossible, but they are highly conjectural. Methodologically, we know too little of early Christian exegetical practice to assume that two scriptural passages could be conflated only when a connecting link in the form of a third could be found. On the rather surer basis of other NT uses of Zech 12.10, N. Perrin argues that that text underlies Mk 14.62; but the argument is not compelling (see Perrin, "Mark 14.62; End Product of a Christian Pesher Tradition?" NTS 12 [1965-66], 150-55; also his *Rediscovering the Teaching of Jesus* [New York: Harper, 1967], 173-85).

[67] See the discussions in Borsch, *Son of Man*, 145-60, 391 n. 4, and Borsch, "Mark xiv. 62 and I Enoch lxii.5," NTS 14 (1967-68), 565-67; Tödt, *Son of Man*, 22-31, 46 f.

[68] Advocates of a relatively late date include E. Schweizer, *The Good News According to Mark*, ET D. H. Madvig (Richmond: Knox, 1970), 326 f; Vielhauer,

ecy of the parousia, the less inclined he will be to dogmatize about its pre-Marcan development.

Mt 26.64 preserves the basic force of the Marcan confession, but there are modifications. The conversion of *egō eimi* into *su eipas* seems to cast only a thin veil over Jesus' affirmation,[69] and probably *plēn* should be taken as an adversative.[70] Matthew retains the orientation to the parousia[71] despite his introduction of *ap' arti*. He uses that phrase elsewhere (23.39;26.29) to note the end of a significant period in the history of salvation,[72] but without emphasis on the time between the period ending and the eschatological consummation. Thus *ap' arti* in 26.64 seems to mean not "from now on" but "at a later time" (viz. at the parousia).[73] The phrase seems to be inserted to bring out the contrast between Jesus' present abasement and his parousia glory; the former condition is about to end.[74] Did Matthew think of Jesus' heavenly SESSION as beginning only with the parousia? As in Mark's case, an unhesitating "Yes" is unwarranted. Matthew's gospel contains the same hints of Christ's pre-existence as Mark's, and Mt 20.20-28 may imply a messianic kingdom inaugurated before the second advent. In addition, far more than Mark, Matthew represents traditions which emphasize the present reality of Jesus' lordship over the church and presence with it (1.23; 18.20; 28.20). At least from the resurrection onward he is omnipotent (28.16). Nonetheless, Mt

---

Aufsätze, 203 f. An especially interesting argument for early dating is offered by J. Jeremias, "Die älteste Schicht der Menschensohn-Logien," ZNW 58 (1967), 171 f.

[69] The recent analysis of M. Thrall (*Greek Particles in the New Testament* [Leiden: Brill, 1962], 74-78) would be more persuasive if the parallel use of *su eipas* in Mt 26.25 were unambiguous. Cf E. Lohmeyer and W. Schmauch, *Das Evangelium des Matthäus* (Meyer, 1956), 355.

[70] See Thrall, *Particles*, 70-74 and W. Trilling, *Das wahre Israel* (Erfurter Theologische Studien; Leipzig: St. Benno, 1959), 67 for arguments on both sides of the question.

[71] G. Strecker (*Der Weg der Gerechtigkeit*, 2nd ed. [FRLANT 82, 1966], 115, 236) underlines this. J. Schniewind (*Das Evangelium nach Matthäus* [NTD, 1964], 263) says the reference is to Jesus' exaltation immediately after resurrection, but adds that the verse ignores the period between resurrection and parousia.

[72] If one may speak of a Matthean idea of *Heilsgeschichte*. In both passages the period conceived to be at an end is that of Jesus' earthly career.

[73] Similarly Grässer, *Problem*, 176; Tödt, *Son of Man*, 84; Trilling, *Israel*, 68. Orientation to the parousia would also be a natural interpretation if one accepted the hypothesis of A. Debrunner that the term is really *aparti* and means "certainly" (Über einige Lesarten der Chester Beatty Papyri des Neuen Testaments," *Coniectanea Neotestamentica XI in honorem Antonii Fridrichsen sexagenarii* [Lund: Gleerup, 1947], 45-49).

[74] Cf Cullmann, *Christology*, 119; Tödt, *Son of Man*, 78; Trilling, *Israel*, 68. So Mt 26.64, like 23.39 and 26.29, asserts the close of a period.

26.64 speaks of Jesus' glorification only in relation to the parousia, presumably because until then his glory will be concealed from his judges.[75]

The basic Marcan meaning of Jesus' prophecy—the vindication of his messiahship—is retained. Indeed, it is enhanced, since in the context of Matthew's entire presentation the final vindication of Jesus will mean the triumph of God's righteousness.[76] Also, the Matthean text seems to bear more of a threatening tone than its Marcan counterpart: "You have said this, but I tell you. . . !"[77] When he comes at God's right hand, Jesus will judge his judges.

Lk 22.69 offers fundamental changes in the Marcan confession, but retention of the basic motif of vindication. There is no longer any allusion to the parousia: *opsesthe* and the picture of an advent on the clouds have vanished, while the addition of *apo tou nyn* shows that the Lucan Jesus is speaking of the age to begin with his resurrection-ascension, the age of the church.[78] In keeping with this, the announcement that the Jewish leaders will perceive Jesus' glorious enthroned state has been eliminated. According to Luke, believers may have such visions before the second coming, but not others.[79]

The questions and answers of Lk 22.67-70 offer a progression in the use of the titles "Christ," "son of man," and "Son of God." Jesus' words about the son of man in vs 69 are seemingly inadequate or ambiguous for his listeners, and so they ask if he means he is God's Son. Perhaps this is only a bit of dramatic rewriting of Mark designed to give each title emphasis.[80] It is also possible that Luke seeks to

[75] In Mt 19.28 and 25.31, the *act* of the son of man's enthronement is dated at the parousia. Both sayings apparently reflect late Jewish apocalypticism (1 Enoch 61.8; 62.2) rather than Jesus' teaching, and perhaps they stand in some tension with Mt 26.64 and other verses in the gospel which suggest that his glorification occurs before his second coming. Yet 19.28 and 25.31 do not exclude the possibility of earlier exaltation; they only direct attention, as does 26.64, to the parousia.

[76] Cf G. Barth in G. Bornkamm *et al.*, *Tradition and Interpretation in Matthew*, ET P. Scott (Philadelphia: Westminster, 1963), 137-53.

[77] The material peculiar to Matthew in Mt 24.30 also points more directly to judgment. Cf Lohmeyer and Schmauch, *Matthäus*, 369; Tödt, *Son of Man*, 82 f.

[78] Cf the sense of the phrase in Lk 1.48; 5.10; 12.52; Acts 18.2. See further H. Conzelmann, *The Theology of St. Luke*, ET G. Buswell (London: Faber & Faber, 1960), 109, 116.

[79] E.g., Stephen and the disciples who bear witness in Acts 2.34; 5.31. Cf the "faith-visions" of Heb 2.9; 12.2; Jn 1.51. Conzelmann (*Luke*, 116) says that this evangelist thought the vision of the ascended Christ was reserved for martyrs like Stephen, but this seems to outrun our slender evidence.

[80] Cf J. M. Creed, *The Gospel According to St. Luke* (London: Macmillan,

show his readers the unpolitical, otherworldly meaning of the title "Christ" when applied to Jesus, despite the charge which the Jewish leaders ultimately prefer (23.2). Luke shows a general concern in this direction, and possibly he thought Ps 110.1*b* particularly apt for expressing the transcendent character of Jesus' office.

No more in Luke than in the other gospels is there indication of a specific function which Jesus will have while seated at God's right hand. The emphasis is on his impending glorification, not on any saving or judgmental work to be performed. Yet, like Acts 7.55-56, perhaps Lk 22.69 was meant to assure Christians who had to endure the world's hatred that Jesus was already (since his resurrection) exalted beside God. That Luke has seen fit to drop the references to the parousia while retaining the vindication motif suggests that, in his view, Christ's vindication is apparent already during the age of the church. This impression will be strengthened by an examination of the passages in Acts which cite Ps 110.

In *Acts 2.33-36* two distinct allusions and one complete quotation of Ps 110.1 may be distinguished. The pentecostal speech of Peter moves elliptically around two foci, the coming of the Holy Spirit and the resurrection-exaltation of Jesus. The interpretation of the Spirit provided here is peculiarly important within Luke-Acts as a whole, and we shall consider in a later chapter the special appropriation of Ps 110 to explain the Spirit's appearance. Still, the fundamental theme of this speech is not the doctrine of the Spirit but the declaration of vs 36 that Jesus of Nazareth is the savior to whom men must now look. Three kinds of witnesses are appealed to for support of this conclusion: the apostolic eye-witnesses (2.32), the Spirit's coming manifest in visible signs (2.16 ff; 2.33), and the scripture texts which are cited throughout the speech. In a way which is quite remarkable, especially in view of other portions of Luke-Acts, the resurrection, ascension, enthronement, and continuing lordship of Jesus seem to be interpreted here as essentially one event.[81] The claim in 2.36 that Jesus is *kyrios* appears to allude directly to the quotation of Ps 110.1*a* in 2.34, but that citation is at once followed by a quotation of the rest

---

1930), 278 Conzelmann, *Luke,* 84 f, 141, 170-72, 188 n. 7; Tödt, *Son of Man,* 102 f.

[81] So H. Conzelmann, *Die Apostelgeschichte* (HNT; Tübingen: Mohr, 1963), 30. U. Wilckens (*Die Missionsreden der Apostelgeschichte* (WMANT, 1961), 150 f) takes a somewhat different view.

of Ps 110.1. The implication is that Jesus is *kyrios* while he sits enthroned at God's right hand. In Acts 2.32-33, the exaltation to God's right hand seems equated with the resurrection, to which the apostles were witnesses. In its form the allusion to Ps 110 in 2.33 is unlike any other in the literature we are considering with the exception of Acts 5.31. The use of *hypsoun* suggests that in Jesus' enthronement he himself is passive and God is the active agent.[82]

This appearance of relative passivity is connected with the problem of what if any function the exalted Christ has in Luke's theological framework. Christ gives the Spirit to the church, but this he has in turn received from the Father (vs 33). Through him men receive forgiveness and salvation (e.g., Acts 2.38; 4.12). Yet in a major way Luke seems to imply that Jesus' kingdom will begin only with the parousia (22.29-30; Acts 1.6-7).[83] Acts represents the exalted Christ as

[82] In contrast to Heb 1.3; 8.1; 10.12; 12.2, "Mk" 16.19, every citation of Ps 110.1*b* in Luke-Acts implies that the session is initiated by God rather than by Jesus. Conzelmann (*Apostelgeschichte*, 30) rightly sees here a subordinationist tendency. Certain scholars have urged that Acts 2.33 and 5.31 allude to Ps 118.16 (OG) rather than to Ps 110.1 since *tē dexia* is instrumental rather than local (e.g., A. Wikenhauser, *Die Apostelgeschichte* [*Regensburger Neues Testament*; Regensburg: Pustet 1961], 46; cf Dodd, *Scriptures*, 99). Such an interpretation is not impossible, but several considerations make it unlikely. An instrumental reading would simply underscore something already plain, viz., that God rather than Jesus is the active agent in the exaltation (cf Wilckens, *Missionsreden*, 151). By contrast, the quasi-spatial sense which results from taking it as a dative of place has clear significance in both verses, defining the character of the exaltation as heavenly. Finally, it seems most natural to relate the *tē dexia* of 2.33 to the *ek dexion mou* of 2.34. Cf E. Haenchen, *Die Apostelgeschichte* (Meyer, 1959), 145 and n. 6. Lindars (*Apologetic*, 171) suggests that both Pss 110 and 118 lie behind Acts 2.33 and 5.31. See further G. Bertram, TWNT 8,607 f n. 34.

[83] The allusions to Christ's kingdom in Lk 1.33 and 19.38 are emphatic but vague about the time of its inception. Cf Lk 23.2, 35-39; Acts 13.21-23; 17.7. On the general Lucan conception of a withdrawal and relative passivity of the exalted Christ during the present age, see H. J. Cadbury, "Acts and Eschatology," *The Background of the NT and Its Eschatology* (Festschrift C. H. Dodd), ed. W. D. Davies and D. Daube (Cambridge: Univ. Press, 1954), 305; Conzelmann, *Luke*, 176 f; Haenchen, *Apostelgeschichte*, 82 f. H. Flender (*St. Luke: Theologian of Redemptive History*, ET R. H. and I. Fuller [Philadelphia: Fortress, 1967], 102) describes the Lucan conception as one of a present reign of Christ which will become visible only at the end of time. On the special tradition expressed in Acts 3.20-21, see J. A. T. Robinson, *Twelve NT Studies* (SBT 34; London: SCM, 1962), 147 f, 151 f; R. F. Zehnle, *Peter's Pentecost Discourse*, 93 f. On the wider question of primitive christological strata representing the exalted Jesus as inactive, see esp. Fuller, *Foundations*, 154, 158 f, 166 f, 173 f, 243; Schweizer, *Lordship*, 57 and n. 3; Hahn, *Titles*, 161-68; R. Leivestad, *Christ the Conqueror* (London: S.P.C.K., 1954), 283 f.

guiding events only to a very limited degree; usually God the Father is represented as the one in control.[84] Luke-Acts often applies the *kyrios* title to Jesus, but not in a cosmological sense.[85] Certainly he is not a king of a sort to threaten Caesar's order.[86] Probably during the interim between resurrection and parousia Luke conceived of Jesus as lord in the sense of ruling over the church as its recognized savior.[87] The church is inspired and directed by the Holy Spirit, but Luke never hints that the Spirit and the risen Christ are one.[88]

The theme of Peter's speech in Acts 2 is not the work of the exalted Christ but the vindication implied by his exaltation. In the beginning (2.22-24) and conclusion (2.36) Peter stresses that Jesus was condemned by men but glorified by God. His acquittal was revealed in the event of his resurrection-exaltation-enthronement. Ps 110 is used as a medium for describing the event (vs 33) and as an inspired text for confirming it (vss 34-36).[89] Secondarily the exaltation of Christ (and the scriptural texts cited) constitute a vindication of Jesus' disciples (cf 2.12-15).

The idea of the defense of Christians comes more to the fore in *Acts 5.31*, where the citation of Ps 110.1*b* appears in a reply of Peter and his fellow disciples to the accusation of the high priest that they have broken the command not to preach in Jesus' name. The burden of the whole reply in 5.29-32 is the necessity of yielding not to the will of man but to that of God (as made known in the events of Christ's death and resurrection). Indeed, the theme of the ineluctability of the divine will seems dominant throughout the chapter. Ananias and his wife cannot stand against it (5.1-11), prison walls cannot obstruct

[84] Luke designates Jesus as *kyrios* when he summons men to obey him in visions and dreams (Acts 9.5, 10-17, 27; 18.9; 20.8, 10; 22.19; 23.11; 26.15). Christian exorcism may be linked with the title as applied to Jesus (Lk 10.17; Acts 19.13,17).

[85] The formula of Acts 10.36 may originally have expressed cosmological lordship, but nothing in Luke-Acts indicates that the evangelist ascribed such lordship to Jesus. Cf Haenchen, *Apostelgeschichte*, 297.

[86] Cf Conzelmann, *Luke*, 187-89.

[87] The *kyrios* title is linked with Jesus in respect to the substance of the church's faith (Acts 16.31; 20.21), baptism (Acts 8.16), prayer (Acts 7.59-60), and obedience (Lk 6.46; 9.61). Cf Haenchen, *Apostelgeschichte*, 82 f; Conzelmann, *Luke*, 176-84.

[88] On the work of the Spirit, see, e.g., Acts 1.8; 5.3; 8.29; 10.19; 11.12; 13.2; 15.28; 16.6-7.

[89] Zehnle (*Discourse*, 34) calls attention to a special indication of the importance of Ps 110.1 in this speech. Luke does not quote the last line of Ps 16.8-11 ("at your [God's] right hand are pleasures forever") in Acts 2.28. Almost certainly this reflects a deliberate decision of Luke to connect God's right hand not only with Jesus' exaltation but specifically with Ps 110.1.

it (5.17-21a), and the apostles' opponents would do well to fear opposing it (5.35-39). When Peter and his fellows proclaim that the Jewish leaders caused Jesus' death, they do so not to incite the vengeance of God or man on those leaders but to bring them to repentance.[90] They, and all the hearers of the apostolic message, should realize that in killing Jesus they opposed God. The disciples must obey God rather than man, and so must the Jewish leaders! Thus the speech of the disciples concludes as it began with the theme of obedience to God (5.32).

The allusion to Ps 110.1*b* in 5.31 is plain enough in view of Acts 2.33-36. The main force of the reference seems one of expressing God's vindication of the Jesus whom men condemned to death. At the same time, this exaltation means not only that God approved of Jesus but also that through Jesus repentance and forgiveness are possible.[91] Like Acts 2.31-36, 5.30-31 implies that no sharp distinction is being drawn between Jesus' resurrection and his exaltation to the right hand. Acts 5.32 confirms this by suggesting that witnesses of the resurrection may be considered witnesses of the exaltation. What the disciples mean by saying that the Spirit is a witness also to these things, including the heavenly SESSION of Christ, is not wholly clear. Perhaps the reader is to recall the quite special connection stated in the Pentecost speech (2.33), though of course the Jewish rulers could not be presumed to be familiar with that statement. More likely, 5.32 means only that the work of the Spirit, evident in the words and miracles of the apostles (as well as their deliverance from prison), confirms the truth of what they say.

Acts 7.55-56 is difficult to interpret largely because it appears to incorporate a peculiar stratum of pre-Lucan tradition. It is fairly clear that the author of Acts interpolated his account of Stephen's speech into a narrative in which the statement of 6.15 was followed directly by the report of his vision.[92] Secondly, the term "son of man" occurs in Acts only in 7.56, and here for the only time in the NT on the lips of someone other than Jesus. Despite indications that Luke found significance in the parallelism of the trials of Jesus and Stephen, it is more plausible to assume that this phrase originated in pre-

[90] Cf Acts 5.28, 30-31, and 3.17-19.

[91] Cf Haenchen, *Apostelgeschichte*, 206; Wilckens, *Missionsreden*, 175 f.

[92] The sequence between the transfiguration of Stephen's face and his looking into heaven is broken. See M. Dibelius, *Studies in the Acts of the Apostles*, ET M. Ling (London: SCM, 1956), 168.

Lucan tradition than in an effort on Luke's part to correlate the vision with Jesus' affirmation to the sanhedrin (Lk 22.69).[93] Further, the assertion that Jesus was standing rather than sitting at God's right hand is unparalleled in the literature from the NT age, and, since nothing here or elsewhere in Luke-Acts explains the significance of the standing posture, the contention of Bauernfeind that this element derives from tradition is persuasive.[94] The term *ouranos* in 7.55 fits Lucan usage, but *ouranoi* of 7.56 does not; this suggests that the latter expression is pre-Lucan.[95] Finally, the sheer redundancy of 7.56 coming after 7.55 is striking and is most readily explained if one assumes that Luke took over most or all of 7.56 from a source. Acts 7.55 can then be taken as from Luke's own hand, prefaced to 7.56 for explanatory reasons.[96]

The significance which Luke attached to Stephen's vision and the allusion to Ps 110.1*b* can be inferred with reasonable assurance. Basically it means the vindication of Jesus and his vindication of Stephen. Jesus is the righteous one whom the Jewish leaders betrayed and killed (7.52). That he now is at the right hand of God means that God has exalted him to that station. The similarities between this account of Stephen and the gospel reports of Jesus' passion have often been remarked—particularly the charge of attacking the temple (Acts 6.13 = Mk 14.58) and the prayer for forgiveness (Acts 7.60 = Lk 23.34). Yet we should also emphasize that the decisive confession of Stephen expresses the same thought as Jesus' trial confession: his glory at God's right hand. Acts 7.56 is the most distinctively Christian statement in all of Stephen's words to the council, and it is not until this word is spoken that his enemies rush upon him.[97] The vision must be regarded as a miraculous revelation granted Stephen to confirm

[93] Cf Tödt, *Son of Man*, 274-76.

[94] Cited in Haenchen, *Apostelgeschichte*, 243 n. 2. See further J. Bihler, *Die Stephanusgeschichte* (Münchener Theologische Studien 16; Munich: Hueber, 1963), 24.

[95] So Tödt, *Son of Man*, 276.

[96] Acts 7.55 explains the vision in terms of a special momentary fullness of the Spirit in Stephen and tells the reader that the son of man (vs 7.56) is Jesus. The phrase about God's glory may be added to present the tautology of 7.56 from being too tedious; it has no other obvious function.

[97] As elsewhere in Acts, a Christian speech is interrupted at a point determined not by historical probabilities but by Luke's literary and theological purposes. Cf Haenchen, *Apostelgeschichte*, 246. By means of the allusion to Ps 110.1, Luke expresses his conviction that the first (and manifestly exemplary) Christian martyr died as a result of confessing the resurrection-exaltation of Jesus.

him in his faith and (through his reporting of it) to inform his hearers that his entire speech has heaven's approval.

What does Jesus do while at the right hand of God? The specification that he was standing is so unusual that we can hardly doubt that it has special meaning,[98] although Luke-Acts provides no firm clues as to what that meaning might be. The answer to this question lies in the twilight zone of pre-Lucan tradition. Hence we can speak only of a spectrum of possibilities.[99] One is that the standing reflects an idea of Jesus as an angelic being, situated before God's throne as one among many divine beings; such a primitive christological view might claim support from Dan 7.10,13.[100] A second possibility, perhaps the most plausible, is that Jesus rises from his throne to welcome Stephen into heaven (cf Lk 16.9). This interpretation could fit Lucan theology as well as the pre-Lucan tradition since the evangelist elsewhere suggests that true believers do not wait for the end of the world before joining Jesus in heaven.[101] A third possibility is that Jesus rises from his divine throne to execute judgment on his foes in his parousia. Stephen's vision is then an eschatological one, foreshadowing the imminent return of Christ. Such an interpretation seems at odds at least with Luke's general eschatological orientation, according to which one would not at all expect the end of the world to follow soon after Stephen's martyrdom.[102] It is problematic even as an interpretation

[98] Dodd (*Scriptures*, 35 n. 1) and Lindars (*Apologetic*, 42 n. 2) dispute this on the ground that *hestanai* often has simply the sense "to be situated." Yet insofar as Jesus' place at the right hand was consciously related to Ps 110.1b (as it clearly was in Luke's case), the psalm text's *kathou* would in all likelihood preclude the casual use of a verb suggesting a standing posture.

[99] See the list in Haenchen, *Apostelgeschichte*, 243 n. 2. Cf C. K. Barrett, "Stephen," 32-35; Bihler, *Stephanusgeschichte*, 131-34.

[100] Cf Bihler, *Stephanusgeschichte*, 24 f. Philo repeatedly cites Deut 5.31 and once interprets God's command to Moses to "stand by me" as indicative of the latter's sharing in the divine nature (*Post* 28). Cf *Gig* 49; *Deus* 23-25. C. Colpe (TWNT 8,466 f) notes Philo's use of *ho hestōs* for God (*Som* 1.246) and raises the intriguing possibility that Acts 7.55-56 is connected with a Samaritan predicate for God. M. H. Scharlemann (*Stephen: a Singular Saint* [Analecta Biblica 34; Rome: Pontifical Biblical Institute, 1968], 15 f) urges that Samaritan ideas about Moses as an intercessor and lord are alluded to by this reference to the son of man standing in Acts 7. The suggestion is highly speculative, but possible.

[101] Lk 16.19-31; 23.43. Barrett ("Stephen," 32-38) suggests that Luke has deliberately worked out an individualistic eschatology: the death of every Christian is to be marked by "a private and personal *parousia* of the Son of Man." He notes the Jewish idea of Elijah as a psychopomp. Cf Iren *Her* 1.30.14 (1.28.7).

[102] This line of interpretation has been pressed vigorously by H. P. Owen ("Stephen's Vision in Acts vii. 55-6," NTS 1 [1954-55], 224-26), who posits a six-stage series of events between Jesus' death and parousia. The discrimination of the

in the pre-Lucan tradition since the context lacks definite evidence that Stephen's vision is eschatological.[103] A fourth possibility is suggested by Lk 12.8: Jesus rises in the heavenly courtroom to act as a witness on Stephen's behalf.[104] This interpretation would essentially be only a special form of the view that 7.55-56 shows heaven's vindication of Stephen.[105]

Some concluding observations may be offered on the references to Ps 110 in Luke-Acts. In all of them, the idea of vindication is dominant. Each allusion or quotation is part of the testimony of believers to unbelievers. The unbelievers refuse to credit the claim that Jesus is the messiah. But, say the believers (in Acts), he is at the right hand of God and of this we have proof (Acts 2.31-36: the apostles as witnesses of the resurrection, the scriptural prophecies, the coming of the Spirit; Acts 5.32: the apostles and the Spirit as witnesses; Acts 7.55-56: the vision granted Stephen). That Ps 110.1b has been fulfilled in Jesus means that he is in fact God's messiah.

In *1 Pet 3.22* the right-hand position of Jesus is spoken of simply as present fact, with the implication that he gained it with or immediately following his resurrection and ascension ("having gone into heaven"). The parousia will reveal his glory (1.7; 4.13), but there is no suggestion in this epistle that the glory itself will ever change. Although the hymn from which the author took this allusion coupled it with a stress on the subjection of angelic powers, the author never speaks of that subjection elsewhere; and perhaps 5.8 is inconsistent with it. Again, despite pleas that his readers mold their lives according to the will of Jesus as lord (1.3; 3.15; 5.4), Jesus is not in this epistle generally represented as the active ruler of his church. Certainly the power and sovereignty of God the Father are much more frequently mentioned (e.g., 1.3; 5.6,10).[106] Within the thought of the epistle as a whole, the primary import of Jesus' glorification at God's right hand appears to be its proof of his vindication by God despite the condemnation and suffering imposed on him by men (2.4; 3.18). It attests his righteousness and their injustice and hence is a proleptic ex-

---

"standing" stage seems particularly precarious, based as it is on this single difficult text.

[103] Cf Tödt, *Son of Man*, 304 f.

[104] On this mode of interpretation, see below, pp. 132-33.

[105] Cf Hooker, *Son of Man*, 197; R. Pesch, *Die Vision des Stephanus* (Stuttgarter Bibelstudien 12; Stuttgart: Katholisches Bibelwerk, 1966), 54.

[106] Cf F. W. Beare, *The First Epistle of Peter*, 3rd ed. (Oxford: Blackwell, 1970), 51-54.

pression of God's final judgment, a subject of special concern to the epistle's author. In harmony with this interpretation is the declaration that to believe in Christ's glory is to believe in God, who gave it to him (1.21).

The allusion to Ps 110.1*b* in *Eus EH 2.23.13* is embedded in the narrative of the martyrdom of James transmitted by Hegesippus. While the account is plainly legendary, it nonetheless provides important evidence about the beliefs of the Jewish Christians who created the legend.[107] According to this story, James, the brother of Jesus and head of the Jerusalem church, was asked by Jewish leaders to stand on the battlement of the temple and dissuade the people from straying after Jesus. His entire speech is as follows:

Why do you ask me concerning the son of man? He is sitting in heaven on the right hand of the great Power and he will come on the clouds of heaven.

The chronicle goes on to say that a number of Jews were persuaded by James's *martyria* to believe in Jesus and that the leaders were thereby persuaded to kill James. Clearly, then, his "testimony" is regarded as a pellucid and sufficient confession of Christian faith.[108] The description of Jesus' exaltation as son of man sitting at God's right and destined to come again seems meant to show God's approval of Jesus in contrast to the rejection of Jesus (or faith in him) by the "scribes and Pharisees," who proceed to murder James. The time of Jesus' enthronement is not indicated. James stresses his present-time exaltation[109] but does not mention any activity of the exalted Christ.[110] The action of Christ which is underlined is his future coming, which Hegesippus elsewhere links with the general resurrection

[107] The legend may have originated in the first half of the second century. For discussion of the historical difficulties of the text and the Ebionite tradition it seems to reflect, see esp. E. Schwarz, "Zu Euseb, KG I. Das Martyrium Jakobus' des Gerechten," ZNW 4 (1903), 48-61; A. Meyer and W. Bauer in H-S 1,419-21.

[108] Cf N. A. Dahl, *Das Volk Gottes*, 2nd ed. (Darmstadt: Wissenschaftliche Buchgesellschaft, 1963), 187 f. Among the hardly coincidental similarities between this passage and the account of Stephen's trial in Acts 7, we may note esp. that both martyr confessions concentrate on the son of man's right-hand exaltation. In its reference to the parousia, James's confession recalls Mt 26.64 rather than Acts 7 (or Lk 22.69).

[109] In contrast to Mk 14.62=Mt 26.64, but like Lk 22.69 and Acts 7.55-56, the confession of James declares that Jesus is now at God's right hand.

[110] Note that James prays not to Jesus but to God (16).

and last judgment (EH 2.23.9; 3.20.4). Like Mk 14.62 and Mt 26.64, this reference to final judgment seems to function above all as a prediction of the future vindication of the witness who has spoken. Hegesippus apparently discerned a proleptic sign of the eschatological vindication (which of course implies condemnation for James's slayers) in Vespasian's assault on Jerusalem (EH 2.23.18).

In *Apoc Pet 6,* Jesus foretells the beginning of the last judgment in the following terms:

> And all will see how I come upon an eternal shining cloud, and the angels of God who will sit with me on the throne of my glory at the right hand of my heavenly Father.[111]

In the Apocalypse of Peter as a whole, the key theme is not the vindication of Jesus or of his church so much as the signs leading up to the parousia and the character of the last judgment (and the resultant punishments and rewards). The purpose of Jesus' enthronement at God's right hand is that he may judge the quick and the dead (1 and 3). No other function is associated with it, and probably the author supposed that Jesus' SESSION would begin only at the great judgment. This is not to suggest that Christ's glorification begins only then. Indeed, in two separate passages in this work Jesus is styled lord and God (16), which implies that he is fully divine even during the period of his incarnation. He is already the king of believers (15) and his ascension into heaven is painted as a triumphal procession of the Son of God leading the righteous (17). His SESSION, then, appears to betoken no new exaltation but only the particular function of the one to whom God commits final judgment. The judgment he pronounces is God's judgment (4, 7, 13), and the Father sets a crown on the Son's head in preparation for the judgment. Christ's heavenly SESSION and judgment obviously manifest the will and glory of God.

A distinctive feature of this reference to Christ's SESSION is that angels are said to share it. Elsewhere documents from the NT age declare that Christ will come with a retinue of angels,[112] but only

[111] Quoted from H-S 2,671 f. The passage displays differences from, as well as similarities to, Mk 14.62=Mt 26.64. Christ now comes on "an eternal shining cloud" instead of "the clouds of heaven," and one may ask if Dan 7.13 is cited at all. The term "throne of my glory" recalls similar phrases in 1 Enoch 45.3; 55.4; 61.8; 62.2-3,5; 69.27,29. Ch. Maurer dates the Apocalypse "around A.D. 135" (H-S 2,664).

[112] E.g., Mk 8.38 (=Mt 16.27=Lk 9.26); Mt 25.31; 2 Thess 1.7. Cf Jude 14; Zech 14.5.

here are they described as sitting with him at God's right hand.[113] If a functional interpretation of Jesus' right-hand SESSION is correct, then probably the SESSION of the angels also points more to their judgmental task than to an increase in their glory (of course the text implies that they do partake of glory). Nothing in the rest of the Apocalypse suggests that the status of the angels approaches that of Christ; their position at his throne signifies rather their participation in the final events: God raises the dead by the hand of Uriel (4), and different angels tally the sins of the wicked, prepare the place of torment, and administer the punishments and rewards meted out to mankind. Christ alone pronounces final judgment; they are the executors of it.

A very similar representation of Jesus' SESSION is offered in *Sib Or 2.238-44:*

> But when he raises the dead, loosing the bond of destiny,
> And Sabaoth Adonai the high-thundering shall sit
> On a heavenly throne and establish a great pillar,
> There shall come on a cloud to the eternal, eternal himself,
> Christ in glory with his blameless angels,
> And shall sit on the right hand of Majesty, judging on his throne
> The life of the pious and the ways of impious men.[114]

Here, as in the Apocalypse of Peter (on which it appears to depend),[115] Christ's right-hand SESSION is connected exclusively with the last judgment. To be sure, he comes "in glory" and with a company of angels, but the primary thought is not his exaltation but his work at the great tribunal. In fact the *kathisei* of line 243 makes it even clearer than in Apoc Pet 6 that Jesus' enthronement begins only at the last judgment.

The angels surely take part in some measure in Christ's glory, and yet they are not explicitly said to sit with him. This may be more than accidental since other parts of Books 1 and 2 of the Sibylline Oracles hardly mention angels, let alone emphasize them. On the other hand, the direct role of God in the judgment is stressed here far more than in the Apocalypse of Peter. Many passages in Book 2 read as if God

---

[113] Is there an allusion to Deut 33.2 OG?
[114] Quoted from H-S 2,715 f.
[115] So James, *Apocrypha,* 521. James dates this passage "not early in the second century," but more recently A. Kurfess has argued for an origin around 150 CE (H-S 2,708).

were the only judge (e.g., 2.217-20), and in this allusion to Ps 110.1*b* Christ and God seem to share jointly in the judging. Thus this description of Christ does not at all detract from the glory of God.[116]

Passages Emphasizing Present Exaltation.—A number of references to Christ's SESSION interpret it mainly as a present state existing from the resurrection forward, not connecting it particularly with his second coming. Not even all these references, however, associate the SESSION with governing activity.

Rev 3.21 is something of a borderline case, having strong affinities with the class of citations dwelling on vindication and judgment. It is a borderline case in another respect also, since one cannot be certain that the author intended an allusion to Ps 110.1. Many scholars, however, have urged that such an allusion is present.[117] It is not said here in so many words that Jesus sits beside God, let alone on his right side. But he sits on God's throne and promises that Christians who "conquer" will sit there with him.[118] That this imagery is not meant to be taken too literally or simplistically is suggested by the fact that Revelation often depicts the heavenly Christ not seated but standing.[119] God is often designated as *ho kathēmenos epi tou thronou* (4.2,9,10; 5.1,7,13; 6.16; 7.10,15; 19.4; 21.5).[120] In chap. 5 Christ is described as a lamb standing *en mesō tou thronou* (cf 7.17), and he goes to God's right hand to take the scroll (5.7; cf 5.1). Here, too, allusion to Ps 110.1*b* might be suspected.[121]

The connotations of Jesus' place on God's throne are rich and complex. Rev 3.21 clearly means to emphasize his glorification after death. The enthronement was a kind of reward granted him for his faithfulness. Of course the prophet regards Jesus' glory as uniquely like God's (5.12-13), but in 3.21 the promise of similar honor is held out to

[116] Sib Or 2 is certainly based on an older Jewish poem and the distinctively Christian lines in it are few. The stress on God as judge is therefore natural. Lines 241-43 mention only "Christ" (not "Jesus Christ"); one wonders if these, too, might not be pre-Christian (perhaps related to the picture of the son of man in 1 Enoch).

[117] E.g., Str-B 4,452; E. Lohmeyer, *Die Offenbarung des Johannes*, 2nd ed. (HNT, 1953), 40; Cullmann, *Christology*, 223; Leivestad, *Christ*, 292.

[118] Note that in 22.1,3 the throne belongs to both God and the Lamb. Cf 12.5. In 3.21 God's throne is also "my throne."

[119] E.g., 5.6; 14.1. Further instances of his sitting, one clearly connected with his parousia, are 19.11 and 14.14. See T. Holtz, *Die Christologie der Apokalypse des Johannes* (TU 85, 1962), 129, 130, and n. 2.

[120] Does Rev 20.11 refer to Christ or to God?

[121] Str-B 4,452; C. Spicq, *L'Epître aux Hébreux* 2 (Paris: Lecoffre, 1952-55), 205 n. 2. Cf Acts 7.55-56!

church members. The symbol of a throne in Revelation also connotes ruling power. Christ, together with God, rules from the heavenly throne. Their government is especially effective or manifest in the series of divine judgments which mark the end of the present world order (11.15). The beginning of the millennial reign of Christ and his saints is also depicted in terms of enthronement (20.4), and this reign consists mainly or exclusively in judgment. Likewise the appearance of the lamb at God's right in chap. 5 signals the breaking forth of divine judgment on earth (6.1 ff). Thus the power symbolized by Christ's sharing of God's throne is primarily connected with eschatological judgment. The exaltation of Christ is bound together with his death through the complex idea of victory (*enikēsa*[122]). Jesus gained his triumph through faithful witness to the point of death, and believers may conquer on the dual basis of his death and their own similar witness (12.11). His death conditions not only his own exaltation to the divine throne but also the church's hope for deliverance and for the judgment of the world.[123]

Polycarp's allusion to Ps 110.1b is also linked with emphatic teaching about the last judgment and the church's hope of resurrection and mercy from the God "who raised up our Lord Jesus Christ from the dead and gave him glory and a throne at his right hand" (Pol *Phil* 2.1). For Polycarp this throne of Christ connotes his power to govern and judge. The two relative clauses which are subjoined to the allusion—"to whom all things in heaven and earth are subjected" and "whom everything that breathes serves"—are evidently intended to interpret it. The notion of the subjugation of enemies is not explicitly present in the context, but the sequence of clauses implies a connection between the present SESSION and Christ's future office as "judge of the living and the dead." Polycarp does not say flatly that Jesus will judge on the last day while still sitting at God's right, but it is clear that his future office as judge is simply an extension of the dominion he has now while so seated. God and Jesus are apparently thought of as ruling jointly over world and church (cf 5.2-3; 6.2; 12.2). It is God who gave Christ his honor and power, but Christ's position does not seem to be less than that of an equal. Later in the epistle Christ is called "the eternal high priest" who builds up the

---

[122] Cf esp. Jn 16.33; 1 Jn 5.4. See Holtz, *Christologie*, 36-39; O. Bauernfeind, TWNT 4,943-45 (=TDNT 4,942-45).

[123] Cf Bultmann, *Theology* 2,174. On the relation between God's rule and Christ's, see Holtz, *Christologie*, 183-85, 202 f.

church according to its prayers (12.2). Evidently Polycarp means that Jesus acts as priest as well as lord while sitting at God's right hand.

The solemn christological affirmations in *1 Clem 36,* which conclude with a quotation of Ps 110.1*b-c,* are symptomatically preceded and followed by teaching about the glory and requirements of God the Father. Jesus' glory is generally defined in this epistle in relation to the Father's. Although Christ is here called "the high priest of our offerings, the protector and helper of our weakness," what seems most important to Clement is that through him "we see mirrored God's pure and sublime face." Christ is the supreme revealer of God's saving purpose and demands.[124] As in Hebrews, the servant posture of the angels (Ps 104.4—Heb 1.7) is a foil for the lordly status of the Son. That status, described in Pss 2.7-8 and 110.1, is one of rank (the Son, seated at God's right) and dominion ("I will give the nations for your inheritance and the ends of the earth for your keeping," "I make your enemies your footstool"). Both quotations, however, stress the work of God. The future dominion Clement envisages is presumably the conversion of all mankind, at least to the point of recognizing God, the savior, and the elect (59.4). Despite his reliance on Jewish traditions and natural theology, Clement's thought and piety center in Jesus as savior.[125] Nevertheless, he does not emphasize any idea of the exalted Christ exercising a ruling office over the world in general or over the church.[126] He characteristically calls God, not Christ, the great *despotēs* of the universe (e.g., 8.2; 20.8; 33.2; 61.1-2; 64.1). Perhaps he thought of church members as governed by both Father and Son,[127] but he usually speaks only of the Father as the one whom Christians must obey.[128] Even the foes mentioned in Ps 110.1*c* seem to be viewed as God's rather than Christ's.[129]

[124] Cf A. W. Ziegler, *Neue Studien zum ersten Klemensbrief* (Munich: Manz, 1958), 47 f.

[125] Cf A. von Harnack, *Einführung in die Alte Kirchengeschichte: Das Schreiben der römischen Kirche an die korinthische aus der Zeit Domitians (I. Clemensbrief)* (Leipzig: Hinrichs, 1929), 72-75; Ziegler, *Studien,* 46 f.

[126] While Christ (like God the Father) is styled *kyrios* (e.g., 16.2; 20.11; 32.2; 64.1), his lordship seems to be regularly connected with redemption, not with creation or government. The precise meaning of "scepter of the majesty of God" (16.2) is unclear.

[127] Note the "commandments of Christ" (49.1); cf 2.1.

[128] E.g., 14.1; 48.1; 56.1; 58.2. The solitary mention of Christ's kingdom (50.3) is textually uncertain and in any event concerns the last judgment, not the present age.

[129] So, e.g., R. M. Grant, "First Clement," in *The Apostolic Fathers,* ed. Grant, 2 (New York: Nelson, 1965), 64.

The declarations about Christ's majesty in chap. 36 balance others which dwell on his earthly meekness (especially those in chap. 16). Still, the SESSION in heaven does not appear to be conceived as a reward granted Jesus after death. Clement presupposes Christ's pre-existence and writes about the divine power which he possessed but refrained from using during his earthly life (*kaiper dynamenos* 16.2). Possibly, then, Clement supposed that even before the incarnation Christ had a glory akin to that of the SESSION. At all events he never indicates when that exaltation began or when, if ever, it will cease.[130] For him Ps 110.1 is essentially an expression of the present glory of Christ as savior of the church.

The allusion to Ps 110.1 in the "longer ending" of Mark at *"Mk" 16.19* portrays the actual events of ascension and enthronement.[131] The writer distinguishes both from the resurrection, which, however, is evidently regarded as the first stage of his divine glorification. There is no distinct reference to parousia or last judgment (16.16 notwithstanding), and so it is impossible to say whether the author of this "ending" expected that Jesus' SESSION would ever terminate. Despite the brevity of the allusion, it bears several meanings. First, the enthronement beside God clearly is regarded as expressive of the glory of "the Lord Jesus." Secondly, along with the ascension it marks the conclusion of his speaking with the disciples and of the resurrection appearances generally. Yet, thirdly, 16.19-20 represent Jesus as simultaneously seated in heaven and actively furthering the labors of his disciples on earth. His work is manifested in miracles which accompany their preaching in fulfillment of the promise of 16.17-18. The implication is that the enthronement of Jesus symbolizes the power (or omnipotence) whereby he accomplishes his will in regard to the church, the hostile powers (16.17-18), and the world (16.15—"all creation"). The major concern of Mk 16.9-20, apart from that of describing appearances and ascension, seems to be one of showing how those events led to the overcoming of unbelief.[132] The signs which attend the apostolic preaching are meant to "confirm" their message. Thus

---

[130] This is related to the decline of futuristic eschatology in the epistle. Cf Harnack, *Schreiben*, 75.

[131] The "longer ending" of Mark cannot be dated with precision, but it may be presumed to have come into existence about 150 CE. Such a date is indicated by a citation in Irenaeus (*Her* 3.10.6 [3.11.6]), the use of the "ending" in Tatian (Arabic version), and a possible allusion in Justin (*Apol* 45).

[132] Within this brief composition *pisteuein* occurs four times, *apistein* twice, and *apistia* once.

the heavenly SESSION is again linked with the idea of vindication, though here it is chiefly the gospel message which is vindicated. Also, the vindication is given not to unbelievers especially but to persons willing to hear the disciples (as well as to the disciples themselves). Again, the vindication is given through earthly miracles, not through the resurrection-ascension itself, a vision of Jesus in heaven, or the parousia. Furthermore the glory of God (as distinct from that of Christ) receives no notice in the whole of Mk 16.9-20, despite the passive *anelēmphthē*[133] and the mention of God's right hand in 16.19. Throughout the passage Christ is described as the initiator of events, and it is in harmony with this that 16.19 represents him as actively taking his heavenly throne (*ekathisen*).[134]

In the Nag Hammadi *Apocryphon of James* we find a quite similar picture, one in which Jesus is described as ascending to his heavenly place at the right hand after an extended period of instructing disciples (550 days!). He tells them:

> But now I am about to ascend to the place (*topos*)
> whence I came.
>
> . . . .
>
> But observe the glory that awaits
> me and when you have opened
> your hearts listen to the hymns
> that await me above in the heavens.
> For it is necessary for me today to
> occupy (the) right side of my Father.
> But I have spoken to you the last word.
> I shall be separated from you.
> For a chariot (*harma*) of spirit took me up
> (14.20-34).[135]

In this text, which may date from the second quarter of the second century,[136] Jesus' PLACE is evidently a heavenly situation which he

---

[133] The appearance of passive forms of *analambanein* in 1 Tim 3.16 and Acts 1.2,11,22 suggests that it had become a stereotyped expression for the ascension, one not necessarily stressing the activity of God the Father.

[134] The wording of Heb 2.4, which emphasizes the direct working of God the Father, may usefully be compared with "Mk" 16.19-20.

[135] This and all other quotations of the Apocryphon are from the translation of M. Malinine *et al., Epistula Iacobi Aprocrypha* (Zurich: Rascher, 1968). On the unusual expression "occupy the right side," see Malinine *et al., Epistula,* 75. The "chariot of spirit" recalls the story of Elijah and the description of Job's ascent to his right-hand throne in the Testament of Job (see above, p. 23).

[136] So W. C. van Unnik, "The Origin of the Recently Discovered 'Apocryphon Jacobi,'" *Vigiliae Christianae* 10 (1956), 156. H.-C. Puech (in Malinine *et al.,*

had before his earthly career and simply resumes after his ascension. That ascension signifies not only his resumption of divine glory but also the conclusion of his post-resurrection revelations. Peter and James are allowed to follow Jesus into heaven in ecstasy and to hear the hymns and rejoicings with which he is welcomed into the celestial regions (15.5-28). They then return to the other disciples and report:

> He has ascended.
> He gave us a pledge (*dexia*) and
> promised life to us all (15.35-37).

The fact that this parting pledge is expressed with *dexia* suggests that Jesus' PLACE is also a token of the salvation made possible through him.

The References in Hebrews.—Most of the quotations and allusions in Hebrews have affinities in function with references to Ps 110.1 in other early Christian writings. Yet they merit consideration as a separate group since this epistle may be considered the crowning document for the study of the early church's use of the psalm—quite apart from its extraordinary interpretations of Ps 110.4. The writer of Hebrews refers to Ps 110.1 more often than any other author in the NT era and gives it several important meanings. Some elements of his interpretation are unique and probably originated with him.

The unusual weight to be put on Ps 110 in the epistle is suggested at the outset by the prominence of two references in the majestic opening chapter. The allusion in *Heb 1.3* is the epistle's first distinct reference to Jewish scriptures, and grammatically it forms the main assertion of 1.3-4.[137] The quotation in 1.13 climaxes a series of scriptural testimonies to the Son's exaltation.[138] The theme of the whole chapter, and the fundamental meaning here given to the SESSION, is the unparalleled glory of the Son. Presumably the use of *megalōsynē* in 1.3 is designed to exhibit the Son's greatness (as well as to

---

Epistula xxx) thinks this dating questionable, but agrees with van Unnik that Egypt was probably the place of origin.

[137] Cf J. Moffatt, *The Epistle to the Hebrews* (ICC, 1924), 1.

[138] Heb 1.3, 13 seems to illustrate a tendency of the author's literary style, the framing of a section of the epistle by the repetition of a theme or key words. A. Vanhoye calls this "inclusion" (*La structure littéraire de l'Epître aux Hébreux* [Studia Neotestamentica 1; Paris: Desclée de Brouwer, 1963]). Although 1.5-14 has the general appearance of a repetition (with scriptural proofs) of the ideas of 1.1-4, the SESSION is the only specific image expressed twice in the chapter.

mitigate the anthropomorphic connotations of Ps 110.1b^{139}). His glory is ontological and in a sense eternal (1.2-3a); yet the author also seems to maintain that only after his earthly career and death did he enter on perfect glory, a state portrayed first by the heavenly enthronement, then by the acquisition of a name above every other (1.3b-4).[140] A cosmic enthronement schema, not originally Christian, apparently underlies the account of the sitting down on the divine throne, the proclamation of the enthronement name (1.4) and rank (1.5), the call for angelic obeisance (1.6), and the repetition of the announcement of exaltation (1.8-13).[141] As direct scriptural testimony to this heavenly enthronement event, Ps 110.1 was invaluable to the author of Hebrews.

Whether or not he kept in mind Ps 110.1a (which he never cites), the writer of Hebrews certainly regarded vs 1b as an invitation addressed directly to the Son by God. The scriptural quotations in Heb 1 are presented as a succession of divine words which the church on earth, as it were, overhears.[142] Ps 110.1b-c is part of the colloquy between God and the Son: as the course of Christ's earthly career is set by his words to God (10.5-7), so his enthronement is accomplished by God's word to him. In 1.3 Jesus is described as seating himself (similarly 8.1; 10.12-13; 12.2), but 1.13 explains that he does so by God's will.[143] The glorification of the Son in Heb 1 constantly points back to the glory of God.[144] It is especially noteworthy that the enthronement of the Son does not seem to imply government. Despite an allusion to the kingdom of the Son (1.8) and one to Melchizedek's kingship (7.1-2), Hebrews never represents the exalted Christ as ruler or judge.[145] His role in sustaining the world is men-

---

[139] So Windisch *Hebräerbrief*, 12, who cites T Levi 3.9 as a parallel. Similar circumlocutions are used in Heb 8.1; 12.2.

[140] On the tensions in the author's christology, which may indicate use of differing traditions, see esp. Windisch, *Hebräerbrief*, 13.

[141] Similar enthronement descriptions are presented in Phil 2.9-11; 1 Tim 3.16; Rev 4-5. See esp. J. Jeremias, *Die Briefe an Timotheus und Titus* (NTD, 1947), 20-22; Käsemann, *Gottesvolk*, 58-71; Michel, *Hebräer*, 116 f.

[142] Cf M. Barth, "The Old Testament in Hebrews," in *Current Issues in New Testament Interpretation*, ed. W. Klassen and G. F. Synder (New York: Harper, 1962), 62.

[143] Likewise in 5.9-10 Jesus is said to have become the source of salvation through his obedience, but this exaltation is also derived from the decree of God (Ps 110.4).

[144] Cf Spicq (*Hébreux* 1,325): the theology of Hebrews is theocentric, not christocentric.

[145] In Heb 7 Christ is compared to Melchizedek not because the latter was king but because he was a priest of whose order marvelous things might be said. Cf

tioned (1.3), but he is not called its master. The angels are inferiors who worship him, but they are not called his servants. Christians have received an eschatological kingdom (12.28), but this idea is not developed nor is it linked with notions of reigning with Christ now or in the future.[146] It seems plain that for the author of Hebrews the ruler of angels, church, and universe is God alone.[147]

The third citation of Ps 110.1 in Hebrews (8.1) appears in the heart of a transitional passage joining the two main parts of the priestly exposition, the first (4.14–5.10; 6.20–7.25) focused on Jesus' priestly rank, the second (8.3–10.25) on his priestly work. As 7.28 draws together the themes of priesthood and sonship, so 8.1 unites those of priesthood and heavenly SESSION. The closing words of 8.1, "in the heavens," suggest the principal concern of this particular citation. The SESSION is recalled now not for its connotation of supreme honor but for its implication that Jesus is located in the celestial sanctuary. This is an essential part of the author's sacerdotal argument: not only does that location show afresh Jesus' superiority to levitical priests; without that heavenly situation he would not be priest at all (8.4). Since the writer appeals to no other scriptural verse to support the conception of Christ's location in heaven, it may not be too much to regard Ps 110.1 as a crucial foundation stone for the two-sanctuary reasoning adumbrated in verses like 4.14, 6.20, 7.26 and elaborated in chaps. 8–10.[148]

In Heb 10.12, by contrast, attention is centered not on where Jesus sits but simply on the fact that he sits. As the context makes plain, this allusion is inserted to support the thesis that Christ completed his sacrificial work once for all in his death. But that single act "he has perfected for all time those who are sanctified" (10.14).[149] By the laws of the old covenant, priests stand daily offering sacrifice;

H. Braun, Qumran und das Neue Testament 1 (Tübingen: Mohr, 1966), 277.

[146] At most, in view of Heb 2.5 ff, one might say Jesus' right-hand SESSION shows that he is destined to be ruler of the future world. Cf Käsemann, Gottesvolk, 77.

[147] So also Moffatt, Hebrews, xxxiii; J. H. Davies, "The Heavenly Work of Christ in Hebrews," Studia Evangelica 4.1, ed. F. L. Cross (TU 102, 1968), 386, 388. Otherwise: Michel, Hebräer, 101 f, 287.

[148] Of course there were other foundation stones, some below the surface. T. Levi 5.1-2; 8.1-17 offers a strong parallel in the depiction of Levi (related to Melchizedek) who is given royal and priestly office in a heavenly temple where God is enthroned. Cf Widengren, "Ideology," 202 f.

[149] The death of Jesus is connected very closely in this epistle with his exaltation into heaven, and his sacrifice seems to be understood as both an earthly and a heavenly event. Cf Käsemann, Gottesvolk, 150.

but, by the terms of the new, Jesus sits because no more sacrifices are needed. The expansion in 10.13 of the psalm verse's *heōs an* into *to loipon ekdechomenos heōs* both calls attention to this part of the psalm verse and interprets it as denoting a waiting period. Like Paul in 1 Cor 15.25, the author finds here a text for the period between Jesus' resurrection and his final return. Yet he describes Christ not as actively subduing his foes but as sitting motionless. Thus Ps 110.1 is brought in here for the sole purpose of demonstrating that Jesus' priestly task has been fulfilled. A second argument from scripture, running to the same conclusion, is presented in 10.15-18: God has granted complete forgiveness (through Jesus' death), and therefore men require no further offerings. Now the full meaning of the allusion in Heb 1.3 becomes clear: "when he had (for all time) made purification for sins, he sat down."

Heb 12.2 discloses yet another facet of the meaning which Ps 110.1 had for this author, its hortatory significance. This is the only citation of the psalm which the author does not set in a doctrinal passage. Heb 12.1-2 forms the rhetorical capstone to the exposition of chap. 11 and a bridge into the direct admonitions of 12.3-29.[150] Jesus is the supreme exemplar of faith and obedient sonship (12.3; cf 5.7-10; 10.5-10). A consensus exists among recent interpreters that a chief theological motif of Hebrews is the conception of believers as the people of God, wandering like ancient Israel between promise and fulfillment, between the exodus and the "rest" in the promised land.[151] The heroes of faith in Heb 11 are brought forward as persons who faithfully sought God's city, and the terms "run the race" and "pioneer" in 12.1-2 show the continuation of the motif of the pilgrim people. The regular corollary of this theme in Hebrews is that Jesus, like Joshua and Moses, is the leader of God's people, the pioneer who goes before them to blaze the trail.[152] Those saints did not reach the perfection they sought (11.16-19, 39-40), but Jesus has been perfected (Heb 1; 2.5-9; 5.7-10) and has sat down. The perfect tense of *kekathiken* contrasting with the aorist *hypemeinen* indicates that, while the suffering of Jesus was a once-for-all event of the past, his heavenly SESSION is past, present, and future.[153]

---

[150] Cf the analyses of Windisch, *Hebräerbrief*, 108 f; Michel, *Hebräer*, 287.

[151] The theme has been most fully explored in Käsemann, *Gottesvolk*. See also Spicq, *Hébreux* 1,269-80.

[152] Cf Windisch, *Hebräerbrief*, 109. On the meaning of "pioneer" and "perfecter" in 12.2, see Michel, *Hebräer*, 431-34.

[153] Spicq, *Hébreux* 2,388. Jesus evidently sits forever or at least until the

Jesus has entered God's rest.[154] As in 10.12, Jesus' sitting posture is emphasized, but now it is contrasted not with the standing of earthly priests or angels but with the race of faith which he has already finished and which his brothers must still run.[155] They are exhorted to "look to Jesus," and this means in part that they are to seek inspiration from meditating on his unique resting at God's right hand.[156] The passage also sets Jesus' present glory over against the hardships and shame of his earthly life. His cross is interpreted as the apogee of his humiliation and sufferings, unique and yet comparable to the sufferings Moses endured (11.26) and the abuse Christians must accept (13.13). His heavenly SESSION seems to be interpreted now as "the joy set before him," a kind of *reward* for his obedience and one which led him to accept his trials.[157] Yet, since Jesus' exaltation is elsewhere shown to be essential for the salvation of man (e.g., Heb. 2.9-10; 5.9-10; 7.29-8.1), probably we should understand that Jesus rejoiced at the prospect of his exaltation partly because he knew that thereby he would bring many brothers to glory.[158]

Some concluding observations about the references to the SESSION in this epistle are in order. All five of them function as testimonies to Jesus' incomparable glory, but each bears a different nuance of meaning. The psalm verse is employed in Heb 1 to show the superiority of Jesus to angels, in Heb 8 and 10 to show his superiority to levitical priests; in Heb 12 it attests the magnitude of his glory but also suggests the glory to which Christians may aspire. The psalm verse's significance and flexibility for the author are again suggested by his linking it with the two chief titles of his christology ("Son" and "priest") and with the concept of Jesus as the leader of the pilgrim people of God. The phrasing of the allusions in each case brings out the key point the author wishes to make: majesty (1.3), location (8.1), inactivity (10.12-13), permanent rest (12.2).

Conclusions.—A red thread running through all the early Christian references to Ps 110.1 is the idea of glory. Jesus' position at God's

---

parousia (9.28).

[154] Cf Windisch, *Hebräerbrief,* 109 f.

[155] Spicq (*Hébreux* 2,388) notes that Jesus' SESSION in 12.2 suggests an athlete's repose after the struggle. Cf Hesiod, *Theogony,* 951-55.

[156] The call to "look to Christ" in his heavenly glory recalls Col 3.1 and Acts 7.55-56. Cf 4 Macc 17.9-10.

[157] Cf 11.26. See Schweizer, *Lordship,* 73; Spicq, *Hébreux* 2,309.

[158] Cf E. Grässer, *Der Glaube im Hebräerbrief* (Marburger Theologische Studien 2; Marburg: Elwert, 1965), 58 nn. 268-69.

right hand is without exception taken to mean his exaltation after death to divine position and honor. It does not simply indicate a heavenly location. Often this is brought out by terms directly referring to Jesus' majesty or supremacy in the immediate environment of the quotation or allusion; this is the case with Col 3.1; Eph 1.20; Acts 2.33-36; Heb 1.3,13; 8.1; 12.2; 1 Clem 36.5; Pol *Phil* 2.1; Apoc Pet 6; Sib Or 2.243; "Mk" 16.19; Apcr Jas 14.30-31. Elsewhere the idea is expressed by an emphasis in the context on vindication (Mk 14.62=Mt 26.64=Lk 22.69; Acts 5.31; 7.55-56; Heg [EH 2.23.13]), or a suggestion that the elevation to the right hand is a reward (Heb 12.2; Rev 3.21), or that it means unique capability (Rom 8.34). In a number of instances, mention of Jesus' PLACE at the right hand apparently serves as a capsule reference to his resurrection, ascension, and continuing exaltation (Mk 14.62 = Mt 26.64 = Lk 22.69; Acts 7.55-56; Heb 1.3,13; 8.1; 10.12; 12.2; 1 Clem 36.5; Rev. 3.21; Apoc Pet 6; Sib Or 2.243; Heg [EH 2.23.13]). At least these passages do not mention resurrection or ascension alongside the heavenly right-hand position. In perhaps two cases the enthronement at the right hand is understood as a particular stage in Christ's glorification, distinguishable from resurrection and ascension (1 Pet 3.22; "Mk" 16.19).

The time at which Jesus is represented as taking the position at the right hand, or at least the time period with which the person who refers to Ps 110.1 is concerned, varies greatly. In Acts 2.33-36; 5.31; all the references in Hebrews; Rev 3.21; "Mk" 16.19; and Apoc Jas 14.30-31, interest is concentrated on the past moment of exaltation (although each passage assumes the continuance of the exaltation into the present and the future). In Rom 8.34; (1 Cor 15.25); Mk 14.62 = Mt 26.64; Apoc Pet 6; Sib Or 2.243; and Heg (EH 2.23.13), the writers are mainly concerned with the parousia and last judgment—though some imply that Jesus has his right-hand situation from the resurrection onward. In Col 3.1; Eph 1.20; Lk 22.69; Acts 7.55-56; 1 Pet 3.22; 1 Clem 36.5; and Pol *Phil* 2.1, the accent falls on the present fact of exaltation.

Ancient Jews and Gentiles alike commonly took the right side and a position at the right hand as symbolic of honor or good furtune, but they did not connect a right-hand seat with any single function. Likewise in the early Christian literature the symbol of Jesus' PLACE or SESSION seems to mean basically honor, not function. A number of the citations examined do imply Christ's present role as lord of church and cosmos (Eph 1.20; Pol *Phil* 2.1) or future judge (Mk 14.62 = Mt 26.64; 1 Cor 15.25; Rev. 3.21; Apoc Pet 6; Sib Or 2.243; Heg [EH 2.23.13]). In Rom 8.34 intercession is mentioned, and in "Mk" 16.19-20 miraculous confirmation of a message. But in all the citations in Hebrews, all those in Luke-Acts, in 1 Clem 36.5, and 1 Pet 3.22, no function at all (whether present or future) is indicated in connection with Jesus' position. The writings in which these citations occur do not in general speak of activity on the part of the exalted Christ. Colossians does represent him as head of cosmos and church, but it does not use Ps 110.1b to express this idea. Moreover, Col 3.1-4 stresses the hiddenness of Christ's glory at present; and Mk 14.62 = Mt 26.64; Acts 7.55-56; and Heg (EH 2.23.13) imply that his glory will remain concealed until his return. It is, therefore, a serious mistake to claim that early Christian references to Ps 110.1b regularly express convictions about Christ reigning as a royal lord in the present era.[159]

Yet the SESSION or PLACE was extremely popular in the early church as a symbol of Christ's glory. If it did not inevitably suggest active lordship, what qualities in this symbol can have so endeared it to the church? It is probably relevant to note that many of the passages we have examined in this chapter betray a concern to affirm the glory of both God the Father and Christ. The very expression "at the right hand of God" implies that Jesus' elevation is relative, always conditioned by the eternal majesty of God. Most early Christians seem to have wanted to understand Jesus' exaltation as supreme and yet not as one which threatened the rank or rule of God the Father.[160] Such a conception could be powerfully and succinctly expressed by means of Ps 110.1b.

The Relation of the Church to Jesus' Exaltation

Christology, by definition, is closely linked with soteriology. Nearly every early Christian reference to Jesus' PLACE or SESSION occurs

---

[159] O. Cullmann has expressed this idea frequently. Apart from his *Christology* (cited above, p. 16 n. 5), see esp. his *The State in the NT* (New York: Scribner's, 1956), 102 f. See also W. A. Visser 't Hooft, *The Kingship of Christ* (New York: Harper, 1948), 78; C. Schneider, TWNT 3,445 (=TDNT 3,442).

[160] In large measure we may suppose that Christians were influenced by Jewish expectations that the eschatological savior would naturally act for, and with the power of, God. Cf P. Volz, *Die Eschatologie der jüdischen Gemeinde im neutestamentlichen Zeitalter* (Tübingen: Mohr, 1934), 223-25. R. P. Martin comes to a similar conclusion regarding Phil 2.11 (*Carmen Christi* [Cambridge: Univ. Press, 1967], 271-83).

in a passage which indicates the significance his exaltation has for men, especially Christians. Certain passages, however, explain this significance in ways that deserve special attention.

Empowerment of the Church.—Early Christians seem to have regularly assumed that the church came into existence through the resurrection-ascension of Jesus. Confident of the power of their lord, Christians were sure of their own power as a gift from him (or, through him, from God).[161] Conversely they typically perceived the signs and successes that they experienced as manifestations of the power of Jesus.[162] In the sense of energizing the church and its preaching, Jesus' SESSION might be regarded as an event visible to all who would use their eyes rightly.[163]

It is along such lines that *Acts 2.33-36* and "Mk" 16.19 are to be interpreted. Acts 2.33 makes the point most plainly: Jesus' elevation to God's right hand leads immediately and inevitably to his pouring out the Holy Spirit on the community of his followers. Where is the connection between Ps 110.1 and the idea of the Spirit? It seems to lie in the quotation from Joel (Acts 2.17-21), which begins with the promise of the advent of the Spirit and ends with "All who call on the name of the lord shall be saved." Here "lord" can only mean Jesus.[164] Thus the citations of Joel and Ps 110 provide crucial underpinning for the conviction that the age of the Spirit dawns when Jesus is proclaimed lord.[165] Luke's doctrine of the Spirit need not be detailed here; but we may observe summarily that for him the Spirit signifies the divine guidance and power given individual Christians and the church generally during the period between Jesus' ascension and parousia.[166] Thus Acts 2.33-36 makes the birth and ongoing career of the Christian community a direct result of Jesus' enthronement at the right hand.

[161] Cf W. Kramer, *Christ, Lord, Son of God*, ET B. Hardy (SBT 50, 1966), 82 (§ 18e).

[162] Cf 1 Tim 3.16; Jn 14.13.

[163] Cf the words of M. Kähler: "Erst mit der Mission in seinem Namen erscheint er [Jesus] auf seinem königlichen Throne in seinem Scheblemini" (*Jesus und das Alte Testament* [Biblische Studien 45; Neukirchen: Neukirchener Verlag, 1965 (=1907)], 75 f). Justin Martyr connected the church's mission esp. with Ps 110.2 (see above, p. 17).

[164] See below, p. 105.

[165] While Luke is not the only Christian who thinks the Spirit's coming depended on Jesus' glorification (cf Jn 7.39; 14.16-17), he shows a particular interest in Acts 2 in representing these events as fulfillment of scriptural promises.

[166] See Conzelmann, *Luke*, 213.

Before proceeding to the "longer ending" of Mark, we may note in passing that the psalm allusions in *Acts 7.55-56* are also related to the church's development. Elsewhere in Luke-Acts divine visions regularly serve to point out the direction in which saving events are to move. That is, they are not in Luke's narrative given by God simply for the consolation of individuals.[167] A major theme in Stephen's speech is the Jews' rejection of God's chosen leaders and prophets, climaxed in the murder of Jesus, and Luke connects Stephen's own death with a general persecution which leads to the extension of the church's preaching beyond Jerusalem. Stephen's witness before the sanhedrin, crowned by his words about a vision of Jesus at God's right hand, thus points toward the progress of the mission from Jerusalem "to the ends of the earth" (Acts 1.8).[168]

In the *"longer ending" of Mark,* a reference to Jesus' SESSION is sandwiched in between accounts of his post-resurrection commission to the disciples (Mk 16.15-18) and a summary account of how it was fulfilled (16.20). As a consequence, the reader is impelled to view Jesus' exaltation as a precondition of the fulfillment of the commission. Mark 16.20 says that the exalted lord worked with the disciples as they preached and confirmed their message by the *sēmeia*—surely extraordinary demonstrations of power—which accompanied it. Since the disciples' lack of faith was particularly remarked in earlier portions of this text, and since the writer does not say that the risen Christ's appearance to the disciples sufficed to remove their unbelief, it is possible that the reader is meant to infer that the disciples' faith was established through the event of Jesus' ascension and enthronement in heaven. Thus the author of this ending may have intended to express something very like the thought of Acts 2; but he does not mention the Holy Spirit or try to explain why the exaltation of Jesus had to precede the disciples' mission.[169]

A special association of Christ's exaltation with potent revelation appears in *Rev 5.* The lamb goes to God's right hand (5.1,7) to take a scroll which contains the mysteries of the future. The breaking of its seals signifies the inauguration of eschatological judgments; it also symbolizes the granting of preeminently needful knowledge to the church. And the disclosure is made possible by Christ's exaltation.[170]

---

[167] See, e.g., Acts 9.5-6, 10.3,9-16; 16.9; 22.17, 21; 27.24. Cf Pesch, *Vision,* 48.

[168] Cf Pesch, 38-40, 58; Bihler, *Stephanusgeschichte,* 182-85; 250.

[169] So one may hesitate simply to equate the views of this text and Acts 2.33-36. But see Daniélou, *Etudes,* 48 f.

[170] Similar imagery appears in Odes Sol 23 and the Nag Hammadi Gospel of

It is impossible to say whether there is any deliberate allusion to Ps 110.1*b* in the fourth gospel's description of the Son as being "in the bosom of the Father." Yet there is a resemblance to the conception of Rev 5 in the evangelist's interpretation of that image indicating Christ's ability to reveal the Father (Jn 1.18) .[171]

Christians at the Right Hand of God?—No text from the NT age expressly says that men have the present or future possibility of sitting with Christ at God's right hand. Yet several passages come extremely close to doing so. We have already surveyed a number of texts from late Judaism and Christianity after the NT period which describe men exalted to heavenly stations more or less similar to such a SESSION.[172] One might suppose that teachings about a future reign of the saints in pre-Christian Judaism[173] and primitive Christianity[174] would readily lead to statements about their possession of seats on God's right hand. Yet only the Testament of Job distinctly develops the idea.

In *Rev 3.21* believers are promised that those who "conquer" shall be seated on Christ's throne, which is also God's throne. The con-

---

Truth 19.34 ff. The idea of persons ascending into heaven and then receiving special revelations was fairly common in late Judaism. A particularly interesting expression of it is T Levi 2.10, since that *Testament* elsewhere uses language recalling Ps 110 (see above, p. 24). On the general subject, see further W. Bousset, *Die Himmelsreise der Seele* (Darmstadt: Wissenschaftliche Buchgesellschaft, 1960) ; G. Widengren, *The Ascension of the Apostle and the Heavenly Book* (Uppsala: Lundequistska, 1950) , and above, p. 54 and p. 56 n. 19.

[171] The "beloved disciple" is in the best position at the last supper to understand Jesus (Jn 13.23-26). Apparently he reclines at Jesus' right side. See R. Bultmann, *Das Evangelium des Johannes* (Meyer, 1941) , 56 f; R. E. Brown, *The Gospel According to John, XIII-XXI* (Anchor Bible 29 A; Garden City: Doubleday, 1970) , 574. Cf Plato, *Phaedo* 89 *A*.

[172] See above, pp. 55-58.

[173] On the conception of a reign of the saints in Judaism, see esp. Volz, *Eschatologie*, 275 f; D. S. Russell, *The Method and Message of Jewish Apocalyptic* (Philadelphia: Westminster, 1964) , 285-303. Some particularly interesting expressions of it: 1QpHab. 5.4; IQM 17.7-8; As Mos 10.8-10; Wis 3.7-10; 5.15-16; 1 Enoch 62.14-16. See further Schweizer, *Lordship*, 22-31.

[174] For the thought of Christians sharing Christ's dominion, see esp. Rom 5.17; 1 Cor 4.8; 6.2-3; 15.50; 2 Thess 1.5 ff; 2 Tim 2.12; Mt 16.18-19; 19.28; 25.34; Mk 10.35-45 par; Lk 12.32; 22.29-30; Rev 2.26-27; 5.10; 20.4,6; 22.5. Useful discussions are offered in K. L. Schmidt, TWNT 1,588-92 [=TDNT 1,587-90]; Bietenhard, *Reich*. Gnostic texts like the *Gospel of Thomas* (logia 2 and 81) and the *Gospel According to the Hebrews* (cited in Clement of Alexandria, *Misc* 5.14.96) regard the salvation-reign as attainable in the present world. See B. Gärtner, *The Theology of the Gospel According to Thomas*, ET E. J. Sharpe (New York: Harper. 1961) , 261-63. Cf Asc Isa 9.10-13,18.

94

querors are those who witness faithfully to Christ (cf Rev 12.11). The prophet seeks to exhort Christians to face the prospect of martyrdom with courage and high hopes. Basically the sharing of Jesus enthronement seems to mean possession of salvation, but it also suggests supreme honor and reward.[175] It is something earned. To be sure, 3.21 represents this enthronement as given rather than taken; but the dominant tone of the promise in its context is indicative of exaltation construed as recompense. Beyond this, the image connotes actual participation in a judgmental reign of Christ at the end of the world.[176] In Rev. 6.9-11 and 7.13-17 some martyrs are depicted in heaven already enjoying immortal bliss; but nowhere in the book are they represented as enthroned with Christ during the present age. One other feature of Rev. 3.21 is noteworthy: the *hōs kagō*, setting the triumph and SESSION of Jesus in parallel with those of Christians. While the author of Revelation elsewhere dwells on the uniqueness of Jesus and his saving work, texts like the present one undeniably suggest a certain parity between Christ and Christians regarding both earthly struggles and heavenly exaltation.[177]

In *Heb 12.1-2* as in Rev 3.21, christology is pressed into the service of exhortation. Believers are summoned to guide their pilgrimage by looking to Jesus, considering both his earthly career and his celestial glory. Their conduct should be modeled on his earthly perseverance; but they are also to meditate on his SESSION, the reward of that perseverance.[178] That the epistle's writer thinks that Christians can hope to share the SESSION is indicated by several facts. In Heb 4 a correspondence is developed between the "rest" (*katapausis*) which God entered (4.4) and that which believers should labor to enter (4.11).[179] In 10.12-13 and 12.2 Jesus' SESSION is interpreted above

---

[175] On the limitation of the promise of Rev 3.21 to an elite group (the martyrs), see M. Riddle, *The Revelation of St. John* (MNTC, 1940), 61-65. Otherwise: Holtz, *Christologie*, 37 and n. 4.

[176] Cf Rev 1.6; 2.26-27; 5.10; 20.4,6. From 22.5 it would appear that the servants of God and the lamb continue to reign forever—though the character of this reign is not specified. Holtz thinks that the emphasis is on glorification rather than on participation in government (*Christologie*, 206).

[177] Cf Lohmeyer, *Offenbarung des Johannes*, 40, 162. Of course the tenses of 3.21 indicate one vital difference: Jesus has been enthroned. Christians will be enthroned. Perhaps the seer also meant to contrast the passivity of believers in their exaltation ("I will grant to sit . . . .") with Jesus' active sitting down ("I sat down") on God's throne.

[178] See above, pp. 88-89. Cf the emphasis on looking to the reward in Heb 11.16, 26; 13.13-14. A particularly good parallel to this mode of exhortation is in Philo, *Mig* 133-34.

[179] Cf the ideas of rest in Mt 11.28-29; Rev 14.13. On the general concept in

all as a resting after the completion of his earthly task. Further, a direct equating of "the place of the right" and "the place of rest (*anapausis*)" is found in a later gnostic work in a description of the hope or present bliss of gnostics.[180] Finally, the orientation of Heb 11.1-12.2 is hortatory and Jesus is presented as the supreme model of faith. His exaltation to the right hand is conceived here chiefly as a reward, and the logic of the whole passage points to an assumption that loyal Christians may expect like reward.[181] In Heb 2.5-13 christology and soteriology outweigh hortatory interests, but even there great stress is put on Jesus' similarity to his "brothers" and on a pattern of suffering—exaltation valid both for him and for them. Yet the author is very reserved in speaking of the future state of believers; certainly he never explicitly promises them heavenly thrones.[182] What will Christians do when they come to their heavenly glory? Unlike the author of Revelation, the writer of Hebrews never suggests that they will reign as kings or priests. The emphasis in 12.2 is on rest and honor. Probably their gaining something like Jesus' SESSION chiefly implies for this writer existence in the saving presence of God.[183] Heb 12.2 also differs from Rev. 3.21 in suggesting, far more than the latter verse, that the promise of glory akin to that of Christ is held out to all Christians, not just to those who die for the faith.

Some passages in Hebrews reflect another pattern of conceptualization, one according to which Christians have already arrived in

---

Hebrews and its religious background, see Käsemann, *Gottesvolk*, 40-45; Michel, *Hebräer*, 185; Vielhauer, *Aufsätze*, 215-34; Gärtner, *Thomas*, 265-67; Grässer, *Glaube*, 105-15. A recent study by O. Hofius (*Katapausis: Die Vorstellung vom endzeitlichen Ruheort im Hebräerbrief* [Wissenschaftliche Untersuchungen zum NT 11: Tübingen: Mohr, 1970]) emphasizes the importance of the "rest" motif in Hebrews but denies Käsemann's conclusion of a gnostic background. Theissen (*Untersuchungen*, 128 f) seems justified in arguing that Hofius has not proved Käsemann incorrect on this point.

[180] "Unbekanntes altgnostisches Werk" (Schmidt-Till, *Schriften*, 360). See Vielhauer, *Aufsätze*, 281 f. Cf Exc Theodotus 18.1.

[181] Evidently the Jewish exemplars of faith also share in the reward (11.40). Cf Asc Isa 9.7-13, 17-18 and Bruce, *Hebrews*, 78 f. The author of Hebrews does not understand himself to be teaching a doctrine of salvation by works: men can approach God only through the work of Jesus (e.g., 10.19-22). Cf Schille, "Basis," 276.

[182] The straightforward assurance of Bruce (*Hebrews*, 353 f) on this point is not strictly warranted by the text.

[183] Since worship seems the essential task of Christians on earth (12.22-24; 10. 22-25; 13.15-16), the author may have conceived the future of believers as a more perfect sharing in the heavenly liturgy.

heaven. Most striking is 12.22-24, where earthly believers are said to be part of the congregation of the heavenly Jerusalem. In view of Eph 2.6 and Col 3.1, it may be supposed that this imagery stems from liturgical traditions, probably baptismal ones.[184] It has firm ties with the author's view that through Jesus' ascension Christians have gained access to the heavenly sanctuary (e.g., 6.20; 9.24; 10.19-22).[185]

One may speculate that behind certain other texts from the NT age there lie convictions about future heavenly rewards at the right hand of God. Thus, given its other similarities to Hebrews, *1 Clement* may at one point (50.3) be understood to allude to such rewards after death.[186] In his letter to the Philippians, *Polycarp* remarks that the saints will reign with Christ (5.2; cf 2.3) and judge the world (11.2). He also states that great Christians of the past who suffered "with Christ" are now "with the Lord in the place which is their due" (9.2). Conceivably the anarthrous *thronos* of Pol *Phil* 2.1 is meant to imply the existence of thrones near God's, thrones prepared for Christians. In the *Apocryphon of James* Jesus tells his disciples that they should ascend into heaven as he does (13.12-13) and that

> I came down to dwell with you
> in order that you also might dwell
> with me (9.2-4; cf 16.10).[187]

Since Jesus ascends to "occupy" his father's right side, a similar station seems to be promised to faithful followers.[188]

Two documents from the first century of the church, *Ephesians* and *Colossians*, clearly imply that Christians on earth presently share Jesus' heavenly enthronement. The more explicit text is *Eph 2.6*, where the author tells his readers that (apparently through baptism) God has raised them from the dead and caused them to sit in the heavenly regions with and in Christ (*synēgeiren kai synekathisen en tois epouraniois en Christō Iēsou*). They are saved already (2.5,8). Whereas the *synezōopoiēsen* of 2.5 may come from Col 2.13 (or some common tradition), the *synēgeiren* and *synekathisen* are unmistakably used to parallel verbs employed in Eph 1.20 to affirm Jesus'

---

[184] Cf Schille, *Hymnen*, 28 and 57.

[185] Cf Käsemann, *Gottesvolk*, 75-98; E. Percy, Die Probleme der Kolosser- und Epheserbriefe (Lund: Gleerup, 1946), 291 f; Bruce, *Hebrews*, 375 f.

[186] Cf 1 Clem 5.4,7; 45.8.

[187] The quotation is from Malinine et al., *Epistula*, 123.

[188] Elsewhere in the Apocryphon (5.1-3; 6.19-20; 7.14-15) Jesus declares that his disciples may become his equals.

resurrection and heavenly SESSION. The language and thought of
Ps 110.1*b* are thus appropriated to designate that condition of believers which Schlier calls *"in-Christus-mit-Christus-in-die-Himmel-
versetzt-worden-Sein.*[189] Somewhat as gnostics might have expressed
it, the author of this epistle declares that Christians have already
taken part in Christ's ascent into heaven.[190] It is true that Eph 2.7
may refer to a future revelation of God's kindness, but there is no
trace of the view expressed in Colossians that for now salvation is
possessed only in hiddenness. Here the heavenly SESSION has become
an image of the salvation extended to all believers. Consistent with
his idea that salvation is by grace, the author feels he can affirm
nothing less than that believers enjoy an essentially unimprovable
situation.

The conception of divine grace in Ephesians includes the gifts
presently characterizing and shaping the life of the church; and these
gifts are especially connected with Jesus' ascension (4.7 ff). In the
context of 1.20–2.6, the presently exercised gifts are represented by
the summary terms "power" and "wisdom." The same infinite force
manifest in Jesus' resurrection and SESSION now energizes believers;
that power not only equips individuals for special ministries but also
furnishes the growth and defense of all believers (3.16-20; 6.10). Yet
in this epistle Christians do not rule or exercise judgment. Christ
alone is made *kephalē* (head) over church and cosmos; the church's
role now, and apparently for all time, is one of subjection to him (cf
5.23). Christ has been exalted over all the supernatural powers, but
they still threaten his followers.[191] Christians do not "stand" now to
"sit" later (cf 6.13*b*); their life in Christ, as depicted in this epistle,
seems both a passive sitting in exaltation and a standing in the midst

[189] Schlier, *Epheser,* 4th ed., 110 f. Eph 1.20-23 and 2.1-10 contain a number of
features in common, suggesting that the author intended readers to see his
ecclesiology as a mirror image of his christology. Both Jesus and Christians were
raised from the dead (1.20; 2.1,5) and set in heavenly places (1.20; 2.6). The
phrase *en tois aiōsin tois eperchomenois* in 2.7 balances *en tō mellonti* in 1.21. The
same divine power at work in Christ's exaltation works in Christians (1.19; 2.5). Cf
Percy, *Probleme*, 275.

[190] Schlier (*Epheser,* 4th ed., 111) cites parallels from the Odes of Solomon
and Origen. An expression in the recently published *Epistle to Rheginus* ("and we
went to heaven with him") seems to allude to Eph 2.5-6. See M. Malinine *et al.,
De Resurrectione* (Zurich: Rascher, 1963), 62, lines 27-28. Cf R. McL. Wilson,
Gnosis and the New Testament (Philadelphia: Fortress, 1968), 120.

[191] Perhaps the author feels that the position of believers "in the heavenly
places" exposes them in special ways to the assaults of the evil powers, which
also inhabit those regions (6.12 ff).

of combat. The present exaltation of the church mentioned in 2.6 is also related, by context, to its possession of knowledge, the revelation of God's mysterious plan to unite everything in Christ and make Jews and gentiles fellow heirs (1.9-10; 3.4-11). The material immediately adjoining 2.6 stresses power rather than knowledge, but for the author of Ephesians the two are intertwined.[192]

According to *Colossians,* the life of believers is hid with Christ in God (3.3), and Christ himself sits at God's right hand (3.1). Like Eph. 1.20–2.6, these statements seem derived from a baptismal ideology which emphasized the unity of the exalted Christ with Christians.[193] The writer did not say directly that Christians share Jesus' heavenly SESSION, but this omission may be purely accidental. The call to set minds on heavenly instead of earthly things leads naturally to injunctions about renouncing worldly passions and conduct in 3.5 ff. The mystical or metaphysical conceptions to which these verses allude are difficult to penetrate,[194] but the author clearly intends the union of believers with Christ to be thought of as a condition chiefly appropriated through faith, baptism, and right conduct. All the hopes (1.27), aspirations, and action of Christians depend on their present unity with Christ (3.17). Perhaps this mode of exhortation bears an escapist tinge. The particular instructions in 3.5–4.6 concern non-believers hardly at all. As by his resurrection Jesus has withdrawn

---

[192] He prays for knowledge of God's purpose and power (1.17-19) and later for power to have knowledge of the purpose (3.16-18). On the general idea, see Schlier, *Epheser,* 4th ed., 78. Irenaeus remarks that Christians cannot fully grasp religious mysteries because they have *not* sat down at God's right hand as Jesus has (*Her* 2.28.7 [2.43.1]). Cf above, p. 56.

[193] Note the similarities between 3.1-4 and 2.12. On the relation to baptism, see Scott, *Epistles,* 62; Schille, *Hymnen,* 57. On the emphasis on baptismal ideas elsewhere in the epistle, see E. Käsemann, *Essays on New Testament Themes,* ET W. J. Montague (SBT 41, 1964), 159-64.

[194] The alternatives "the things above" and "those on earth" which Col 3.2 presents as objects of *phroneite,* seem roughly equivalent to "the things of the Spirit" and "the things of the flesh" in Rom 8.5 ff. Clearly "the things above" in Col 3.1-2 (the phrase occurs only here in the epistle) have both ethical and quasi-spatial meaning; the phrase indicates how Christians are to live and where their true life is. For partial parallels, see further Mt 6.19; Jn 8.23-24; 3.31; 1 Cor 15.47; Phil 3.19; Jas 3.15. A passage in Philo (*Praem* 152) offers some remarkable similarities to both Eph 2.6 and Col 3.1-4 (in all three passages, it is difficult to differentiate sharply between the mystical, the metaphysical, and the metaphorical). Lohmeyer supposes that Col 3.1-4 implies that each Christian on earth has a heavenly *Doppelgänger* (*Die Briefe an die Kolosser und an Philemon,* 12th ed. [Meyer, 1961], 134), but this seems fanciful.

from the sensible world into hiddenness, the members of his body are obligated to separate themselves from the world.[195]

The situation of believers with Jesus also means their possession of heavenly glory, but this will be concealed till the parousia (Col 3.4). Yet the hiddenness of their glory does not lessen its reality and certainty. Whatever its more specific teaching, the heresy combated in this document denied the certainty or adequacy of the deliverance given in Christ, on this ground urging submission to angelic beings.[196] To refute such ideas, the author of Colossians insists on the utter sufficiency of Christ's redemption and—as an extension of that idea— the absolute security of believers. At the eschatological disclosure of Christ, they will undoubtedly appear as sharers of his glory (3.4).[197]

One might surmise that the notions of Christians already seated with Christ in heaven are a relatively late development, derived from earlier convictions about sitting with him after death (as in Rev 3.21). Yet Ephesians and Colossians must be dated at least as early as Hebrews and Revelation. Further, we have seen that a subsidiary tendency within Hebrews suggests that believers are already united with the heavenly Jesus. Finally, the thought of being seated with Christ in heaven seems an extension of the idea of dying and rising with him, and that idea is probably pre-Pauline.[198] The idea of a present enthronement of believers with Christ may, therefore, be as old as that of an enthronement to be gained only in the future. It may be even older.

The early church evidently saw value, but only limited value, in affirming that Christians sit or will sit at God's right hand. Basically the image was a vivid expression of the glory and joy Christians conceived to be essential to their faith. Even in Eph 2.6 the image seems less an expression of ecclesiastical triumphalism than one of awe at the boundless grace of God. The hortatory settings of Rev 3.21; Heb 12.2, and Col 3.1 show that the SESSION promise was used largely to stimulate renunciation and devotion. Another concern which

---

[195] To be sure, Colossians roundly condemns the asceticism of the heretics it opposes. On the general relation between doctrine and conduct, see E. Lohse, "Christologie und Ethik im Kolosserbrief," *Apophoreta* (Festschrift E. Haenchen), ed. W. Eltester (Berlin: Töpelmann, 1964), 156-68.

[196] See esp. Käsemann, *Essays*, 167 f; F. Francis, "Humility and Angelic Worship in Col 2.8," *Studia Theologica* 16 (1962), 109-34.

[197] For similar ideas of the eschaton as involving a revelation of the saints in glory, see Rom 8.19-23; 1 Thess 4.14; 1 Clem 50.3; Wis 3.1 ff; 4 Ezra 7.26, 28; 13.12, 37 ff, 48-49; Asc Isa 4.16. Cf W. D. Davies, *Paul,* 318 f.

[198] Cf Percy, *Probleme,* 288-92.

probably favored the development of the symbolism was that of indicating how Christians might enjoy fellowship with the exalted Jesus.[199] Yet the paucity of texts that even approach saying that Christians may share Christ's SESSION suggests that the idea awakened deeply rooted hesitation and protest. Perhaps it did so by tending to erase any distinction between the glory of Jesus and that of his followers. We have earlier noted that Ps 110.1b was peculiarly suited for affirming the glory of Christ without diminishing that of God the Father. It was not well suited for maintaining the distinction between Christ and Christians, once applied to the latter.

The Suggestion of a Distant Christ.—All early Christian references to Ps 110.1b imply an understanding of Jesus' SESSION as transcendent, heavenly. How far did this suggest a separation between Jesus and his followers (at least those still alive on earth)?[200] If Christ is always conceptualized as in heaven and believers as on earth, it is meaningful to speak of a gulf between them even if no one would try to measure it in miles. The greatness of the sense of separation might be indicated by statements of relative intimacy or direct interaction between Christ and Christians.

In Luke-Acts, for example, Jesus' heavenly position appears to be understood both in a quasi-spatial sense and in terms of a lack of ongoing communication. The ascended Jesus is no longer on earth; he remains in heaven during the period before the parousia (Acts 1.1-11; 17.31). After his ascension Jesus shows himself to his disciples only in visions and dreams, and Luke's terminology for these shows that he does not regard them as of the same nature as the resurrection appearances in Lk 24 and Acts 1. Jesus is in heaven, the church on earth.[201] In keeping with his use of spatial language to describe Jesus' ascension (Acts 1), Luke goes further than any other NT writer in suggesting that Jesus' PLACE is a sort of physical location (Acts 7.55-56).

[199] Particularly Rev 3.21 seems to reflect this concern, following directly as it does on 3.20, with its promise of intimate communion.

[200] Cf above, p. 57.

[201] Acts 18.10 is hardly an exception to this pattern; it is a stereotyped promise of protection. Cf C. F. D. Moule, "The Christology of Acts," *Studies in Luke-Acts* (Festschrift P. Schubert), ed. L. E. Keck and J. L. Martyn (Nashville: Abingdon, 1966), 179 f. For somewhat different assessments, see H. Schlier, *Besinnung auf das Neue Testament* (Freiburg: Herder, 1964), 231; Conzelmann, *Luke*, 176 f. A brief but suggestive study dealing with Luke's emphasis on the absence of Jesus is Eric Franklin's "The Ascension and the Eschatology of Luke-Acts," *Scottish Journal of Theology* 23 (1970), 191-200. Cf above, p. 71 n. 83.

The epistle to the Hebrews also suggests a quasi-spatial separation between Jesus, seated in heaven, and his brethren, struggling on earth.[202] Yet—in some contrast to Acts—Hebrews assigns positive significance to this separation: Jesus is now in the heavenly regions acting on behalf of the followers who remain on earth.[203] Likewise in Rom 8.34 Christ's intercession at God's right hand seems consciously contrasted with the intercession of the Spirit in the hearts of believers (Rom 8.26-27). The efficacy of Jesus' intercession is all the greater for its being *extra nos*. Yet, leaving Colossians and Ephesians out of account, Paul never mentions Jesus' situation at God's right apart from this passage; contrariwise, he often speaks of life "in Christ" and of Christ living and working within Christians. So his use of the SESSION idea does not prevent him from making emphatic declarations about the immanence of Christ in the church.[204]

The gospel of Matthew, despite its twofold reference to a christological understanding of Ps 110.1*b* (Mt 22.41-46; 26.64), gives special prominence to assurances that Christ is "with us" not only during the incarnation (Mt 1.23) but also during the career of the church (18.20; 28.20). The risen Jesus claims omnipotence as he addresses his disciples on earth (28.18), and no mention is made of a withdrawal by ascension.[205] Whether Mark conceived Jesus to be "located" at a distance from Christians between resurrection and parousia is unclear. But the Marcan appendix (16.19-20) conjoins—with a nonchalance which mocks any idea of simple location—a description of the heavenly SESSION of Jesus and a forthright reference to his "working with" his disciples as they preach on earth. In Apcr Jas 14.30-31, on the other hand, Jesus' ascent to the right hand of God signifies separation from the disciples and the end of special post-resurrection revelations.

Where the other Christian writings which cite Ps 110.1*b* stand on this issue of separation cannot be decided with confidence, often be-

[202] Among other things, Jesus' ascension means separation from sinners (Heb 7.26). Cf Michel, *Hebräer*, 279-81.

[203] See below, 149-50 f. Cf Spicq, *Hébreux* 2,165.

[204] Two qualifications may be in order. Paul sometimes suggests that Christians will enjoy deepest fellowship with Christ only after death (e.g., 1 Thess 4.17; Phil 1.23; 2 Cor 5.6). Secondly, Rom 8.34 probably pertains chiefly to the last judgment and so does not bear too directly on the apostle's ideas about Christ's relation to Christians during the present age. Cf M. Dibelius, *Botschaft und Geschichte* 2 (Tübingen: Mohr, 1956), 137.

[205] Yet in the Matthean version of some parables the absence of Christ becomes a "creative factor" (so K. Stendahl, "Matthew," *Peake's Commentary on the Bible*, ed. M. Black and H. H. Rowley [London: Nelson, 1962], 794).

cause the writings are so brief. But since 1 Peter, 1 Clement, Barnabas, the Apocalypse of Peter, and Sibylline Oracle 2 regularly seem to represent Christians as presently related to God instead of Christ, they also imply that the SESSION connotes separation.

Thus a number of texts from the NT period suggest that Jesus' heavenly situation marks a significant distance between him and his followers. This links up with our earlier observation that his SESSION is not always, or perhaps even regularly, understood to mean active rule or relationship with the church.[206] For some early Christians it seems to have meant that between his ascension and parousia Christ is essentially inactive, that during this stage of salvation history believers have to do primarily with God the Father or the Holy Spirit.

Yet the church's relation to God was regularly understood to be determined through what Jesus had done during his earthly life (and, usually, through what he would do at the last judgment). His exaltation to the right hand of God could never be interpreted as radical remoteness or non-involvement.[207] Whether they regarded Jesus as relatively active or inactive during the present age, early Christians recognized him as the agent of salvation, the source of the life and hope they had in God. To say "Jesus is at the right hand of God" was therefore akin to saying, "Now we're safe no matter what happens."[208]

Conclusions.—Belief in Christ's right-hand PLACE or SESSION could easily lead to major soteriological and ecclesiological conclusions, and it did so already in the early Christian period. Several early Christians used the image to affirm that the church lives by the power and guidance of the exalted Christ. Some suggested that believers already participate in his heavenly SESSION during their earthly lives; others, that they will do so after death. Finally, the conception of Jesus' position beside God in heaven seems sometimes to have been connected with views of him as relatively detached from the present life and trials of the church.

[206] Above, pp. 90-91.
[207] Contrast the type of transcendence evidently symbolized by Apollo's bow: his essential aloofness from human concerns. See W. F. Otto, *The Homeric Gods*, ET M. Hadas (Boston: Beacon, 1964), 77-79.
[208] Cf H. R. Niebuhr, *The Responsible Self* (New York: Harper, 1963), 177.

CHAPTER 4

Psalm 110.1 as Support for Christological Titles

Besides being connected with various christological ideas, Ps. 110.1 is also associated significantly with four christological titles. The best-known case is the synoptic pericope concerning the messiah as "son of David" (Mk 12.35-37 par), but other titles and passages require consideration as well. It may be noted at the outset, however, that no single title appears regularly in the vicinity of the references to this part of the psalm.

Lord

The term *kyrios* appears in the OG text of Ps 110.1, and it is used as a christological title near references to that verse in Acts 2.33-36; 7.55 [?]; Pol *Phil* 2.1, and "Mk" 16.19. Moreover, the argument of Mk 12.35-37 par pivots on the psalm's phrase *tō kyriō mou*. One need not be surprised, then, that a number of scholars have perceived a special link between the psalm and this title. Some, like Dodd, maintain that the church's use of the title for Jesus is ultimately based on the psalm:

There can be little doubt that various Hellenistic usages affected the development of the idea of Christ as *Kyrios* in early Christian theology and even in the New Testament itself. But since the title "Lord" is given to Christ in a testimonium [Ps 110.1] which is as clearly primitive as anything we have, it seems unnecessary to go farther for the origin of the usage, however it may have been extended and enriched in meaning from other sources.[1]

Hahn, while denying that the psalm gave the initial impetus to Chris-

[1] Dodd, *Scriptures*, 121. Similar positions are taken by W. Foerster, TWNT 3, 1088 and 1094 (=TDNT 3,1089 and 1094) ; Daniélou, *Etudes*, 46 n. 9.

tian use of the title, maintains that it was a major factor in the development of that usage.[2] What can be said of such theses?

Positive evidence of a linking of title and psalm certainly exists. Acts 2.36 marks the climax of an argument that Jesus is both *kyrios* and Christ; and that conclusion immediately follows a quotation of Ps 110.1a-c. Since the title *kyrios* is used of Jesus in Acts 2.20-21) where Joel's prophecy of the outpouring of the Holy Spirit is quoted,[3] one may find in that prophecy and Ps 110.1 (quoted in 2.34-35) substantiation of the crucial nexus of thought underlying the entire speech: the connection between the exaltation of Jesus as lord and the coming of the Spirit. Thus Acts 2 reflects an early conviction that the psalm verse proves the legitimacy of entitling Jesus *kyrios*. An echo of this conviction may be present in Acts 7.55, if the true reading of that passage contains *Iēsoun ton kyrion*.[4]

The same idea lies beneath Barn 12.10-11, where Ps 110.1 and Isa 45.1 are cited together, probably from a testimony collection. That collection will have linked the two verses primarily because of a common term, *kyrios;* both were viewed as scriptural evidence that Jesus merited that title.[5] In Pol *Phil* 2.1 and "Mk" 16.19 the title is applied to Jesus in the immediate neighborhood of references to his heavenly right-hand SESSION. In both cases the context emphasizes his lordly status and activity.[6] Does this demonstrate that Polycarp and the writer of the Marcan longer ending were thinking specifically of Ps 110.1a? Neither quotes it, and the idea of the SESSION might have suggested lordship by itself. Later generations of church writers often cited the psalm text to justify christological use of the title, and they frequently urged that the twofold use of *kyrios* in vs 1a implies the similarity in dignity of God and Christ (see above, p. 21).

Yet all this does not prove that Ps 110 inspired the first Christian use of the title. Indeed, several considerations weigh heavily against that supposition. To begin with, if it were correct, why did the whole NT age produce only five Christian citations of vs 1a of the psalm?[7]

---

[2] *Titles*, 103-14.

[3] See Haenchen, *Apostelgeschichte*, 142. Cf Acts 9.13-14,20-21; 22.16.

[4] Attested by D *h p*. On the centrality of the *kyrios* title in Acts, see Zehnle, *Discourse*, 68.

[5] See above, p. 38. Since Barnabas elsewhere applies the title to Jesus freely (e.g., 1.1.3,4; 2.6; 5.1; 14.5), probably he agreed with the compiler of the testimony collection that such application was supported by Ps 110.1.

[6] Within "Mk" 16:9-20, Jesus is referred to as *kyrios* only in vss 19 and 20, in connection with his ascension and post-ascension signs.

[7] One may note further that vs 1a is never cited in isolation from the rest of the

Dodd, to be sure, argues throughout his *According to the Scriptures* that NT authors quoted Jewish scriptures with due attention to context; hence, on his view, authors who cited the middle or end of vs 1 may also have intended to "point to" the opening words of the verse. It cannot be said, however, that Dodd's general thesis about contextual exegesis in the early church has won wide acceptance.[8] Early Christian exegetes show little sign of interpreting contextually the snatches of Ps 110 which they cite: none before Justin Martyr seems to pay any attention to vss 2-3 and 5-7, and only the author of Hebrews cites vs 4. Of course, when a writer called Jesus *kyrios* he *may* have had Ps 110.1a in mind; and when one cited vs 1b or 1c of the psalm, the thought of vs 1a *may* not have been far behind. But these are bare and barren speculations.[9] The theory that Ps 110.1a is at the root of Christian use of this title for Jesus must be defended on the basis of passages which explicitly connect the two. Of the texts we have considered above, Acts 2.33-36 is the oldest, and it probably dates from near the end of the first century (although it may rely on older sources). Since Christian use of both psalm and title seemingly antedates Paul, the evidence of Acts regarding the origin of the title's use has only limited value. Further, the text of Ps 110.1a does not speak absolutely of a second *kyrios* besides God, but only of "my Lord"—the lord of the psalmist. Neither the Hebrew original nor the OG would readily beget the notion that the second "lord" is divine (see above, p. 21).

It has sometimes been urged that Mk 12.35-37 par has direct bearing on our question. Lindars, for example, maintains that the argument in the pericope depends on the chain of ideas in Acts 2.33-36 and that it presupposes that the psalm's *tō kyriō mou* is equivalent to the absolute *kyrios* title which the church applied to the heavenly

---

verse. This suggests that it was not well known by itself.

[8] See, e.g., Dodd, *Scriptures*, 126. For criticism of the thesis, see M. D. Hooker, *Jesus and the Servant* (London: S.P.C.K., 1959), 21 f. R. T. Mead ("A Dissenting Opinion About Respect for Context in Old Testament Quotations," NTS 10 [1963-64], 279-89), J. A. Fitzmyer ("The Use of Explicit Old Testament Quotations in Qumran Literature and in the New Testament," NTS 7 [1960-61], 297-333), and A. C. Sundberg ("On Testimonies" NovT 3 [1959], 268-81) offer a number of examples of non-contextual interpretation in the NT.

[9] How dubious such reasoning can be, is illustrated by Dodd's assertion that 1 Cor 15.20-28 implies the ascription of the *kyrios* title to Jesus on the basis of Ps 110 (*Scriptures*, 121 f). The idea of Christ's lordship is present (esp. in 15.25), but the title is not. Further, it is surely conceivable that Paul simply took over a traditional custom of according this title to Jesus, without ever pondering what scriptural basis it might have. Certainly he never cites Ps 110.1a.

Christ.[10] The implication is that the link between title and psalm is at least as old as the pericope. This argument, however, is not without its weaknesses. The sense of Jesus' words in the pericope depends on there being serious difficulty in reconciling the doctrine of the messiah as David's son with the psalm evidence that David called him "my lord." The assumption made is that no man would call his son (or descendant) "my lord." [11] In fact, the logic of the pericope is threatened, if not annihilated, when one supposes that "David's lord" is here equated with "the Lord." [12] So this pericope does not assume Christian faith in an exalted *kyrios*.[13] Finally, it cannot have been invented (by early Christians) to justify the application of *kyrios* to Jesus because its center of interest is not that title but rather "son of David." [14]

We have now surveyed all the citations of Ps 110.1 which are related by context to explicit use of the *kyrios* title. Given particularly the evidence of Acts 2 and Barn 12, and considering the very widespread use of the title and the psalm verse, it does seem likely that many early Christians found support for the title in the psalm. We may, indeed, surmise that many found such support in Mk 12.35-37 par, even though the original sense of Jesus' saying was not connected with the title.[15] Still, this is not to agree with those who claim that the psalm gave birth to Christian use of the title or that the majority of believers in the NT era closely associated the two. If either of these propositions were true, it would be strange that citations of vs 1a of

[10] Lindars, *Apologetic*, 47. Cf Hahn, *Titles*, 103-6.

[11] So, e.g., Lohmeyer, *Markus*, 262; Cullmann, *Christology*, 204.

[12] I shall argue below that "son of David" in this pericope is a title of exaltation, not of lowliness or merely human origin (as in Rom 1.3-4). If this is correct, then "the lord" (understood as referring to the exalted Christ) is not incompatible with it.

[13] Hahn (*Titles*, 105) contends that the pericope must have been created by the hellenistic community since the Hebrew psalm's *'adōnî* is not a known messianic title. (Cf Fuller, *Foundations*, 82 n. 19; S. Schulz, "Maranatha und Kyrios Jesus," ZNW 53 [1962], 125-44.) The argument is not conclusive since (1) contemporary Judaism sometimes interpreted the psalm messianically (see above, pp. 28-30); (2) our knowledge of the Palestinian church's theological vocabulary is too limited for us to say that it could not have used the title *'adōnî* of Jesus. On point (1), cf Lohmeyer, *Markus*, 262 n. 3; Cullmann, *Christology*, 203. On point (2), cf G. Dalman, *The Words of Jesus*, ET D. M. Kay (Edinburgh: Clark, 1902), 324-31; Stendahl, *School*, 79.

[14] So also Vielhauser (*Aufsätze*, 164), though he, too, thinks that the pericope presupposes use of the absolute *kyrios* title for Jesus.

[15] So also R. P. Gagg, "Jesus und die Davidssohnfrage. Zur Exegese von Markus 12,35-37," *Theologische Zeitschrift* 7 (1951), 18-30.

the psalm are so rarely to be found in the vicinity of the term *kyrios*. The most reasonable conclusion would seem to be that the psalm verse played a real but modest part in encouraging Christian usage of the title. This complements our earlier conclusion that early Christian references to Jesus' position at the right hand of God do not uniformly connote the *idea* of lordship.[16]

Son of Man

Six passages link this title and the SESSION: Mk 14.62 = Mt 26. 64 = Lk 22.69; Acts 7.56; Barn 12.10-11; Heg (EH 2.23.13).[17] Only Barnabas seeks to show that the title does not fit Jesus; all the other passages apply it to Jesus' post-resurrection glory. These five texts, however, are not independent witnesses to an association of title and psalm. The Matthean and Lucan trial confessions probably use "son of man" simply because the Marcan one did. The use of the title in Acts 7.56 probably reflects pre-Lucan traditions (see above, pp. 73-74). But Luke wrote of Stephen's trial and death with many backward allusions to Jesus' passion, and his retention of "son of man" may only show that he thought that Jesus' confession had made the title appropriate for later martyrs. Hegesippus also probably attests a special tradition which emphasized the title,[18] but his narrative suggests deliberate modeling after Mt 26.64 and Acts 7.

Before referring directly to Ps 110.1, and after quoting other Jewish scriptural texts, Barnabas writes (12.10):

See again Jesus, not as son of man but as Son of God, revealed in a type in the flesh.

The term "son of man" may here be understood as a title, and Barnabas may intend these words to be connected with Ps 110.1. If both these assumptions are valid, then two remarkable things must be noted. First, "son of man" here means "merely a human being," in flagrant contrast to the phrase's sense in the gospels.[19] Second, it is

---

[16] Our discussion has necessarily left out of account other possible sources of Christian use of the *kyrios* title. Cf Kramer, *Christ*, 84 (§ 18 f).

[17] Holtz (*Christologie*, 19) suggests that Rev 1.13 ff. reflects a tradition which linked "son of man" with Ps 110.1.

[18] So H. J. Schoeps, *Theologie und Geschichte des Judenchristentums* (Tübingen: Mohr, 1949), 79-82.

[19] Similarly Ignatius, *Eph* 20.2; Justin, *Dial* 100; Irenaeus, *Her* 3.16.5 (3.17.5); 5.21.3. See C. Colpe, TWNT 8,480 f.

likely that Barnabas knew a special tradition (probably Christian) relating the title and the psalm.

The title *may* have been in Paul's mind as he wrote 1 Cor 15.25; the Adamic speculation presupposed by the context, and the merging of the ideas of Pss 8 and 110, suggest it. In Heb 2.6 ff, there is a quotation of Ps 8 which includes the phrase "son of man," and this passage seems to be a continuation of the subjection theme raised in Heb 1.13 with a quotation of Ps 110.1. Again, in Eph 1.20-22 the two psalms are paraphrased in a manner which indicates that Jesus might have been conceived as the exalted "son of man" as in Lk 22.69. Still, the writers of these three passages never use "son of man" explicitly as a christological title, and it must remain doubtful whether they connected it with the psalm.[20]

Thus a real but relatively minor association was established in the NT age between this title and Ps 110.1. Their combination in an early report of Jesus' trial confession and the similarity between Ps 8.7 and Ps 110.1 were presumably the main causes of the association. There is no evidence that Ps 110 encouraged or decisively shaped Christian interpretation of this title. The reverse is also true.

Son of God

Barn 12.10 argues directly from Ps 110.1 that Jesus is the Son of God rather than the son of David (or any other man). In Mk 12.35-37 (= Mt 22.41-46 = Lk 20.41-44) almost the same argument appears, but this passage leaves the reader dangling with the question, "How is he [the messiah] David's son?" Probably each of the synoptic versions of the argument is meant to imply that the Christ is the Son of God, but only Barnabas draws that conclusion openly.

In Mk 14.61-62 (= Mt 26.63-64 = Lk 22.67-70), Jesus' declaration about the son of man who will sit on God's right is conjoined with the question, "Are you the Son of God?" But the latter title is no more closely linked with Ps 110 in this passage than are the titles "son of man" and "Christ."

In Heb 1 the main christological title is "the Son," and references to it are located near the references to the psalm in 1.3 and 1.13. Moreover, in 1.3-4 the enthronement at the right hand of God is directly connected with the obtaining of a name more excellent than that of any angel, viz. "the Son."[21] A similar use of "the Son" occurs

[20] Cf E. Schweizer, TWNT 8,372.
[21] Michel, *Hebräer*, 105.

in 1 Cor 15.28, at the climax of a train of thought closely bound up with an allusion to the psalm in 15.25. Both Heb 1 and 1 Cor 15, then, connect references to Ps 110.1 with the title "the Son," and both imply that the title connotes divine sonship.[22] Likewise 1 Clem 36.4 prefaces quotations of Pss 2.7-8 and 110.1 with notice that these are words of God spoken to his Son.

We have now examined all the citations of Ps 110.1 which are linked contextually with titles signifying divine sonship.[23] They imply a significant but not major tradition of interpreting such titles and the psalm verse together.

Son of David

Context joins this title and Ps 110.1 in Mk 12.35-37 (=Mt 22.41 45=Lk 20.41-44), Barn 12.10-11, and the account of James's death in Hegesippus (EH 2.23.13-14). Only in the last (and latest) of these passages is the title used positively and without qualification. By contrast, the synoptic pericope and Barn 12 make problematic the entire early Christian tradition of styling Jesus "the son of David."

1. *The Meaning of Jesus' Argument About the Son of David.*—The authenticity of Mk 12.35-37 has often been challenged or denied, but one essential feature of the pericope makes its historicity highly probable. In their Marcan form the words attributed to Jesus here raise but do not distinctly answer the question about the applicability of the title "son of David" to the messiah. It is difficult to imagine any of the evangelists (or any other early Christian) creating such a logion; hence it is most reasonably credited to Jesus himself.[24] The Marcan setting of the saying may, however, be artificial: the persons whose messianic views are attacked by Jesus here may not have been open foes (the scribes) but neutral bystanders or even close disciples.[25]

[22] Hahn (*Titles*, 307-17) plausibly argues that behind these two passages, and certain others, there is a distinctive tradition of using "the Son" instead of "the Son of God."

[23] In Acts 7.56, P⁷⁴ reads "Son of God" instead of "son of man." On Ps 110.3, see above, pp. 21-22.

[24] Similar arguments for the pericope's authenticity on the ground of its ambiguity are set forth, e.g., by Lohmeyer, *Markus*, 263; Taylor, *St. Mark*, 493; E. Lövestam, "Die Davidssohnfrage," *Svensk Exegetisk Årsbok* 27 (1962), 81 f; Borsch, *Son of Man*, 394 f.

[25] Note that Mark 12.35 does not specify Jesus' hearers; 12.37b refers vaguely to a crowd. The holders of the messianic dogma attacked by Jesus are represented by Mark as "the scribes," by Matthew as "Pharisees." Luke does not identify them.

In the logion, Jesus quotes and interprets Ps 110.1 as calling into question the common idea that the messiah is David's son. He does not clearly repudiate that opinion, but he declares it misleading in one or two directions. First, the messiah is David's lord according to the psalm. This must mean that he is superior to David, and the implication is that the messiah's kingdom will not be a mere renewal of David's. In the context of Jesus' other teaching, we should probably infer a second sense in which the messiah is David's superior. Probably the meaning is that the messiah's rule will not be worldly or militaristic, as David's was (cf Ps Sol 17.21 ff). Throughout his ministry Jesus seems to have regularly discouraged hopes that he would exercise political or military power akin to that which David or the Hasmoneans wielded. His words in this pericope may therefore carry a deliberate rejection of the mundane interpretation of Ps 110 perhaps favored by Hasmoneans and other post-exilic Jews.

Given the polemical intent of the logion, it is hard to define much positive content in its interpretation of the psalm. Yet at least this is clear, and it is of high importance: Jesus taught that the psalm applied to the messiah. This pericope may be the only one in the entire synoptic tradition which can be regarded as directly expressing Jesus' understanding of messiahship. Jesus is represented as having quoted Ps 110.1 in its entirety, and we have no reason to think that he actually quoted less (though his argument turns on vs 1a). It may be inferred, then, that Jesus attached messianic meaning to the latter portions of the verse as well. The enthronement at God's right hand must, for him, have been a transcendental event. Perhaps, although we cannot confidently ascribe Mk 14.62 to him, that text's reference to the eschatological coming of an enthroned son of man is substantially faithful to Jesus' own expectation.[26] Likewise Jesus may have taken Ps 110.1c to pertain to a messianic victory over foes. While not a zealot, his hope of the end-time arrival of God's kingdom surely included the forcible termination of all earthly governments and of Satan's kingdom. Moreover, while Jesus does not here claim to be the messiah, he must have felt that the one described in Ps 110.1 would vindicate his ministry. Judging from this logion, Jesus did not

[26] Cf R. Bultmann, *Theology* 1, 28. Borsch (*Son of Man,* 396 f) takes a quite similar view, although I cannot discover why he thinks that the pericope implies both a heavenly and an earthly messiah. I cannot here enter into the intricate problem of whether any of the synoptic sayings concerning the son of man are authentic. My point is simply that Jesus probably found in Ps 110.1b reference to a non-earthly enthronement of the messiah.

use the psalm as a basis for elaborating a positive messianic doctrine of his own, but only for demonstrating the insufficiency of a contemporary doctrine. His final question (Mk 12.37) has perplexed many Christian minds, and it is not unlikely that Matthew correctly reports that none of his original hearers could solve the puzzle (Mt 22.46). The whole point of his words seems to be that there can be no simple reconciliation of the titles "son of David" and "David's lord." [27]

The Argument About the Son of David in Pre-Marcan Tradition.— The interpretations of the logion about the psalm and the son of David during the period of pre-Marcan transmission cannot be traced with assurance. One can hardly discern stages in the formation of the pericope itself; most interpreters assume that Mark took it over from the tradition as he found it.

Several scholars have argued on good grounds that the pericope was incorporated into a cycle of *Streitgespräche* sometime before Mark wrote.[28] This would imply that the saying was judged an important proof of Jesus' debating skill, especially in connection with the Jewish scriptures. But the particular answers, if any, which early Christians at this stage gave to the question "How is he David's son?" cannot well be decided.[29] Early church documents indicate that there existed

---

[27] K. Schubert (*The Dead Sea Community*, ET J. S. Doberstein [London: Black, 1959], 139 f) contends that the explanation of Jesus' words lies in *4Q Florilegium* 1.10–14, which represents the messianic "branch of David" as also the Son of God (using a quotation of 2 Sam 7.14). But the synoptic pericope does not plainly approve of either "son of David" or "Son of God." Cf H. Braun, *Qumran*, 1.73.

[28] The fullest argument for the cycle's existence and analysis of its content is offered by M. Albertz, *Die synoptischen Streitgespräche: ein Beitrag zur Formengeschichte des Urchristentums* (Berlin: Trowitzsch, 1921), 16-36. See also his *Die Botschaft des Neuen Testaments* I/1 (Zollikon-Zurich: Evangelischer Verlag, 1947), 65-71, 172 f. Taylor (*St. Mark*, 101) generally agrees with Albertz, though he thinks Mark himself composed the cycle sometime before writing his gospel. For arguments against the cycle's existence, see W. L. Knox, *The Sources of the Synoptic Gospels* 1 (Cambridge: Univ. Press, 1953), 85-92.

[29] A number of scholars urge that the early church would have interpreted the pericope to mean that Jesus is "son of David" in his earthly career and "Son of God" thereafter (a two-stage christology expressed more directly in Rom 1.3-4). So, e.g., Hahn, *Titles*, 251-53; Bornkamm *et al.*, *Tradition*, 33 and n. 1. Fuller (*Foundations*, 188 f) basically concurs, though he thinks that Rom 1.3 reflects a somewhat more advanced christology than our pericope. D. Daube (*The New Testament and Rabbinic Judaism* [London: Athlone, 1956], 158-69) and J. Jeremias (*Jesus' Promise to the Nations*, ET S. H. Hooke [SBT 24, 1958], 52 f) agree that Rom 1.3-4 is the key to unlock the pericope, and they view Jesus' argument as essentially a puzzle about the reconciliation of scriptural passages. Yet the pericope mentions only one scripture (Ps 110); the view that the messiah is

a wide range of feeling about the title "son of David," including enthusiastic approval (e.g., Matthew), relative indifference (e.g., Hebrews, gospel of John), and downright hostility (Barnabas). The ambiguity of the pericope would probably allow persons of every inclination regarding the title to claim that the pericope agreed with them. But evidence on how that final question was in fact understood during the pre-Marcan period is simply unavailable. At most one can say that Christians accustomed to applying Ps 110.1b-c to Jesus will have probably considered the logion a cryptic reference to his heavenly exaltation.

The Meaning of the Argument in Mark's Gospel.—In this gospel Mk 12.35-37 is the climactic debate confrontation between Jesus and the Jerusalem leaders. Formally, there is no exchange between opponents, as in the pericopes in 11.27–12.34. Yet Jesus is presented as criticizing the teaching of the scribes, a class regularly pictured as hostile in the gospel; and the last words of 12.37 indicate that Jesus is still teaching openly. The paragraph certainly implies that the scribes could not (or did not) reply to Jesus' questions. It is clear, then, that Ps 110.1 functions here as a text by means of which Jesus proves his exegetical and theological superiority to the scribes. Nevertheless Mark will hardly have regarded the story simply as one more demonstration of Jesus "beating the rabbis with their own stick." [30] The evangelist *must* have been concerned about the subject matter of Jesus' words since it is messiahship! Besides 14.62, this is the only passage in the gospel portraying Jesus as speaking publicly on that issue. Mark must have regarded such words as a key self-disclosure.

What substantive meaning will he have found in them? Our best clue is Mk 14.62, which contains the gospel's second and final reference to Ps 110.[31] There Jesus lays claim to being messiah, Son of God, and son of man; and his SESSION is a heavenly one to be manifested at his parousia. We may reasonably suppose that it is along

---

David's son is only attributed to men. So Bultmann, *History*, 405. While Mk 12.35-37 raises questions which *might* have been answered in some sectors of the early church by the christology represented in Rom 1.3-4, it is to be noted that the latter passage affirms Jesus' right to both "Son of God" and "son of David" titles; the Marcan pericope does not even mention the former title and only poses a question about the latter. Cf Suhl, *Funktion*, 89-91; Vielhauer, *Aufsätze*, 187 n. 81.

[30] So Lindars, *Apologetic*, 47.

[31] H. Waetjen ("The Ending of Mark and the Gospel's Shift in Eschatology," *Annual of the Swedish Theological Institute* 4 [1965], 120) detects in Mk 16.5 "a reflection of Jesus' elevation to lordship at God's right hand." This must be considered at best a very doubtful allusion to Ps 110.

such lines that Mark thought the mysterious words in 12.35-37 should be interpreted. The failure of the scribes to answer Jesus' challenge to their doctrine is matched by the blind condemnation which follows his trial confession. After 14.61-62, 12.35-37 adds nothing to the gospel in terms of theological doctrine. But, coming two chapters before the trial confession, the debate story adds drama and a measure of suspense. Just as the message of the messiah's suffering is not fully stated early in the gospel but emerges only gradually, so also the meaning of his glory is brought out in stages (e.g., at Mk 9.1-8; 13.26-27; 14.28, 62; 16.7). The saying in 12.35-37 essentially raises a question about the superiority of the messiah to the son of David expected within Judaism, and the reader is left uncertain how that superiority is to be specified. So Mark's dominant motive for including this saying about David's son was probably a literary one, that of creating a tension in the gospel not to be resolved before Jesus' trial.[32]

It is difficult to decide whether Mark was interested in applying the "son of David" title to Jesus. David is mentioned in two other passages in the gospel (2.25; 11.10), but the title occurs only in 12.35-37 and 10.47-48. In the latter passage, it appears on the lips of Bartimaeus, but with no indication that the beggar's terminology has Mark's endorsement.[33] Evidently the evangelist interpreted 12.35-37 chiefly as an assurance that Jesus' divine dignity outstrips Jewish notions of the messiah as David's son.[34]

[32] Cf P. Carrington, *According to Mark* (Cambridge: Univ. Press, 1960), 264-66. The issue of overriding concern to Jesus' opponents in the temple debates, as in his trial, is that of the authority he claims. In 12.35-37, as in 11.27-33, Jesus in effect evades the question they desire to pose; he answers it in 14.62.

[33] Bartimaeus also calls Jesus "rabboni," which suggests a distance between his estimate of Jesus and that of Mark. Cf J. Schreiber, "Die Christologie des Markusevangeliums." ZTK 58 (1961), 164. W. Wrede (*Vorträge und Studien* (Tübingen: Mohr, 1907], 174 f) argued that Mark opposed the "son of David" title, citing the admittedly odd word order of *pothen autou estin hūios* in 12.37 (changed by both Matthew and Luke). That phrasing, he felt, emphasizes the *autou* and implies that Jesus is not David's son but God's. This is a large inference from a minor grammatical peculiarity, and Mark seems hardly the author to express things by such a nicety of syntax. It is just possible, however, that this word order reflects a pre-Marcan interpretation of the pericope which was hostile to the title. The references to David in Mk 2.25 and 11.10 do not show that the evangelist was especially interested in it. Cf Lohmeyer, *Markus*, 225, 231, 262.

[34] C. Burger (*Jesus als Davidssohn* [FRLANT 98, 1970], 42-71) makes a strong case that Mark carefully distributes references to Jesus' relation to David in connection with his arrival in Jerusalem (10.47-48; 11.10; 12.35-37). Burger believes that Mark's attitude to the "son of David" title was essentially that of Rom 1.3-4, one of restrained approval. In view of the meager data in the gospel, however, the line between relative approval and plain indifference is hard to draw.

The Meaning of the Argument in Luke 20:41-44.—As with Mk 12.35-37, the literary context of the pericope in Luke (rather than its wording) makes it a debate-like confrontation between Jesus and his opponents, one which he wins on the basis of his deeper grasp of Ps 110.1. For Luke also the final question of Jesus may have pointed beyond the title "son of David" to those of "Son of God" and "son of man." The latter two figure importantly in Luke-Acts, although perhaps neither is a particular favorite of the author's.[35] At least the Lucan trial confession (22.67-70), which contains the gospel's only other reference to the psalm, employs "Son of God" and "son of man." Luke-Acts regularly employs Ps 110.1 in passages emphasizing the vindication and enthronement in glory given Jesus immediately with (or following) his resurrection.[36] In view of this, Luke can hardly have failed to perceive in the logion about the messiah as son of David a thinly veiled hint of Jesus' impending messianic exaltation.

Acts 2.33-36 seems to furnish clues for the right interpretation of our pericope no less important than those in Lk 22.67-70. We have already seen that this passage in Acts is the only one within the NT which indubitably joins Ps 110.1a and the absolute christological title kyrios. Since Lk 20.44 runs *Dauid oun auton kyrion kalei*, the evangelist may already intend readers to note the connection in the gospel logion. More interesting yet is the fact that in Peter's Pentecost speech the name of David occurs with unusual prominence.[37] Pss 16 and 110 are attributed to him, but Peter stresses that their fulfillment came not with David but with Jesus (in his resurrection-exaltation). Jesus is vastly superior to David, but he is also David's descendant. Since David was a king, Jesus receives the heavenly throne which was promised David by God (Acts 2.30, 34). Apart from Lk 18.38-39 and 20.41 (where he follows Mark closely), Luke never uses the title "son of David." Yet he strongly emphasizes Jesus' descent from David (Lk 1.27; 2.4; 3.31; Acts 13.23), his saving relation to the people David ruled (Lk 1.32; Acts 15.16-17), and the fulfillment of David's prophecies in him (Acts 13.33-37; cf Lk 24.44). Possibly Luke avoided the specific title because it had for him disagreeable political connotations, or because it suggested that Jesus was merely a second David.[38] In

---

[35] "Son of God" receives no distinctive emphasis apart from Lk 1.32,35 and Acts 9.20. Cf Hahn, *Titles*, 305 f. On "son of man," see Colpe, TWNT 8,462.

[36] See above, pp. 69-76. Cf Burger, *Davidssohn*, 115 f.

[37] It occurs three times (*'Iēsous* occurs four times).

[38] Cf Burger, *Davidssohn*, 112-14. The specific phrase "son of David" is used as a title only once in pre-Christian Judaism (Ps Sol 17.21), and it does not occur in

any event, Lk 20.41-44 will have suggested to this evangelist both the positive ties joining Jesus with David and the resurrection glory which makes him incomparably greater.[39]

The Meaning of the Argument in Matthew 22.41-46.—Like Luke, Matthew left the pericope in the Marcan setting of temple confrontations between Jesus and his foes. But he radically altered its form to bring out more sharply its controversy character. Mark's monologue has become a dramatic dialogue between the messiah and his archenemies, the Pharisees. The term marking their uniting together (*synagein*) suggests that he turns on them en masse—just as they had earlier come as a body to attack him (Mt 22.15,34).[40] Jesus' dexterity in debate is shown by his beginning with seemingly easy questions (22.42) which lure the Pharisees into answering, thence proceeding to questions for which they have no answer (22.43-46).[41]

Matthew's reshaping of the Marcan pericope also suggests a subtle change of its christological meaning. Jesus' opening question, "What do you think about the messiah?" suggests a concern with the general issue of the messiah's nature.[42] The placing of this question back to back with "Whose son is he?" intimates further that the two questions are really one: the mystery of the messiah's nature is the mystery of his origin. Given Matthew's general hostility to the Pharisees (as well as 22.43-46), their response that the messiah is the son of David must have been for him (the evangelist) unsatisfactory. Assuming this, Jesus' question *tinos huios estin* implies, by its form and context, the possibility that the Christ is the son of someone else.[43]

Yet this must be reconciled with Matthew's keen desire to depict Jesus as David's offspring. He is the only canonical evangelist directly to label him "the son of David" (Mt 1.1), and he uses the title far more than any other NT author. He quadruples the number of

early Christian writings apart from the synoptics and Barn 12.10-11. (See Hahn, *Titles*, 242.) Luke may have neglected it simply because many of his contemporaries were unfamiliar with it.

[39] Suhl (*Funktion*, 91 f) thinks that Luke took a more negative view of the "son of David" title. See further S. E. Johnson, "The Davidic-Royal Motif in the Gospels," JBL 87 (1968), 144-48.

[40] The term for their coming together also recalls, perhaps deliberately, Ps 2.2 OG. So W. C. Allen, *The Gospel According to St. Matthew* (ICC, 1907), 242.

[41] Suhl argues persuasively that Matthew employs the "son of David" title in ways that bring out the true and false responses to Jesus of different groups of people ("Der Davidssohn im Matthäus-Evangelium," ZNW 59 [1968], 57-81.

[42] Debates or discourses in Matthew are often opened with "What do you think . . . ?" constructions (Mt 17.25; 18.12; 21.28; 22.17; cf 26.53; 26.66).

[43] So Wrede, *Vorträge*, 174.

beggars who address Jesus with it (9.27-28; 20.30-31), and puts it on the lips of the Canaanite woman (15.22). When Jesus enters Jerusalem, the crowd cries, "Hosanna to the son of David! Blessed be the one who comes in the name of the Lord!" (21.9), and the title is taken up again by inspired children (21.15). The full messianic signification is perhaps plainest in 12.23, where multitudes respond to a miracle with the exclamation, "Is this not the son of David?" That the title usually bears full messianic weight seems certain, despite its application at one point to Joseph (1.20).[44] The geneaology and infancy narratives stress Jesus' descent from David (1.6,17,20); his rank as the true king of Israel is underscored, especially in the passion narrative (2.2; 21.5; 27.11,29,36,42). Matthew may reckon Jesus "greater than Solomon" (12.42) specifically in the sense of being a greater "son of David."[45] Matthew, then, will certainly not have understood 22.41-46 as a denial of Jesus' claim to this title. He must have believed that the riddle implies Jesus is David's son and also another's.

Now, far more clearly than either Mark or Luke, Matthew is anxious to make "Son of God" central to christology. Jesus is God's Son from birth (e.g., 2.15)[46] and is recognized as "the Son of the living God" by Peter (16.16). In this gospel the "bolt from the Johannine blue" has a unique and exalted conclusion (11.28-30) and is complemented at the end of the gospel by an assertion about Jesus' omnipotence and a trinitarian formula (28.18-20). As in Mark, Jesus' trial prophecy of the parousia revelation of his SESSION is connected by context with the title "Son of God." Given this strong emphasis on Jesus' divine sonship, it seems most likely that the evangelist saw in 22.41-46 an indirect declaration that Jesus is both son of David and Son of God. The first title will have connoted for him that Jesus is God's appointed savior for Israel, as promised in the scriptures; the second, that he is lord and savior for all peoples.[47] Nothing in the gospel suggests a

---

[44] Joseph is *a* son of David, Jesus is *the* (eschatological) son of David. So E. Lohmeyer, *Gottesknecht und Davidsohn*, 2nd ed. (FRLANT 61, 1953), 68.

[45] Lohmeyer (*Gottesknecht*, 65) may underestimate the degree to which Matthew related Christ to David as king of Israel.

[46] Cf Hahn, *Titles*, 306.

[47] Although Matthew sometimes appears to use *kyrios* as an absolute christological title (7.21-22; 8.25; 14.28,30; 25.37,44; 28.6), one may doubt that he uses it in this manner in 22.41-46. It is nonetheless intriguing to observe that the Canaanite woman and some beggars address Jesus as *kyrie huios David* (15.22; 20.30-31). Cf Strecker, *Weg*, 2nd ed., 123 f; Burger, *Davidssohn*, 89.

temporal resolution of the pericope's riddle along the lines of Rom 1.3-4.[48] Rather, Jesus properly bears both titles from birth.[49]

The Meaning of the Argument in Barnabas 12.10-11.—The same essential argument linking the "son of David" title and Ps 110.1 makes its final appearance in the NT age in the epistle of Barnabas. The epistle contains no parallel to Mk 14.62 par, but probably Barnabas also applied the psalm verse to Jesus' post-Easter exaltation.[50] He employs it in 12.10-11 to argue for Jesus' divine status and nature.

The quotation of Ps 110.1 is immediately preceded by a discussion of how scriptural passages concerning Moses point toward the divinity of Jesus (12.2-9). Jesus is not the son of man but the Son of God (12.10a). The psalm quotation is prefaced by a notice that David spoke these words to warn in advance against the error of certain "sinners" who would claim that the messiah is David's son. After quoting the psalm (and Isa 45.1), he concludes the section: "See how David says he is Lord, and does not say Son." In contrast to the ambiguous wording of the argument in each of the synoptic gospels, Barnabas' language expresses forthright and total rejection of the "Son of David" title. Apparently the objection is not because it has political associations but because it implies that Jesus was merely human.[51] Perhaps this is related to the fact that Barnabas speaks of

[48] See, however, R. Hummel (*Die Auseinandersetzung zwischen Kirche und Judentum im Matthäusevangelium* [BEvT 33, 1963], 121 f, 141 f), who argues persuasively that Matthew connects "son of David" particularly with the earthly Jesus' special mission to Israel, a mission which in a sense came to an end with his death and resurrection.

[49] So Strecker, *Weg*, 2nd ed., 119 f; Suhl, *Funktion*, 93 f; R. Walker, *Die Heilsgeschichte im ersten Evangelium* (FRLANT 91, 1967), 52 n. 34; 128 f. J. M. Gibbs argues that the title "son of David" is shown to be "inadequate" in Mt 22.41-46; Jesus' *position* as "son of David" (meaning that he is Israel's king) is not denied ("Purpose and Pattern in Matthew's Use of the Title 'Son of David,'" NTS 10 [1963-1964], 460 f). I do not see that Gibbs has shown that Matthew regards "son of David" as inadequate in any respect.

[50] Elsewhere Barnabas mentions Jesus' resurrection, ascension, and parousia in traditional fashion (15.5,9).

[51] A similarly sharp contrast between "Son of God" and "son of David" is drawn in the Pseudo-Clementine *Homilies* 18.13. Cf Schoeps, *Theologie*, 246 f. A less sharp contrast is drawn in Clement of Alexandria, *Misc* 6.132.4. In the relatively late Dialogue of Adamantius (4.46, PG 11.1849), an unorthodox speaker denies that Jesus is the son of David on the basis of Mk 12.35-37 par. On the possibly docetic tendency of the tradition represented in Barnabas, see Prigent, *L'Epître de Barnabé*, 124-26. R. A. Kraft argues for a different conclusion in his review of Prigent's book (JTS 13 [1962], 407); see also now Prigent-Kraft, *Epître de Barnabé*, 173.

David only as a prophet, never as a king (10.10; 12.10-11; cf 6.4,6; 9.1).

What can be deduced about the background of this passage? It may be significant that Barnabas interposes the Isaiah reference in the middle of his argument from Ps 110; he seems in no hurry to conclude the latter. It is almost certainly significant that the argument then presented (12.11c) is loose, so loose as to seem only a casual reference to exegesis long familiar. Such observations lead to the conclusion that Barnabas derived the argument about the title from earlier tradition. Yet he apparently lifted the psalm citation from a collection of testimonies which sought to establish another point: that Jesus is "lord" (see above, p. 38). Also from tradition must come the association of the psalm text and the "Son of God" title (12.10a). And, finally, Barnabas seems to work in a Christian environment in which the synoptic gospels' interpretations of "son of man" and "son of David" are unknown or uncongenial. Did Barnabas take the argument directly from one of those gospels? This seems inherently unlikely. The wording of his argument is closest to that of Mk 12.35-37, but Barnabas does not elsewhere evidence acquaintance with Mark.[52]

In contrast to the synoptic pericope, Barnabas gives no hint that the argument comes from Jesus himself. Those who wrongly style the messiah David's son are simply designated *hamartōloi*. Since David is said to have spoken prophetically to ward off their future error (12.10a), Barnabas is probably thinking of opponents of his own time.[53] All in all, it seems most likely that Barnabas extracted the argument not from any of our gospels but from some traditional source; the latter, however, may have borrowed some wording directly from Mark.[54]

The Psalm and the Title in Hegesippus.—No shadow of the argument we have been considering appears in Hegesippus' account of the trial of James, but it is striking to find James's confession about the son of man enthroned at God's right hand directly followed by the cry (of some believing hearers), "Hosanna to the son of David!" Elsewhere Hegesippus reports that Jesus' relatives were interrogated

---

[52] H. Köster has shown that there is no need to suppose that Barnabas used any of the synoptics (*Synoptische Überlieferung bei den Apostolischen Vätern* [TU 65, 1957], 157).

[53] Perhaps they were simply non-Christian Jews, for whose ideas Barnabas shows a general hostility.

[54] Or perhaps the Testimony collection and Mark depended on a common source for the argument. Cf Köster, *Überlieferung*, 145 f.

by Domitian about their Davidic descent. They admitted it and declared that they hoped in a heavenly kingdom to come at the end of the world when Christ would appear as universal judge (EH 3.20.1-4). It seems that the Jewish Christians whose faith is described in both passages conceived the title "son of David" to express both physical origin and eschatological glory.[55] As in Barn 12.10-11, we seem to be in touch here with a tradition of linking Ps 110.1 with the titles "son of David" and "son of man"—though the tradition of Hegesippus gives both titles highly positive meaning (at least the latter title plainly does not mean simply human sonship).[56] We have also argued that the question about David's son in each of the synoptic gospels is fundamentally answered in Jesus' trial confession. The trial confession of James is modeled on that of Jesus,[57] and it elucidates the sense which "son of David" had in this tradition.

Conclusions.—We have now examined all the texts from early Christianity connecting Ps 110 and the title "son of David." All but the latest (that of Hegesippus) present variant forms of a single argument. But the argument is not used to justify the application of the title to Jesus. Barnabas uses it to denounce the title. Mark uses it but seems indifferent to the title. Luke uses it, but only in other passages does he indicate Jesus' positive relation to David (without stressing the title). Matthew can equate "son of David" and "messiah," but he does not justify that equation from the argument about Ps 110.1.

Why, then, was the argument preserved, especially in its inconclusive synoptic form? Scholars have sometimes argued that the early church's fondness for Ps 110.1 sprang from Jesus' use of it in the son of David argument. Proof or disproof in such matters is impossible, but two considerations militate against this theory. First, the argument seems to have made relatively little impact on early Christianity. Nowhere except in these four passages is there definite allusion to it (Jn 7.42 is not proof to the contrary); and the popularity of the "son of David" title in the early church is strange indeed if this argument was widely studied. Secondly, the argument may not have been regularly credited

---

[55] Cf the political interpretation of S. G. F. Brandon, *Jesus and the Zealots* (Manchester: Univ. Press, 1967), 121-25, 188 f.

[56] Lohmeyer (*Gottesknecht,* 83 f) suggests that this passage reflects a special tradition of using "son of David" to interpret "son of man" and "servant of God."

[57] Note the remark of Hegesippus that James died for the same offense (i.e., the same witness to the glory of the son of man) that Jesus did (EH 4.22.4).

to Jesus: Barnabas and certain later writers allude to it without suggesting that it originated with him.

Our evidence does not suggest that the early church used Ps 110 because of the argument about the son of David, but rather that it retained that argument because it was accustomed on other grounds to using Ps 110. Once *that* usage was established, early believers would presumably have been glad to retain an argument (particularly in a form linking it with Jesus himself) which declared the psalm messianic.[58] All passages discussed in this section agree that Ps 110.1 describes the heavenly glory of the messiah, in contrast to the worldly expectations of the Jews. This positive meaning of the son of David argument was consistently preserved and built upon by each of the synoptic evangelists and Barnabas. Thus concern with the title "son of David" was probably something of a red herring in the development of Christian use of the argument: the real source of its popularity was its unequivocal affirmation of the heavenly majesty of the messiah as described in Ps 110.1.

[58] Cf J. A. Fitzmyer, "The Son of David Tradition," *Concilium* 20 (1966) , 75-87.

CHAPTER 5

Psalm 110.1 in Affirmations About the Subjection of Powers to Christ

Warfare is a dominant theme of Ps 110. In its first verse God promises a ruler that his foes shall be utterly defeated; and vss 2,5 and 6 vividly sketch the violent fulfillment of the promise. In late Judaism ideas of militant saviors seem to have flourished in many circles. The hope of a messianic "son of David" often included the idea that he would crush in battle the foes of God and Israel. The messiah of Israel mentioned in the Qumran scrolls, for example, is such a figure (1QS^b 5). On the other hand, an eschatological victory over sinners or gentiles could be conceived as executed by God himself or a heavenly being like the son of man (1 Enoch 62.2-3). In 11QMelch we find Melchizedek pictured as a heavenly warrior who will carry out the judgment of God by slaughtering the powers of darkness ("Belial and the spirits of his lot") .[1]

Given such precedents for conceptualizing salvation in warlike fashion[2] and the militant language of Ps 110, it is no surprise that some early Christians interpreted the psalm as an oracle about the subjection of Christ's foes. What is surprising is rather their quite limited use of the psalm for this purpose. Chart 5 summarizes the wide diversity of ways in which early Christian literature connected Ps 110.1

---

[1] D. Flusser hazards the suggestion that this document alludes to Ps 110.1,5-6, although he is unable to point to close verbal resemblances ("Melchizedek and the Son of Man," *Christian News from Israel* 17 [1966], 23-39). Michel thinks that 11QMelch may reflect a fusion of ideas of a priestly messiah and a son of man who acts as judge (*Hebräer*, 559) .

[2] For surveys of the general subject, see esp. H. Windisch, *Der messianische Krieg und das Urchristentum* (Tübingen: Mohr, 1909) , 1-28; Moore, *Judaism* 2,323-71; Volz, *Eschatologie*, 272-320; Mowinckel, *He That Cometh*, 311-21; 393-99; 403-10.

Chart 5: Psalm 110.1
In Affirmations About the Subjection of Powers to Christ

(A question mark in parenthesis indicates that the presence of the subjection idea in the passage is doubtful. Numbers and small letters indicate portion of Ps 110.1 to which reference is made. An asterisk marks a direct quotation.)

Text	Reference	Objects of Subjection	Time of Subjection	Primary Function of Quotation or Allusion
(?) Mt 26.64	1b	men	parousia	predict vindication of Jesus
(?) Mk 14.62	1b	men	parousia	predict vindication of Jesus
(?) "Mk" 16.19	1b	demons	present	describe Jesus' heavenly enthronement
(?) Acts 7.55-56	1b	men	parousia	affirm Jesus' vindication and glory
(?) Rom 8.34	1b	spiritual powers	present/last judgment	affirm Jesus' heavenly intercession
1 Cor 15.25	1c	all powers	present/future	argue about resurrection of believers
Eph 1.20	1b	all powers	past/present	affirm glory and power of Christ
Heb 10.12-13	1b-c	foes of Christ	future	argue that Jesus' sacrifice is perfect
1 Pet 3.22	1b	spiritual powers	past/present	affirm Jesus' heavenly glory
Rev 3.21	1b	evil powers	past	exhort believers to faithfulness
1 Clem 36.5-6	1a-c*	evil men	future	affirm Jesus' heavenly glory
Pol *Phil* 2.1	1b	all powers	present	affirm Jesus' heavenly glory and rule
Apoc Pet 6	1b	all men	last judgment	describe last judgment
Sib Or 2.243	1b	all men	last judgment	describe last judgment
(?) Heg (EH 2.23.13)	1b	men	parousia	affirm Jesus' heavenly glory

and ideas of subjection. In several passages listed such ideas are only implicit, if they are present at all. In many others the thought of subjection is a decidedly secondary theme. The identification of the persons or powers subjected to Christ varies widely, and the same is true of the time of subjection. The most important passages for understanding the connection between the subjection motif and the psalm seem to be those that directly refer to the last clause of the psalm's first verse (1c), and I shall accordingly analyze these first.

Subjection Argued from Psalm 110.1c

The oldest passage to be considered, *1 Cor 15.25*, implies that writer and readers are already familiar with the application of Ps 110 to

Christ's victory over his foes. The allusion to vs 1c is introduced merely with *dei gar*, although the context shows that this allusion together with the citation of Ps 8.7 in 1 Cor 15.27 is vital for Paul's train of thought. He aims at establishing that death, along with every other power (15.24), will ultimately be overcome by Christ. The Corinthians seem to have doubted not Christ's past resurrection but their own future resurrection; believing that they already enjoyed the fullness of salvation, they did not expect anything of ultimate consequence from the future.[3] Against this view, Paul in 15.20-28 contends that there is a divinely appointed sequence of eschatological events, one whose finale has not yet arrived.[4] Ps 110.1c must have seemed invaluable to the apostle precisely because he could find in its "until" a clear scriptural prophecy of a time gap between the onset of Christ's reign and the consummation.[5] Such an idea was lacking in Ps 8.7, which, however, Paul also cites because of its authoritative assurance that *all* powers will be put beneath Christ's feet (see above, pp. 36-37). The defeat of the last enemy, death (15.26), coincides (at least roughly)[6] with the resurrection of the dead; but this will all be followed by the subjection of the Son to the Father.[7] The kingdom of Christ is here represented exclusively in terms of a subjugation of powers to him (note the sixfold use of *hypotassein* in 15.27-28). The powers chiefly in view seem to be supernatural ones, but 15.27 emphasizes that "all things" are subjected. This must mean all creatures, including church members. Surely the thought is that they, at least, shall be subjected not by destruction or absorption[8]

---

[3] Cf 1 Cor 4.8; 2 Tim 2.18. Among recent discussions, see esp. J. C. Hurd, *The Origin of I Corinthians* (New York: Seabury, 1965), 284 f; W. Schmithals, *Gnosticism in Corinth*, ET John E. Steely (Nashville: Abingdon, 1971), 155-59, 357-62; Wilcke, *Zwischenreich*, 56-63.

[4] That the thought of progression governs the passage's argument is shown by Paul's description of events besides that of the resurrection. Cf the emphasis on a God-determined sequence in 15.35 ff. Cf H. D. Wendland, *Die Briefe an die Korinther* (NTD, 1965), 127-30.

[5] See esp. F. Godet, *Commentary on St. Paul's First Epistle to the Corinthians*, ET A. Cusin, 2 (Edinburgh: Clark, 1887), 361. The direction of Paul's interest in Ps 110.1c is interpreted somewhat differently in F. Maier, "Ps 110.1," 142-45; H. Conzelmann, *Der erste Brief an die Korinther* (Meyer, 11th ed., 1969), 323.

[6] Conzelmann, *Korinther*, 324 f.

[7] Thus the *achri hou* of 15.25, derived from Ps 110.1c, undergirds the assertion that Christ's reign shall have a termination as well as the claim that the terminus has not been reached.

[8] A view maintained, e.g., by W. L. Knox, *St. Paul and the Church of the Gentiles* (Cambridge: Univ. Press, 1939), 128. In favor of the easier view that

but in obedience and worship. Yet the subjection in the foreground of 1 Cor 15.24-28 is that of the supernatural beings, most of all death; and this subjection seems to end in extermination.[9]

Heb 10.12-13 likewise implies an established tradition of using Ps 110.1 to describe the subjection of Christ's enemies. The reference to this subjection is not only brief but almost incidental, since the real concern lies in arguing that Jesus' death put away sin once for all (see below, pp. 151-52). Here Jesus' SESSION signifies not a period of active rule but rather one of passive waiting for his foes to be subdued (presumably by God). The reference to enemies in 10.13 is so vague that their identity—if the author even asked himself about the matter—is left wholly uncertain. Apostates, according to this epistle, are God's enemies and face dreadful judgment; but they are never described as Christ's enemies. The only mention of a super-human antagonist of Christ is in Heb 2.14, but there the devil is said to have been vanquished already through Jesus' death.[10] This author, then, refers to a tradition of using Ps 110.1 to describe Christ's future victory over his foes, but his own interests lie elsewhere. He assumes that the psalm verse refers to an eschatological delay stretching into the future, but his attention is primarily focused on Jesus' sacrifice in the past.[11]

---

1 Cor 15.28*b* means that God practices his lordship fully is Conzelmann, *Korinther*, 326 f.

[9] With the uses of *katargein* in 1 Cor 15.24,26, compare those in 2.6 and 6.13. Other passages offering complex ideas of subjugation are Rom 16.19-20 and Phil 3.21. Cf W. Thüsing, *Per Christum in Deum* (NTAbh 1; Münster: Aschendorff, 1965), 240-52.

[10] So Moffatt, *Hebrews*, 140.

[11] Hahn (*Titles*, 103, 131-33) contends that Heb 10.12-13 and 1 Cor 15.25 mark a distinctive stage in the development of christology, one which affirmed Christ's SESSION as present fact and yet maintained an "eschatological reservation" based on Ps 110.1*c*. He argues that a completely "de-eschatologized" outlook appears only with the deutero-Pauline text Eph 1.20-22. This hypothesis seems dubious for several reasons. (1) Two brief NT passages seem too slender a base for identifying a special stage in the general development of christology. (2) The species of "realized eschatology" reflected in Eph 1.20-22 may not have appeared later than the "eschatological reservation" view expressed in 1 Cor 15; the enthusiasts Paul combats in Corinth may have subscribed to just such an interpretation of Ps 110.1 as Ephesians presents. (3) At most Ps 110.1*c* can have been only one of several factors which restrained early Christians from totally renouncing futuristic eschatology (cf Vielhauer, *Aufsätze*, 171; Fuller, *Foundations*, 213; E. Schweizer, TWNT 8,371). (4) The interpretations of the eschatological delay in 1 Cor 15.25 and Heb 10.12-13 are so different that one suspects they are entirely independent. It may be noted that Justin Martyr (*Apol* 45) and Irenaeus (*Proof* 85) also take the psalm clause as testimony to an eschatological delay, but perhaps they do so following Paul's example.

In *1 Clem 36.5-6,* Ps 110.1*b-c* is quoted as the last in a chain of scriptural testimonies to Christ's divine glory (see above, p. 82). Then Clement pauses momentarily to explain something about the meaning of the psalm:

Who, then, are the foes? Those persons who are wicked and oppose his will.

Little reading between the lines is needed to detect that Clement has human beings, particularly the rebels in the Corinthian church, in mind.[12] He does not say how or when they will be subjected. Possibly he was thinking of present-time submission through repentance or end-time destruction (cf 1 Clem 8; 41.3). Here, too, the very brevity of the reference to the defeat of the foes implies that the general idea and its association with the psalm were taken over from tradition.

All three passages thus far discussed (1 Cor 15.25; Heb 10.12-13; 1 Clem 36.5-6) imply the existence of a fixed custom in the early church of linking Ps 110.1*c* with the subjection idea. It is worth noting, however, that several direct quotations of Ps 110.1*c*, those in Mk 12.36 par; Acts 2.34-35; Heb 1.13 [13], and Barn 12.10, seem not at all connected with that theme.

Subjection Affirmed or Implied on the Basis of Psalm 110.1b

Several important passages definitely or possibly connect ideas of Christ as lord or conqueror with statements about his SESSION. Although these passages do not directly refer to Ps 110.1*c*, their authors may have had it in mind.

In *Rom 8.34* a reference to the SESSION is immediately followed by an extended declaration that, despite all natural and supernatural threats, "we are more than conquerors through him who loved us" (8.35-39). Although the imagery of 8.33-34 is primarily judicial rather than military, probably readers are intended to see a relation between Jesus' exalted PLACE beside God and their own security.[14] Both 1

---

[12] So, e.g., Grant, "First Clement," 64.

[13] Several scholars argue that Heb 1.13 refers to subjugation, since 1.14 speaks of angels as ministering spirits, and 2.5 ff develops the thought of the subjugation of the future world to the Son. See esp. Cullmann, *State,* 112 f. Yet these texts do not say that the angels were formerly the Son's foes or that they are presently his servants. See further the criticisms of C. Morrison, *The Powers that Be* (SBT 29, 1960), 45-47. Cf Spicq, *Hébreux* 2,21; Schille, "Basis," 275 f; Michel, *Hebräer,* 94, 103.

[14] Cf the view of the hostile powers in 8.31-39 advanced by Boismard (*Hymnes,* 92): "Contre leurs revendications, le Christ est notre avocat."

Cor 15.24-28 and Rom 8.31-39 are broad landscapes of eschatological things, both are mainly concerned with the threat of death, both cite Ps 110.1. It is likely, then, that Rom 8.34 was also meant to imply the defeat of enemies. The time of their defeat seems to be in the future; perhaps the primary reference is to the last judgment (see above, pp. 59-60).

Eph 1.20-23 states directly that in setting Christ at his right hand God exalted him "far above every rule and authority and lordship." Ps 8.7 is then quoted and interpreted to mean that Christ has been made "head over all things" (1.22). He is thus lord of the universe since the time of his resurrection-ascension. There is no suggestion of a process of subjugation of foes in either the present or future. A very similar view comes to expression in *1 Pet 3.21-22*: by virtue of his past elevation to God's right hand, Christ already is supreme over "angels, authorities, and powers." In both passages the primary objects of subjection seem to be angelic powers. In *Pol* Phil *2.1* Christ's reception of "glory and a throne at the right hand" involves his sharing with God the Father in the present rule of the world and the future last judgment of all men.[15] In these three passages, all of which probably derive from hymnic *Vorlagen,* the subjection theme is developed in the direction of asserting Christ's present lordship over all creation. The idea of destroying enemies has receded. This development is probably related to the use in each passage of Ps 8.7 alongside Ps 110.1.

A second group of passages may be distinguished by their association of Jesus' SESSION with his parousia of final judgment.[16] Jesus' trial confession in *Mk 14.62 (=Mt 26.64)* assures his judges that they will

[15] Cf W. Bauer, *Die Briefe des Ignatius von Antiochien und der Polykarpbrief* (HNT: Die apostolischen Väter 2, 1920) , 286.

[16] Cf Rom 8.34. It may be significant that one Greek deity often described as sitting beside Zeus (*paredros Dios*) was *Dikē,* the goddess of penal justice. (For the NT era, see esp. Philo *Conf* 118; *Mut* 194; *Jos* 48. Cf G. Schrenk, TWNT 2,183 [=TDNT 2,181]). Dio Chrysostom (*Disc* 1.74; J. W. Cohoon, *Dio Chrysostum* 1 [LCL, 1932], 38-39) relates Heracles' vision of a divine woman representing true royalty; Justice sits at her right hand (*ek dexiōn kathēmenē Dikē*). Cf above, p. 53. Did early Christians ever correlate Jesus sitting as judge at God's right hand with the Greek idea of *Dikē?* Certainly they typically associated Jesus' vindication and judgment with the triumph of divine righteousness. The references to *dikē* in Acts 28.4 and 25.15 (variant) might allude to such a correlation. (Cf the observations of H. J. Cadbury in *The Beginnings of Christianity* 5, ed. K. Lake and H. J. Cadbury [New York: Macmillan, 1933], 364 and n. 3.) Does Paul's replacement of *dikē* (Hos 13.14 OG) by *nikos* in 1 Cor 15.55 also allude to this correlation?

see the son of man exalted at the right hand of power and coming on the clouds of heaven. This clearly implies their own condemnation.[17] Although *Acts 7.55-56* describes a vision of Jesus at God's right hand in the present age, the passage *may* obliquely allude to the inevitable final divine judgment awaiting those who condemn Stephen (see above, pp. 75-76). Since it refers not only to Jesus' present-time SESSION but also to his final return, the trial confession of James in Heg (EH 2.23.13) plainly hints at the future condemnation awaiting his slayers. Hegesippus indeed seems to regard Vespasian's invasion of Palestine as heaven-sent punishment for the killing of James (EH 2.23.18; cf 2.23.19-20); possibly he thought it a proleptic manifestation of the last judgment. In both Apoc Pet 6 and Sib Or 2.243-44, Jesus' SESSION is represented as beginning at the last judgment, and that judgment involves good and evil men alike.

Two last passages must be mentioned, though their conceptions of subjection differ considerably from those in the texts already discussed. *Rev 3.21* speaks of Christ having "conquered" and sat down on his father's throne. His conquest is evidently conceived in terms of his fearless witness to the point of death, a witness Christians should imitate. No persons or powers subjected are mentioned here, but probably the devil and possibly other supernatural enemies are implied (cf 12.11). Anticipating the final total destruction of the forces of evil (Rev 20), Jesus and his followers overcome them "in principle" by accepting martyrdom (cf Jn 14.30; 16.33; Heb 2.14).

The author of the "longer ending" of Mark may have intended his readers to regard Jesus' ascension and SESSION ("*Mk*" *16.19*) as a victory over his foes. In "Mk" 16.17-18 Jesus promises miracles of triumph over evil powers, and in 16.20 the narrator reports that such miracles actually supported the preaching of the disciples because their ascended lord worked with them.[18] The implication is that demonic powers responsible for disease were subdued if not completely eliminated.

Summary and Conclusions

Numerous early Christian allusions to Ps 110.1 and one quotation of it (1 Clem 36.5-6) relate it to ideas about the subjection of powers to Christ. Yet, as Chart 5 shows, these passages betray widely diverging

---

[17] Cf Rev 1.7 and see above, pp. 67, 69.
[18] Cf the thought and language of Lk 10.17-20.

views of the time of subjection (past, present, future) and the persons or powers subjected (angels, demons, men, creatures generally). Sometimes the identity of those subjected is left vague (notably in the case of Heb 10.12-13).[19] Further, in many of these passages the subjection of powers or persons to Christ is at most a secondary concern. In only three instances is the psalm's text the basis of argument: twice regarding an eschatological delay (1 Cor 15.25; Heb 10.12-13), once regarding the fate of particular opponents (1 Clem 35.5-6).

The connection of Ps 110.1 with this theme (and with Ps 8.7) must have been established at a very early date. It is assumed in 1 Cor 15.25 and present in the *Vorlagen* behind Eph 1.20-23, 1 Pet 3.21-22, and Pol *Phil* 2.1. It seems likely that early Christian ideas about the subjection of all things to Christ were inherent in, or a direct extension of, early convictions about his vindication and exaltation. Primitive Christian hymns and confessions typically assert his unqualified supremacy over other powers (Phil 2.9-11; Col 1.15-20; etc.). As a major symbol of Jesus' exaltation, the SESSION must have been naturally drawn into passages dealing with subjection; the wording of Ps 110.1c could only strengthen this tendency. Given this matrix for its use, however, it is not too surprising that a wide variety of subjection ideas are associated with the psalm verse. The primary interest motivating its usage lay not in identifying Jesus' foes or the time of their defeat but in stressing the absoluteness of his exaltation and the utter security of those he willed to save.

---

[19] Cullmann (*State*, 102 f, 112 f) claims that early Christians regularly interpreted the "enemies" of Ps 110.1 as angels. In view of 1 Clem 36.5-6 and those allusions connecting the psalm text with the last judgment, this seems very questionable. Justin Martyr in one passage interprets the foes mentioned in the psalm as demons (*Apol* 45), but elsewhere (*Apol* 28) he suggests that the text also refers to wicked men.

CHAPTER 6

Psalm 110 in Affirmations About Jesus' Intercession and Priestly Office

Intercession and Psalm 110.1: at God's Right Hand

The connection between Ps 110 and the priestly work and office of Jesus is drawn with unique power in the epistle to the Hebrews, but traces of similar connections and conceptions may be found elsewhere in the early church's literature.[1]

The idea of Jesus or the son of man acting in heaven as intercessor, witness, or judge to men is firmly embedded in the synoptic tradition.[2] This heavenly action seems limited in time to the last judgment. In 1 Jn 2.1 Jesus is depicted as a present-time heavenly paraclete who deals with the sins of believers.[3] Linked with this tradition are Lk 22. 32 and Jn 17, which represent Jesus interceding for disciples on earth before his death.[4]

---

[1] Among recent discussions, see esp. O. Moe, "Das Priestertum Christi im Neuen Testament ausserhalb des Hebräerbriefs," TLZ 72 (1947), cols. 335-38; G. Friedrich, "Beobachtungen zur messianischen Hohepriestererwartung in den Synoptikern," ZTK 53 (1956), 265-311; A. J. B. Higgins, "The Old Testament and Some Aspects of New Testament Christology," *Promise and Fulfillment,* ed. F. F. Bruce (Edinburgh: Clark, 1963), 128-41; A. J. B. Higgins, "The Priestly Messiah," NTS 13 (1967), 211-39; J. Behm, TWNT 5,798-812 (=TDNT 5,800-814); Cullmann, *Christology,* 83-107; Hahn, *Titles,* 229-39; Zorn, *Fürbitte.* See below, p. 140 n. 53, for references in ancient sources.

[2] Mk 8.38 par; Mt 10.32-33 par. In Mt 7.21 ff and 25.31 ff, Jesus acts as both star witness and judge. Cf also 2 Tim 2.12; Rev 3.5. There is some similarity between such texts and Mk 14.62=Mt 26.64, though in the latter passage the issue is chiefly the vindication of Jesus himself.

[3] Rather strangely 1 Jn 2.2 proceeds at once to allude to Jesus' death as the source of forgiveness. Cf R. Bultmann, *Die drei Johannesbriefe* (Meyer, 1967), 29 f; O. Betz, *Der Paraklet* (Leiden: Brill, 1963), 155.

[4] Nothing in Jn 17 indicates that it represents post-Easter intercession on Christ's part, and several verses make plain its orientation to the moment of his

Rom 8.34 plainly assumes a connection between the PLACE at God's right hand and (efficacious) intercession. There are no very close parallels in Jewish literature, but some apparent precedents do exist. Philo interprets Abraham's vision of the three visitors as one of God and his two chief powers; the power of mercy stands on the right and the power of government (or punishment) on the left.[5] Very comparable is the pharisaic notion of the divine *middot* of mercy and judgment; the former is God's right hand (the stronger hand), the latter is his left.[6] How a pagan background might prepare one to grasp the thought of Rom 8.34 is suggested by an inscription of King Antiochus I of Commagene.[7] After death the king expected to be transported to the heavenly thrones of Zeus, where he would be able to intercede with all the gods on behalf of his successors. Looking forward to this beneficial glorification, the king built a mountaintop shrine at which images of himself and several deities were set upon thrones.

In Rom 8.34 Jesus is described as the one "who is at the right hand of God, who makes intercession for us." The time of intercession seems to be the last judgment.[8] The pleading is on behalf of Christians, whose salvation is thus assured. The precise nature of the intercession is not explained, but presumably it is to guarantee forgiveness of sins.[9] At least the relative clauses of this verse are probably pre-Pauline both in content and wording.[10] Yet Paul probably discerned rich meaning in the assertions. In Rom 8.26-27 the decisive point is that the Spirit of God intercedes for believers, not that their prayers as such have efficacy. In 8.31-39 the absolute confidence of Christians

---

departure from the world (17.1,11-13,15,20). Jn 16.26-27 can be read as a deliberate repudiation of ideas of Jesus as heavenly advocate. See R. Bultmann, *Johannes,* 453 f.

[5] *Abr* 124. Cf QE 2.68; *Gaius* 95; *Deus* 73; *Jos* 229.

[6] See M. Buber, *Two Types of Faith,* ET N. Goldhawk (New York: Harper, 1961), 152-54. Cf b. Sanhedrin 38b. See also the references to the Midrash on the Song of Songs and the Apocalypse of Abraham on p. 54 (above). Philonenko (*Testament,* 45) suggests that T Job 33.3 (which refers to Ps 110.1b) alludes to Job 16.19 and the conception of a heavenly witness.

[7] The text is in W. Dittenberger, *Orientis Graeci Inscriptiones Selectae* (Hildesheim: Olms, 1960 [=1903]), 1,593-603 (=383). The inscription is dated in the first century BCE.

[8] See above, pp. 59-60. Cf O. Michel, *Der Brief an die Römer* (Meyer, 1957), 186; L. Mattern, *Das Verständnis des Gerichtes bei Paulus* (ATANT 47, 1966), 95 n. 210; K. Kertelge, *"Rechtfertigung" bei Paulus,* (NTAbh 3, 1967), 125, 128-34.

[9] Is Christ's intercession directly related to that of the Spirit (Rom 8.26-27) or to Christian prayer? Cf N. Johannson, *Parakletoi* (Lund: Gleerupska, 1940), 234 f.

[10] See above, p. 40.

resides not in anything they may do or have done but in the objective acts of God and Christ. Hence it is extremely appropriate that in 8.34 the apostle quotes a traditional confession that the case of the defense at the last judgment will depend on Christ alone.[11]

The closest NT parallel to Rom 8.34 is *Heb 7.25*, where Jesus is represented as "forever able to save those who draw near to God through him since he always lives to intercede for them *(entygchanein hyper autōn)*." This assertion is, as we shall see later, more closely connected with Ps 110.4 than with Ps 110.1. Yet that Jesus intercedes at God's right hand is implied since this activity is obviously heavenly and Jesus' heavenly situation is so often described in this epistle by references to Ps 110.1*b*.[12] The intercession seems to be conceived as continuing throughout the period between ascension and parousia (cf 9.24). The content of Jesus' petition is not precisely indicated, but the first half of 7.25 suggests that it embraces everything needed to give believers access to God. Perhaps the author connects it with the prayers they offer. Yet this idea of eternal intercession is something of a "foreign body" in the epistle's theology. This fact, as well as the resemblance to other passages depicting Jesus as heavenly intercessor, suggests that 7.25*b* is a traditional formulation.

Are similar ideas expressed in other passages from the early Christian period? An allusion to Ps 110.1*b* which *may* have intercessory connotations appears in *Acts 7.55-56*. Christ's standing posture, unparalleled among other early citations of the psalm, has been taken to indicate that Jesus rises to act as a witness or intercessor on Stephen's behalf.[13] Alternatively one might suppose that he rises as a witness in relation to the Jewish judges about to condemn the martyr, denouncing them[14] or perhaps pleading for their forgiveness (to answer, by anticipation, the prayer of 7.60).[15] Such intercessory interpretations

---

[11] Cf K. Niederwimmer, "Das Gebet des Geistes," *Theologische Zeitschrift* 20 (1964), 252, 260-63; Mattern, *Verständnis*, 96.

[12] See, e.g., Spicq, *Hébreux* 2,233.

[13] Cf C. F. D. Moule, "From Defendant to Judge—and Deliverer," *Studiorum Novi Testamenti Societas Bull.* 3,40-53; Michel, *Hebräer*, 340 n. 4; Cullmann, *Christology*, 183. See above, pp. 75-76.

[14] Cf Pesch, *Vision des Stephanus*, 55-58.

[15] Possibly Stephen's attack on the earthly temple (Acts 7.47-50; cf 6.13-14) presupposed an idea of a heavenly sanctuary, the model of the tabernacle of Moses. If this idea is present in the tradition (Luke evinces no interest in it), Stephen's vision may have been interpreted as one of God and Christ in the celestial sanctuary, with Christ as a priestly figure. Cf Dahl, *Volk Gottes*, 196; W. Manson, *Hebrews*, 31-36. More recently Dahl has suggested that, for Luke himself, behind Acts 7.44-50 lies the notion that the answer to David's prayer con-

bring one onto the thin ice of speculation. Yet the "standing" invites conjecture, the tie between the ideas of Jesus' right-hand position and intercession is established for the earliest period by Rom 8.34 and Heb 7.25, and these particular suggestions for the sense of the tradition behind Acts 7.55-56 are as plausible as any others.

One other passage in the NT may relate Jesus' right-hand position to intercession: *1 Pet 3.21-22*. The allusion to Ps 110.1*b* appears close to a description of baptism as a *syneidēseōs agathēs eperōtēma eis theon*. What is the meaning of *eperōtēma?* It occurs nowhere else in the NT and is used so rarely elsewhere that a relatively certain interpretation is impossible. The two principal interpretations are (1) "request" or "appeal" (in the sense of an appeal to God for, or on the basis of, a good conscience) and (2) "pledge" or "undertaking" (as a baptized person's pledge to be faithful to God). Scholars have advanced impressive arguments for both interpretations, though perhaps today the second attracts the larger number of expert voices. Still, no decisive evidence excludes the first.[16]

Now, if the meaning "appeal" was actually in the author's mind, he may have associated *eperōtēma* with his allusion to Ps 110. Just as salvation in Noah's time was grounded on divine action (waiting) during the days before the flood, so in the time of the church men find hope of salvation in baptism—regarded as an appeal for God's eschatological judgment of righteousness based on the divine action in Christ's resurrection and intercession at the right hand of God. One other element in the vicinity of 1 Pet 3.21-22 supports this line of exegesis. The final clause in 3.18, "that he might bring us to God," recalls the idea of access to God mentioned in Eph 2.18; 3.12; Heb 4.16; 7.25; 10.22; 12.22; and it may have specifically priestly overtones.[17] "Put to death in the flesh, but made alive in the Spirit"

---

cerning God's resting place (Ps 132.5) is given in vs 11 of the same psalm (cited in Acts 2.30 apropos of Jesus' ascension). See his article "The Story of Abraham in Luke-Acts," *Studies in Luke-Acts* (Festschrift P. Schubert), ed. L. Keck and J. L. Martyn (Nashville: Abingdon, 1966), 146. From this one might infer that Acts 7.55-56 represents the fulfillment of the aspirations which the Jerusalem temple failed to meet.

[16] Advocates of "appeal" include C. Bigg, *The Epistles of St. Peter and St. Jude* (ICC, 1905), 165; H. Windisch and H. Preisker, *Die katholischen Briefe*, 3rd ed. (HNT, 1951), 73; H. Greeven, TWNT 2,685 f (=TDNT 2,688 f); Bauer *et al.*, *Lexicon*, *s.v.* Scholars favoring "pledge" include G. S. Richards, "1 Peter iii 21," JTS 32 (1930-31), 77; B. Reicke, *The Disobedient Spirits and Christian Baptism* (Copenhagen: Munksgaard, 1946), 182-86; E. Selwyn, *St. Peter*, 205-6; Dalton, *Proclamation*, 224-26; Beare, *First Peter*, 3rd ed., 175.

[17] Cf Selwyn, *St. Peter* 196; Fuchs, *Freiheit*, 117.

connects this saving action with Jesus' resurrection-ascension as well as with his death. Perhaps, then, both the writer of 1 Peter and the *Vorlage* he used related the allusion to Ps 110.1*b* with the *hina* clause of 3.18.[18] It is fairly clear that the guiding theme of 3.10–4.6 is the righteousness which men must have before God. What could be more appropriate than an interpretation of baptism in 3.21-22 which made it the channel whereby men gain righteousness? [19]

Thus, while other passages in early Christian literature describe Christ as priest or intercessor, only these four passages (Rom 8.34; Heb 7.25; Acts 7.55-56; 1 Pet 3.21-22) seem to connect intercession with his station at God's right hand.

Psalm 110.4: a Priest Like Melchizedek

The sacerodotal interpretation of Jesus in Hebrews may be presumed to have a complex background, one related not only to the traditions already discussed in this chapter but also to broader tendencies in Jewish and Christian thought concerning priestly salvation and Melchizedek. A number of remarkable things are said about Melchizedek in ancient Jewish and Christian literature, and he enjoys extraordinary prominence in two documents recently discovered at Qumran and Nag Hammadi. Fortunately, however, a number of fairly up-to-date monographs and articles about Melchizedek are available,[20] and accordingly we need not enter upon an extended treatment of this subject.

Messianic Priest Conceptions.—Evidence from various quarters indicates that many Jews after the Babylonian exile set their hopes in a priestly savior.[21] Haggai and Zechariah exalt the role of Joshua, the

---

[18] Bultmann takes the clause as an integral part of the original confession ("Liedfragmente," 3).

[19] It seems evident that the primary stress of 3.18-22 lies not on what men do but on what God does for them.

[20] See esp. F. J. Jérôme, *Das geschichtliche Melchisedech-Bild und seine Bedeutung im Hebräerbriefe* (Freiburg: Caritatisdruckerei, 1920); G. Wuttke, *Melchisedech der Priesterkönig von Salem* (BZNW 5, 1927); Käsemann, *Gottesevolk;* O. Michel, TWNT 4,573-75 (=TDNT 4,568-71); M. Simon, "Melchisédech dans la polémique entre Juifs et Chretiens et dans la légende," *Revue d'histoire et de philosophie religieuses* 17 (1937), 58-93; G. T. Kennedy, *Saint Paul's Conception of the Priesthood of Melchizedech* (Washington: Catholic Univ. Press, 1951); H. Rusche, "Die Gestalt des Melchisedek," *Münchener Theologische Zeitschrift* 6 (1955), 230-52; J. Fitzmyer, "Now this Melchizedek . . ." *Catholic Biblical Quarterly* 25 (1963), 305-21; Theissen, *Untersuchungen*, 17-20, 130-52.

[21] Cf Volz, *Eschatologie*, 190-93; J. Jeremias, TWNT 2,934 f (=TDNT 2,932 f); J. Klausner, *The Messianic Idea in Israel*, ET W. F. Stinespring (New York: Mac-

high priest; one passage (Zech 6.9-14) originally seems to have pictured his being crowned together with the messianic Zerubbabel.[22] The priestly rulers in Jerusalem during the Persian and early hellenistic periods and the Hasmonean rulers after them may or may not have had eschatological dreams associated with their reigns, but certainly the priestly office was the foundation on which all of them based their government. In the Testaments of the Twelve Patriarchs, Judah and Levi are ranked above all their brothers in regard to Israel's hopes of salvation; and certain passages set Levi—as a priestly figure, and perhaps a messianic one—above Judah.[23] The sectarians at Qumran evidently expected two messiahs, one a David-like warrior and the other a high priest descended from Aaron. It may be that the writers of the scrolls differed among themselves in messianic doctrine, but our data tend to show that they considered the priestly messiah superior to the other.[24] In the messianic revolt of Bar-Kochba a certain priest named Eleazar enjoyed special prominence. The apocalyptic and rabbinic literature mention a number of heavenly intercessors who plead on behalf of Israel or the righteous. Among them the angel Michael was perhaps the favorite.[25] Philo of Alexandria declares that Moses had to be priest as well as king, philosopher, prophet, and legislator.[26] The road to the divine through the Aaronic cultus, while perhaps not the highest for Philo, is yet recognized as genuine and described at length.[27] There is no uniformity in these and other Jewish

---

millan, 1955), 514-16; B. Vawter, "Levitical Messianism and the New Testament," *The Bible in Current Catholic Thought,* ed. J. L. McKenzie (New York: Herder & Herder, 1962), 83-99; A. J. B. Higgins, "Priestly Messiah."

[22] See P. R. Ackroyd, "Zechariah," *Peake's Commentary on the Bible,* ed. M. Black and H. H. Rowley (London: Nelson, 1962), 649.

[23] The chief passages of relevance are T Reub 6.7-8; 10-12; T Sim 7.1-2; 2.9-10; T Levi 5.1-2; 8.1-17; 18.2-15; T Judah 21.2; T Naph 5.1-4; 8.2; T Gad 8.1; T Jos 19.11-12; T Benj 11.2. Cf G. R. Beasley-Murray, "The Two Messiahs in the Testaments of the Twelve Patriarchs," JTS 48 (1947), 1-12.

[24] 1Q S^a 2.12,18-20. See esp. K. G. Kuhn, "The Two Messiahs," *The Scrolls and the New Testament,* ed. K. Stendahl (New York: Harper, 1957), 54-64. Some scholars deny that the eschatological priest is conceived as a messiah (e.g., C. T. Fritsch, "The So-Called Priestly Messiah of the Essenes," *Jaarbericht van het vooraziatsch-Egyptisch genootschap Ex Oriente Lux,* Deel VI [Leiden, 1967], 242-48).

[25] Note, e.g., b. Ḥagigah 12b. See W. Lueken, *Michael* (Göttingen: Vandenhoeck & Ruprecht, 1898); Moore, *Judaism* 1,438 f; cf J. Daniélou, *The Theology of Jewish Christianity,* ET J. A. Baker (London: Darton, Longman & Todd, 1964), 121-27.

[26] *Mos* 2.2-5, 187.

[27] One notable treatment is offered in *Mos* 2.71-135. See further *Spec* 1.97, 116; *Praem* 56; *Fug* 108 ff.

expressions of priestly hope regarding the identity or precise functions of the saving priest or intercessor. But he regularly appears as mediator between God and man, enabling men to approach the divine. As Käsemann remarks, "the figures vary, but the schema remains." [28]

Melchizedek in Pre-Christian Judaism in General.—Melchizedek was one of the priestly figures in whom late Judaism hoped. Our evidence is scattered and at times fragmentary, but it suffices to show that the ancient priest-king of Salem was the subject of widespread speculation in the period immediately preceding the Christian era. [29] In the post-biblical era the earliest extant Jewish allusions to Melchizedek may be in those passages of 1 Maccabees and the Testaments of the Twelve Patriarchs which appear to defend the Hasmonean rule with the precedent of Melchizedek's. [30] There is an obvious lacuna in Jubilees at the beginning of 13.25, just where the reader would expect a narrative of the main events of Gen 14. Since the latter part of Jub 13.25 assumes that priests have a right to tithes, Abraham's meeting with Melchizedek was probably part of the original book. Since other texts in Jubilees apparently praise the Hasmoneans, it may well be that the missing statements about Melchizedek were highly laudatory. [31] We seem to have a similar gap in Philo's *Questions on Genesis;* but other passages of his display a consistently favorable, sometimes panegyrical, attitude toward Melchizedek. In *Abr* 235 he is *ho megas hiereus;* in *Cong* 99 he is the self-taught holder of the priesthood; [32] in *LA* 3.79-82 he is king of peace and righteousness, God's own priest, the *orthos logos* who brings men salvation (symbolized in his gifts of

[28] *Gottesvolk,* 130. Käsemann thinks the root idea is one of an incarnate *Urmensch* who as such has the rank of a highpriestly messiah.

[29] In the Hebrew scriptures he is mentioned only at Gen 14.18-20 and Ps 110.4. Although earlier generations of scholars tended to date both passages in the post-exilic period, the consensus now favors a much earlier origin for each. See G. von Rad, *Genesis: A Commentary,* ET J. Marks (Philadelphia: Westminster, 1961), 174-76. H. E. del Medico has advanced the radical theory that neither passage meant to refer to a person named "Melchizedek" but rather allude to the title "king of righteousness" ("Melchizedek," *Zeitschrift für die alttestamentliche Wissenschaft* 69 [1957], 160-70). While this notion gets some support from the targum on the psalm and *Aboth R. Nathan* 34.4, there are so many other rabbinic and early Christian references to "Melchizedek" as a personal name that we must assume that this was at least the dominant interpretation in the early Christian period.

[30] See pp. 24-25 above.

[31] Cf R. H. Charles, *The Book of Jubilees* (London: Black, 1902), 100 f and lxxiii.

[32] Cf E. R. Goodenough, *Light,* 151, 155-57.

wine and bread).[33] Josephus says only that Melchizedek was made the first priest of God because of his righteousness, that he built a temple in Jerusalem, and that he persuaded Abraham to accept gifts from the king of Sodom (*Ant* 1.[10.2] 180-81; JW 6.[10.1]438). Ps-Philo never mentions Melchizedek or the events of Gen 14.[34]

Melchizedek at Qumran.—The recent publication of 11Q Melchizedek has revealed that Melchizedek was the subject of some remarkable reflection at Qumran. In the fragmentary document he appears with commanding prominence.[35] The work, which has been dated in the first half of the first century CE or shortly before, is an eschatological midrash containing a series of scriptural quotations interspersed with "pesher" explanations. Although some of the language and themes of the document have parallels elsewhere in the Dead Sea scrolls (especially in 4Q Flor and 1QM), the emphasis on Melchizedek is unique.[36] Here he is a divine being, exalted among or above the angels in heaven,[37] who will perform decisive saving work on behalf of the sons of light at the end of days.[38] The Jubilee and release year

[33] Cf E. Stein, *Philo und der Midrasch* (Giessen: Töpelmann, 1931), 31.

[34] M. R. James, *The Biblical Antiquities of Philo* (London S.P.C.K., 1917), 103.

[35] The *editio princeps* was published by A. S. van der Woude, "Melchisedek als himmlische Erlösergestalt in den neugefundenen eschatologischen Midraschim aus Qumran Höhle XI," *Oudtestamentische Studiën* 14 (1965), 354-73.

[36] Before 11Q Melchizedek appeared, there was no evidence from Qumran of special interest in Melchizedek, either positive or negative. Elsewhere in the scrolls he is mentioned only in 1Qap Gen 22.14-17, where his meeting with Abraham is paraphrased with minor changes from Gen 14. It may be significant that in *that* document Melchizedek's name is written as one word, while in 11Q Melchizedek it is two words. These facts suggest that 11Q Melchizedek represents only a minority opinion at Qumran.

[37] See esp. line 10. Cf J. Fitzmyer, "Further Light on Melchizedek from Qumran Cave 11," *JBL* 86 (1967), 25-41. J. Carmignac ("Le document de Qumrân sur Melkisédeq," *Revue de Qumran* 7 [1970], 343-78) denies that line 10 pertains to Melchizedek and contends that the document simply uses "Melchizedek" as a symbolic name for the human Davidic messiah elsewhere mentioned in Qumran writings. I think it more natural to read line 10 as a reference to Melchizedek as a divine or angelic being, but Carmignac's interpretation is certainly possible. M. de Jonge and A. S. van der Woude ("11Q Melchizedek and the New Testament," *NTS* 12 [1965-66], 301-26) think that 11Q Melchizedek may identify Melchizedek with the archangel Michael, an idea set forth explicitly in certain medieval Jewish texts. Fitzmyer is agnostic on the point. Certainly there is striking similarity in the traits ascribed to Michael in 1QM 17.6-7 (cf 9.15-16), those ascribed to the "prince of light" in 1QM 13.10; 17.6 (?) ; 1QS 3.20; CD 5.18, and those attributed to Melchizedek in 11Q Melchizedek: all three figures are angelic leaders or allies of the "sons of light" in the end-time war against Belial and his hordes.

[38] Those to be saved are "men of the lot of Melchizedek" and the time of re-

legislation of Lev 25 and Deut 15 is interpreted as pertaining to an eschatological return of exiles or captives (presumably to Palestine). Melchizedek is somehow connected with this and perhaps makes atonement for sins (lines 4-9).[39] The salvation-peace prophesied in Isa 52.7 is also related to him, possibly because he produces it or because he preaches and teaches about the times of wrath and mercy (lines 15-24). Most clearly, however, Melchizedek is portrayed as the executor of God's judgment against the hosts of Belial through a crushing end-time victory (lines 9-14).[40] Nowhere in all this does a clear allusion to Gen 14 or Ps 110 appear. Perhaps those texts were referred to in fragments of the work not recovered; but it is also possible that the writer deliberately ignored them.[41] Finally, it may be noted that it is uncertain whether Melchizedek was related to the expectations of an eschatological high priest expressed in other Qumran documents.[42]

Rabbinic and Samaritan Traditions About Melchizedek.—Nor was the rabbinic tradition indifferent to Melchizedek. Almost all the references to him in rabbinic literature are distinctly favorable or markedly hostile. He is often identified with Shem and praised as the first priest of God in Jerusalem.[43] Sometimes he is represented as a teacher or inspired author. The bread and wine mentioned in Gen 14 signify his revelation of torah to Abraham (Genesis Rabba 43.6). He also

demption is "the year of good favor for Melchizedek" (lines 8-9).

[39] The subject and nature of the atoning work are obscure.

[40] In this "reign of judgment" he is assisted by (other?) angels—the "holy ones of God" (lines 9,14).

[41] On the apparent absence of allusions to Ps 110 at Qumran, see p. 27 above. J. A. Sanders suggests that the general train of thought of the psalm underlies the whole of 11Q Melch, but this impression is hard to verify. See Fitzmyer, "Light," 31 f, 37. A positive link with the psalm is also argued by W. H. Brownlee, "Jesus and Qumran," in *Jesus and the Historian,* ed. F. T. Trotter (Philadelphia: Westminster, 1968), 64-70.

[42] Cf de Jonge and van der Woude, "11Q Melchizedek," 322. R. Meyer ("Melchisedek von Jerusalem und Moresedek von Qumran," VTSup 15 [1965], [Leiden: Brill, 1966], 228-39) has recently argued that the "Moresedek" at Qumran was possibly regarded as the earthly counterpart of the heavenly Melchizedek of 11Q Melchizedek. He also offers the interesting suggestion that both Hasmoneans and Dead Sea sectarians appealed to Melchizedek, since the Zadokite priesthood in the post-exilic era had already connected their authority with his. Cf the theory of Tournay mentioned above, p. 19 n. 3.

[43] E.g., Midrash Tehillim on Ps 76. Certain liturgical texts in the Apostolic Constitutions identified by Bousset as of Jewish origin describe Melchizedek as a true priest (see Goodenough, *Light,* 323 326, 330 f). Curiously the Targums Onkelos and Ps-Jonathan avoid calling him "priest" (see discussion in J. A. Fitzmyer, *The Genesis Apocryphon* [Biblica et Orientalia 18; Rome: Pontifical Biblical Institute, 1966], 157).

taught Abraham the practice of charity[44] and gave counsel to Rebeccah.[45] The rabbis credited him with having written some of the canonical psalms (b. Baba Bathra 14b-15a) and having admonished the nations as a prophet for 400 years.[46] The Talmud names four messiahs: the son of David, the son of Joseph, Elijah, and the priest of justice. Ginzberg and Kohler urge that the last may be Melchizedek.[47] But the rabbis also spoke against Melchizedek. I have already mentioned the opinion of R. Ishmael, who taught that God deposed Melchizedek from the priesthood.[48] His view probably reflects opposition to early Christendom's appropriation of Melchizedek as a type of Christ.[49] Similar downgrading appears in a report from Epiphanius that "the Jews declare Melchizedek to have been the son of a prostitute."[50] Another rabbinic opinion expresses hostility not toward Melchizedek but probably toward Christians who revered him as one of the uncircumcised pious before Abraham: it affirmed that Melchizedek was born circumcised.[51]

Alexander Polyhistor reports a Samaritan tradition that Melchizedek met Abraham at Mt. Gerizim (Eusebius, *Prep* 9.17.5-6 [*GCS* 43.1, 503]). Much later Epiphanius reports an opinion that Melchizedek's parents were Heracles and Astarte, and he apparently attributes this view to Samaritans (*Her* 55.2). Conceivably these scraps of evidence reflect an established Samaritan association of Melchizedek with worship at Gerizim; if so, the author of Heb 7 was probably not the first to argue Melchizedek's superiority to the levitical priests at Jerusalem.[52]

Melchizedek in Early Christian Traditions Apart from Hebrews.—
Early Christianity described Jesus as priest or high priest rather frequently, but (leaving Hebrews out of account) these titles seem to

[44] Midrash Tehillim on Ps 37.
[45] Midrash Tehillim on Ps 9.
[46] Ginzberg, *Legends* 5,192.
[47] *Ibid.*, 142; K. Kohler, JE 8,450. Cf Klausner, *Messianic Idea*, 515.
[48] See above, pp. 28-29.
[49] This is the view, e.g., of Ginzberg, *Legends* 5,226. See above, 30. Other opponents than Christians have been suggested: Alexandrian Jews (K. Kohler, JE 8,450); Hasmoneans (Petuchowski, "Melchizedek," 127-36); Samaritans (Theissen, *Untersuchungen*, 135).
[50] *Heresies* 55.6. Cf Spicq, *Hébreux* 2,209 n. 1.
[51] Genesis Rabba 43.6-8; Midrash Tehillim on Ps 7. Cf Justin Martyr, *Dial.* 19.4; 33.2; Tertullian, *Jews* 2.14. M. Simon ("Melchisédech") presents a careful analysis of the development of thought about Melchizedek in the framework of Jewish-Christian debate.
[52] See Theissen, *Untersuchungen*, 17 f, 130-35.

have been applied only with regard to his heavenly post-resurrection position and work.[53]

Hebrews is the only Christian work before Justin Martyr which mentions Melchizedek. Justin remarks that, like Jesus himself, Melchizedek was priest of the uncircumcised (*Dial* 33.2; cf 63.3; 83.2; 118.1). Theophilus of Antioch (*Autolycus* 2.31) says nothing about a relation to Christ but reports that Melchizedek was a righteous king and the first priest of God. Tertullian contends that his possession of the priestly office shows that divine law existed before Moses (*Jews* 2.7-8). Clement of Alexandria is the first Christian writer to find in Melchizedek's gifts to Abraham a prefiguration of the eucharist.[54] Jerome reports that Origen and Didymus regarded Melchizedek as an angel (*Epistle* 73.2). Other Christians thought him a manifestation of the Son of God or the Holy Spirit (Epiphanius, *Her* 55.5, 7; 67.3,7). A rich configuration of legends is offered in the "Melchizedek fragment," apparently a Jewish-Christian work, perhaps tinged with gnosticism.[55] After a miraculous conception and birth, Melchizedek acts as priest and king at Adam's grave in the middle of the earth. He is preserved by Michael in paradise at the time of the flood, and it is said that at last he shall rule over all as high priest and word of God. The work is not fully consistent, but it apparently applies this eschatological promise to a second Melchizedek (the first eventually dies). A kindred concern to find in Melchizedek a priestly (and non-Aaronic) link between Jesus and the primeval age is attested in the narratives about him in the Ethiopic Book of Adam and Eve and the Syriac Book of the Cave of Treasures. In these works, which also betray both Jewish and Christian traits, God appoints Melchizedek as priest to offer bread and wine perpetually over Adam's grave at Golgotha. Melchizedek gives the wine of salvation to Abraham, and the symbolism is climaxed in an account of the messiah's death. While the Adam-Christ typology is the one most emphasized in the story,

---

[53] 1 Clem 36; 61.3; 64.1; Ign *Phld* 9.1; Justin, *Dial* 96.1; Epistle of the Apostles 51; Mart Pol 14.3. Rev 1.13 may reflect a priestly christology. Cf Theissen, *Untersuchungen*, 33-52.

[54] *Misc* 4.[25] 161.3. Clement also mentions a group of "mystics" who said that Moses received the name "Melchi" after his ascension into heaven (*Misc* 1.[23]153.1). Were they identifying Moses with the heavenly Melchizedek? Cf Goodenough, *Light*, 292 f.

[55] Ginzberg, *Legends* 5,226. For translations and introductory discussions, see W. R. Morfill and R. H. Charles, *The Book of the Secrets of Enoch* (Oxford: Clarendon, 1896), 85-93; Vaillant, *Secrets*, xiii, 64-85, 114-19.

a close link between Melchizedek and Christ is also underscored.[56]

A recent discovery, comparable in importance to 11Q Melchizedek, is that of the still unpublished first tractate of the gnostic codex 9 from Nag Hammadi.[57] Like its Qumran counterpart, this document is in fragmentary condition. In it Melchizedek is called "Holy One of God Most High" and "true high-priest of God Most High," and he figures as a key heavenly personage along with Jesus Christ. Melchizedek is chiefly mentioned in the document in two types of contexts, one type referring to baptism and sacrifices and the other type referring to a victory he wins over hostile supernatural and earthly foes. No other Nag Hammadi writing mentions him by name, though another writing refers to "the kings and priests of righteousness" who will appear in the last days to perform purifying acts (the terminology recalls Gen 14.18-20 and Heb 7.1-2).[58] Melchizedek has an important role in the Pistis Sophia as a "heavenly helper," one of those in "the place of the right hand" (allusion to Ps 110.1?). He is the "great receiver of light" who brings purified light into the "treasury of light" (i.e., brings men's soul to heaven).[59] Both in this work and in the Second Book of Jeû (codex Brucianus) he bears the additional name of Zorokothora. In the latter, too, he is a mysterious power of the realm of light; and Jesus prays to God to send Zorokothora-Melchizedek in secret with the "water of the baptism of fire" as a sign that Jesus' disciples have received forgiveness.[60] In the gnostic Dialogue between John and Jesus, John asks about the meaning of the affirmation that Melchizedek is parentless, without beginning or end of days, and holds an eternal priesthood like the Son of God (cf Heb 7.3). Jesus' answer is not preserved.[61] Finally, we must note that several scholars detect within Heb 7.1-3 itself allusion to secret doctrine about Melchizedek.

---

[56] See E. A. W. Budge, *The Book of the Cave of Treasures* (London: Religious Tract Society, 1927); S. C. Malan, *The Book of Adam and Eve* (London: Williams & Norgate, 1882).

[57] The following description is based on a paper by Birger A. Pearson ("The Heavenly World According to the First Tractate of the Unpublished Gnostic Codex IX from Nag Hammadi") given at the congress of the International Association for the History of Religions at Stockholm in August 1970. Professor Pearson (who kindly supplied me with a copy of his paper) argues that the treatise has special affinities with 11Q Melchizedek, the Pistis Sophia, the Second Book of Jeû, and the Melchizedekian heresy as described by Epiphanius in *Her* 55.

[58] A. Böhlig and P. Labib, *Die Koptisch-gnostische Schrift ohne Titel aus Codex II von Nag Hammadi* (Berlin: Akademie-Verlag, 1962), 67 and n.

[59] Schmidt and Till, *Schriften*, 34-46 (21 f), 194-95 (125 f), 291 (188 f).

[60] *Ibid.*, 110-11 (310 f).

[61] H-S 1,333.

The well-balanced, sonorous phrases, the careful choice of words, and the failure of the rest of Heb 7 to develop the ideas of 7.2-3—all this does seem to point to a special tradition of teaching about Melchizedek, teaching very possibly of a gnostic or proto-gnostic character.[62]

From various church writers between the third and seventh centuries we learn of a certain Melchizedekian heresy, the general tendency of which was to exalt Melchizedek above Christ.[63] Hippolytus connects the movement with a certain Theodotus, a banker, who claimed that Jesus was the inferior image and descendant of Melchizedek (Ref 7.36.1). Ephiphanius, who provides the fullest account of it, says that a potter named Theodotus concluded from Ps 110 that Melchizedek was a heavenly power, and from Heb 7.1-3 that, lacking parents and genealogy, he was superior to Christ. The Melchizedekites, he reports, regard Melchizedek as a priestly advocate through whom offerings to God must be made (Her 55). It was a minor heresy, never condemned by pope or council; apparently it never attracted a great champion or large following. It seems to have been a gnostic movement, and some scholars have maintained that it was conceived within pre-Christian Judaism.[64]

Summary.—Despite the sparsity of information about Melchizedek in the Jewish scriptures—or perhaps partly *because* of that exiguity—the mysterious priest-king fascinated and impressed considerable numbers of Jews, Samaritans, Christians, and Christian gnostics in the period of Christian origins and in those periods adjoining it. That he could be identified as a savior or otherwise related to the ultimate ground of salvation is shown by the Samaritan tradition locating him at Mt. Gerizim, Philo's description of him as an embodiment of the logos, the rabbinic interpretation of his gifts to Abraham as equivalent to torah, and the picture of him as supreme among the heavenly hosts in 11Q Melchizedek. Certain Christian (especially gnostic) materials also connect him intimately with salvation—notably the "Melchizedek fragment," the Book of Adam and Eve, the Book of the Cave of Treasures, the first tractate from Nag Hammadi Codex 9, the Pistis

---

[62] Wuttke, *Melchisedech*, 6 ff; Käsemann, *Gottesvolk*, 134. Cf O. Michel, *Hebräer*, 259-63.

[63] See the convenient summary in Kennedy, *Melchizedech*, 126-28.

[64] See M. Friedländer, "La secte de Melchisédech," *Revue des Etudes Juives* 5 (1882), 1-26; R. T. Herford, *Christianity in Talmud and Midrash* (London: Williams & Norgate, 1903), 39 f. On the other hand, G. Bardy ("Melchisédech dans la tradition patristique," *RB* 35 [1926], 497) argues that the heresy was essentially christological.

Sophia, the Second Book of Jeû, and the reports of the Melchize-dekites. A wide range of saving functions are assigned him: revelation of divine truth, militant victory over foes of God and men, bearing of souls to heaven, sacrifices, giving of sacraments (baptism, eucharist). Some traditions represent him as an angelic or heavenly being. Others seem to regard him as merely earthly and human. In Hebrews Melchizedek is not a redeemer, and he performs no saving acts. Yet he is a kind of symbol of ultimacy, a prototype of the eschatological redeemer. The epistle seemingly regards him as an earthbound man of the past; but the priest whose prototype he is lives forever in heaven. Thus in various ways Hebrews seem to reflect and stand critically over against a variety of traditions concerning Melchizedek. To specify precisely which traditions (among those we have examined) the epistle's author knew, and which he did not, is impossible.

Psalm 110 and the Priestly Christology of Hebrews

While perhaps acquainted with a number of esoteric traditions, the author of Hebrews has seen fit to emphasize the scriptural foundations of his christology, above all those in Ps 110.[65]

Apart from an anticipatory reference in Heb 1.3, the citations of the psalm which bear on the priesthood of Jesus are set prominently at the beginning and end of the main argument and at strategic points within it.[66] Given the author's literary artistry in arranging materials, it seems advisable to examine his citations in the order in which they appear.[67]

Heb 1.3 does not term Jesus "priest," and its allusion to Ps 110.1*b* does not in itself express sacrificial ideas. Nonetheless, it is significant that the clause "he sat down at the right hand of the majesty on high" is immediately preceded by "having made purification for sins." Syntactically the latter clause (like the other participial clauses of 1.3) leans on the finite *ekathisen*. Temporally, the reader is clearly meant to regard the acts of purifying and sitting as sequential. Further, these two clauses announce the chief themes of the epistle's christology, i.e., atonement and exaltation. None of the other declarations in 1.1-4 will receive comparable elucidation. The dominant concern of Heb 1 is the glory of Jesus as unique Son, but 1.3 hints that he is also a priest.

---

[65] His references to the psalm are summarized on Charts 3 and 4 (above, pp. 46-47).

[66] Cf Schille, "Erwägungen," 108.

[67] This method will be suspended when we come to Heb 7, for reasons to be explained.

When, beginning in 4.14, the author of the epistle launches into his extended exposition of Christ's office as high priest, it can hardly be doubted that he is presenting doctrine which is arcane and perhaps novel. This is teaching "hard to explain," indigestible to those unable to go beyond elementary things (5.11–6.1).[68] That this doctrine requires justification is indicated by the author's careful and lengthy argumentation from scriptural texts.

In *Heb 5.6* we find the first citation of Ps 110.4. It will be quoted twice more in chap. 7 where it supplies much of the driving pulse of the argument. Indeed, the psalm verse seems an indispensable arrow in the author's quiver, and a prod to his thought as well as a tool of persuasion. Yet, these things being so, it is likely that a major concern in 5.6 is simply to introduce this text as a testimony about Jesus— more is at stake than simply proof that his appointment resembles that of a levitical priest.[69] That proof is not unimportant, however. The psalm's fourth verse is construed as evidence that Jesus did not arrogate priesthood to himself but was directly summoned to the office by God.[70] In this respect the psalm verse shows Jesus' similarity to the levitical priests; in Heb 7 it will be used to argue their radical dissimilarity.

An interest in linking the titles "Son" and "priest" is apparent in the conjunction of psalm quotations in 5.5-6 (cf 1.5). The whole of 5.5-10 looks like a deliberate restatement of the enthronement description in Heb 1. The single long sentence of 5.7-10, with its introduction by a relative pronoun and its kerygmatic contrast of the period of Jesus' earthly trials and that of his exaltation, forms a striking parallel to 1.3-4. The climax of this chain of statements (5.10), like 1.13, is a citation of a verse from Ps 110 (though a different verse).[71] The

---

[68] This is not to say that the author's priestly thought is completely novel. He seems to assume that his readers will not question the application of Ps 110.4 to Jesus any more than they object to the title "high priest" in 2.17. Moreover, we have seen that the community addressed may have known confessions or hymns on which 5.6-10 and 7.26-28 are based (above, p. 43). On the general topic, see H. Zimmermann, *Die Hohepriester-Christologie des Hebräerbriefes* (Paderborn: Schöningh, 1964); F. Schröger, *Der Verfasser des Hebräerbriefes als Schriftausleger* (Biblische Untersuchungen 4; Regensburg: Pustet, 1968), 120-27, 142 (the latter emphasizes the epistle's use of Jewish scriptures rather than other sources).

[69] Just as in Heb 1.5-14 the writer has more in mind than a warning against overrating angels.

[70] Cf M. Dibelius, "Der himmlische Kultus nach dem Hebräerbrief," *Botschaft und Geschichte* 2 (Tübingen: Mohr, 1956), 160-76; Friedrich, "Lied," 95-115.

[71] In both 1.1-14 and 5.5-10, citations of Ps 110 stand at the beginning and at

general similarity of 5.5-10 and 1.1-13 is so great as to imply that the author understood Jesus to have received divine sonship and priesthood at the same time (the ascension).[72] The parallelisms of chaps. one and five and of the divine oracles quoted in 5.5-6 further indicate a conscious interest in associating the two titles.[73] The declarations in 5.10 and 6.20 that Jesus is *archiereus* "after the order of Melchizedek" point back to 5.6. For the interpretation of Jesus' saving work, the author obviously prefers the title "high priest" to "priest" since in the Jewish cultus only the high priest entered the inner tent to offer blood for the sins of the people (9.7).[74] Yet Ps 110 uses the term "priest" and the author of the epistle, although he probably wished that it read "high priest," regularly retains the former in his direct quotations.

While the allusion in *5.10* appears in close proximity to the quotation in 5.6, the intervening verses give it additional meaning. Here the title "high priest" is set in apposition to "the source of eternal salvation to all who obey him." The world *aitios* recalls the *archēgos* of Heb 2.10 (cf 12.2) and points to Jesus as pioneer among the sons of God. Yet *aitios* probably also means "source" in this context.[75] In his priestly work Jesus is more than the first to be perfected: he is the bringer of sanctification to men on the basis of his death (10.14). The clause "being designated by God," as in 5.4-6, points to God as the final author of Jesus' priestly status. Finally, 5.7-9 indicates that Jesus was given this rank after an earthly career of suffering and obedience; it thus reaffirms that ascension and priesthood hang together.

The same association is suggested in *6.20,* where the Melchizedekian

---

the end of a series of key christological assertions. In both passages, and only in them, the same words about divine sonship are quoted from Ps 2.7.

[72] So Käsemann, *Gottesvolk*, 59; cf Bornkamm, *Studien*, 201-3. Otherwise: Spicq, *Hébreux* 2,111 and 119; A. Cody, *Heavenly Sanctuary and Liturgy in the Epistle to the Hebrews* (St. Meinrad [Ind.]: Grail, 1960), 90.

[73] These are the primary titles of the author's christology; "Son" predominates in 1.1–4.13, "priest" (or "high priest") in 4.14–10.23.

[74] The author uses *archiereus* for Jesus in 2.17; 3.1; 4.14-15; 5.5,10; 6.20; 7.26, 28; 8.1; 9.11 (cf 9.25-26). Apart from quotations of, and definite allusions to, Ps 110.4, he calls Jesus *hiereus* only in 8.4 and 10.21 (allusion to Zech 6.11). The attempt by Schille to distinguish sources on the ground of the alternation of "priest" and "high priest" seems too simple (so E. Grässer, "Der Hebräerbrief, 1938-1963," *Theologische Rundschau* 30 [1964], 154). In most of the "priest passages" (7.1-25; 8.4-9; 10.1-14) the author aims at contrasting Jesus with levitical priests in general; hence *hiereus* is naturally employed.

[75] Bauer, *Lexicon, s.v.*

priesthood is predicated of Jesus just as he enters the inner (heavenly) sanctuary as "forerunner on our behalf." That phrase is close in sense to the *aitios* of 5.10 and the *archēgos* of 2.10 and 12.2. As other passages in the epistle show, Jesus enters the sanctuary through his death; and the *hyper hēmōn* emphasizes the purification which he is thereby enabled to give men so that they may draw near to God.[76] Heb 6.20 thus, like 5.10, joins the phrase "according to the order of Melchizedek" with the saving work of Jesus. This is the more striking because hereafter that phrase will be linked with his priestly office, not his work.[77]

The main intent of *Heb 7* is to show that Jesus' priestly office is genuine and superior to that of the Levites. The two points are argued largely on the basis of Ps 110.4. The psalm verse has a dominant place in the thought of 7.11-25, but it also appears at the very end of the chapter and it glitters behind the fabric of 7.1-10, verses depending more conspicuously on Gen 14.18-20. The chapter begins as a kind of explanation of a question raised by the psalm citations in chaps. 5 and 6: who is Melchizedek and what is his *taxis*? Further, despite the use of the Genesis narrative, only selected elements in it are picked up or even mentioned; while virtually every syllable in the psalm verse is probed for significance.[78] The reader is never allowed to forget that the object of interest is not Melchizedek in himself but the one whom the psalm oracle likens to him.

More than any other early Christian text (with the possible exception of Mk 12.35-37 par and Barn 12.10-11) Heb 7 seems to have its thought molded by Ps 110. It is therefore highly desirable to analyze the structure of its argument and seek to define primary and secondary elements.

The core assertion is presented in 7.16: Jesus is priest *kata dynamin zōēs akatalutou*. Here, and here alone in the chapter, the author explains why Jesus is a priest. But in what sense does he possess "indestructible life"? Surely the basic conviction behind the phrase is that of Jesus' resurrection-exaltation.[79] Granting, however, that Jesus

[76] Cf 10.14; 2.10-11. See the *religionsgeschichtliche* analysis in Käsemann, *Gottesvolk*, 79-82.

[77] Is this because in Heb 7 Melchizedek moves to the foreground and the author did not wish to suggest a parallel between his priestly *activity* and that of Jesus?

[78] On the general method of exegesis employed in Heb 7, see Schröger, *Verfasser*, 156-59 (he sees a parallel in rabbinic concern to interpret one scriptural text in the light of a second).

[79] One might see in 7.16 secondary references to the life which Jesus makes possible for believers (cf 2.14-16; 10.38; 12.9) and to the power of eternal life he

is immortal, why does this qualify him as priest? The answer is provided in 7.17 with a quotation of the divine words in Ps 110.4. The thought is evidently that the psalm proves that there exists an authentic priesthood independent of Aaron's to which only persons who never die may belong. Since Jesus is eternal, he may belong. But *must* he? Yes, because the psalm oracle is meant for him (7.13). That idea of the psalm verse's application to Jesus is the second foundation block of the whole chapter, and it was set in position already in 5.6-10.[80]

There is another side to 7.16-17. "According to the power of an indestructible life" is opposed to "according to a legal requirement." The latter phrase must, in the context (cf 7.5-6 and 11-14), allude to the acquisition of priestly office by tribal lineage. Melchizedek, having no parents at all, had no genealogy to qualify him. Despite his descent from Judah (7.14), Jesus too is *agenealogētos* in the sense most important for this author: his claim to priesthood does not rest on a family tree.[81] For this epistle's author, the meaning of Ps 110.4 was fundamentally "You are a priest because—like Melchizedek—you are forever."

This exegesis is confirmed by Heb 7.3, where a long introductory portrait of Melchizedek is finished with "resembling the Son of God, he remains a priest *eis to diēnekes*." Commentators usually discern an argument from silence here: Genesis does not mention Melchizedek's death, and the author (quite in accord with rabbinic as well as Philonic hermeneutics) thence deduces that he never died. It is noteworthy, however, that this argument would prove at best only his immortality, not his perpetual priestly office. *That* conclusion follows more readily from Ps 110.4, and the likelihood that the author has it in mind is favored by the equivalence of *eis to diēnekes* and *eis ton aiōna*. But we can take a further step. The fact that Melchizedek continues a priest forever is the chief, if not the only, characteristic which he shares with Jesus.[82] Although the entire description of Melchizedek in 7.1-3 attests his greatness, the only respect in which he directly resembles Christ is his possession of an unending priesthood.

---

had even before his resurrection. Cf Spicq, *Hébreux* 2,258 and 394. On the conception of the life-power of Jesus' blood in 9.11-22, see esp. E. F. Scott, *The Epistle to the Hebrews* (Edinburgh: Clark, 1922), 151-53.

[80] In this passage, as in 7.16, the ideas of accession to priesthood and of resurrection-ascension are joined.

[81] Cf Michel, *Hebräer*, 261; Spicq, *Hébreux* 2,210.

[82] Similarly Spicq, *Hébreux* 2,210 n. 2. Cf Schille, "Erwägungen," 85.

After the fundamental identification of Melchizedek in 7.1-3, vss 4-10 seek to show how he (and, by implication, Jesus) surpasses the levitical priests. Three proofs of superiority are adduced: the tithe Abraham paid, the blessing Melchizedek gave, and the latter's everlasting life. The assurance that, in contrast to mortal levitical functionaries, Melchizedek "lives" [83] (vs 8) must stem from Ps 110.4 and the silence of Genesis about his death.[84]

The same basic theme recurs in 7.23-24. Jesus surpasses levitical priests because their mortality requires them to succeed one another; he, by contrast, needs no replacement, being *eis ton aiōna*.[85] Again, everything turns on the yoked premises of the resurrection-ascension and the application of Ps 110.4 to Jesus.

A subsidiary argument, urged in 7.20-22, focuses on the swearing mentioned in the psalm verse *(omnynai)*. Jesus, as opposed to priests of the older order, was appointed by a divine oath; hence he is superior to them. God's act of swearing seems to suggest to the author the higher seriousness and finality with which the new priesthood was established.[86] The conclusion of 7.22 indicates that the unchangeable guarantee rests not merely on the scriptural verse but on the person to whom it is addressed. Essentially the oath of Ps 110.4 is taken not as a warranty given Jesus but as one given believers that he is "the surety of a better covenant." The psalm word and Jesus are joined into a single guarantee for faith. And this double assurance recalls the "two unchangeable things" of Heb 6.18, suggesting that the entire discussion of the pledge to Abraham (6.13-18) looks forward to 7.20-22 and Ps 110.4. This suggestion gains force from the strong similarity in the descriptions of Jesus in 6.19-20 and 7.19*b*, 22.[87]

In 7.28 the phrase "the word of the oath, which came later than the law" must refer to Ps 110.4. Beyond recalling the thought of 7.11-12,

[83] Since Melchizedek's condition is here contrasted with that of mortals, the simple verb "live" must here mean "live forever."

[84] The use of *martyrein* in 7.8 suggests that the author thinks of the positive statement of the psalm. Cf Schröger, *Verfasser*, 143.

[85] The phrase is surely taken from the psalm verse.

[86] Hebrews mentions three oaths, all sworn by God (3.11=3.18=4.3; 6.13-17; 7.20-21=7.28). In each the author perceives special solemnity and finality—"he will not change his mind." Possibly the author thinks of these divine words as unalterable specifically in contrast to the mosaic legislation about Levi.

[87] See esp. H. Köster, "Die Auslegung der Abraham-Verheissung in Hebräer 6," *Studien zur Theologie der alttestamentlichen Überlieferungen* (Festschrift G. von Rad), ed. R. Rendtorff and K. Koch (Neukirchen: Neukirchener Verlag, 1961), 105-8; Spicq, *Hébreux* 2,181. Cf Schille, "Erwägungen," 105 f.

20-21, this closing verse only adds the idea that the priest appointed forever is a Son perfected forever, a concept related less to our psalm than to verses in the epistle like 2.10 and 5.9.[88]

The arguments examined thus far are directed at proving that Jesus is priest and that he is a more glorious one than the levitical priests. Yet the author also desires to demonstrate that the inferior priesthood is inadequate, incapable of mediating salvation. The main argument to this end is offered in 7.11-19. The contention of 7.11-14 is that the very pronouncement of the divine oracle in the psalm (assumed to be later than the Mosaic legislation—7.28) signifies the insufficiency of the former priesthood.[89] The oracle was spoken to a non-Levite, and hence the levitical ordinances are demonstrably futile. Perhaps behind this argument lies a polemic against persons who disputed Jesus' sacerdotal rank on the ground that he was of Judah's tribe.[90]

The second argument about the Mosaic law turns on its failure to bring men to perfection (7.18-19). Presumably this is connected with later words about the old sacrifices as able to cleanse externals only (9.9-10,13,23; 10.1-4). This argument, while harmonizing well with 7.11-14, does not directly appeal to Ps 110.4 (unless 7.19*b* is an allusion).

In 7.25 we have an extension of the reasoning about Jesus' immortality as priest: he is always (*eis to panteles*) able to save those who approach God through him since he always lives (*pantote zōn*) to intercede for them. That Ps 110.4 is still in mind seems evident. We have already seen that this verse has a close parallel in Rom 8.34 (see above, p. 132). But it introduces a source of unresolved tension into the epistle's theology. The author's dominant view of the atonement seems to be that it was accomplished once for all in Jesus' death

[88] However, 7.19 shows that the author connects imperfection with the levitical law and perfection with the order announced in the psalm.

[89] On the general hermeneutical principle used, see G. B. Caird, "The Exegetical Method of the Epistle to the Hebrews," *Canadian Journal of Theology* 5 (1959), 44-51. The epistle's author does not explain why, if a later priesthood invalidates an earlier one, the priesthood of Melchizedek was not called into doubt by Aaron's. But in fact the Melchizedek of Hebrews, while certainly having priestly office, performs no priestly work (apart from the blessing of Abraham, and perhaps the receiving of tithes). Cf Spicq, *Hébreux* 2,179.

[90] The question of these "heretics" might even have resembled Mk 12.37: "David calls the messiah 'priest' (Ps 110.4), so how can he be his (David's) son?" The epistle's author, however, mentions Jesus' descent from Judah not to connect him with royal messianism but only to show that the levitical priesthood's law is shattered by the new order. Cf Friedrich, "Lied," 114 f; N. A. Dahl, "A New and Living Way," *Interpretation* 5 (1951), 405 and n. 18.

(see esp. 1.3-4; 7.27; 9.25-28; 10.12-14). In 10.12-13 and 12.2 the heavenly SESSION seems to involve Jesus' passivity. Yet in 7.25 and occasionally elsewhere (2.17-18; 4.14-16; 8.2; 9.24; 12.24; 13.8,13) the author implies that Jesus has an ongoing priestly ministry in heaven on behalf of believers. Why should he need to intercede after offering an utterly adequate sacrifice? Moreover, if the intercession is central to the author's soteriology, why does he mention it directly only once and never discuss it systematically—as he does Jesus' death? Also, one may note that this intercession reference is really only a passing remark, made in the context of a discussion not of Jesus' priestly work but of his priestly office.[91] The intercession can hardly be for minor or occasional sins only,[92] however, since the author declares (7.25) that it is a matter of salvation (*sōzein*).

One may attempt some kind of theological harmonization—e.g., Jesus' pleading reminds God of the everlasting validity of his death-oblation, or the intercession is merely a symbol of the eternal efficacy of the death.[93] The spiritual reassurance which a liturgical image of Jesus as eternal advocate might provide can easily be imagined. But I suspect that 7.25 is best viewed as a foreign element, or "seam" indicative of the uniting of two fundamentally different ideas of Jesus' priestly work: one that it is consummated in his cross, the other that it is a post-resurrection celestial ministry. The latter view has many Jewish and Christian parallels, and may well have been part of the theological tradition assumed by the author and his readers. The writer retained the older christological view but failed to fuse it perfectly with his understanding of Jesus' death.

In two other passages Ps 110 figures prominently in the author's exposition concerning Jesus' priesthood, but these involve the psalm's first verse rather than its fourth. Heb 8.1 and 10.12-13 have already been discussed in connection with their bearing on the glory of the exalted Jesus, and 10.12-13 has some relation to the motif of the subjection of foes. Yet these verses are chiefly important in the epistle for their contribution to its sacerdotal argument.

---

[91] The writer's main concern in 4.14–7.28 is with Jesus' priestly office, in 8.1–10.25 with his saving work. Cf O. Kuss, "Der theologische Grundgedanke des Hebräerbriefs," *Münchener Theologische Zeitschrift* 7 (1956), 263.

[92] Cf Bultmann, *Theology* 2,166 f; Grässer, *Glaube,* 161.

[93] See, e.g., Käsemann, *Gottesvolk,* 154; Spicq, *Hébreux* 1, 311-16; 2, 136 f and 268. Cf W. Stott, "The Conception of 'Offering' in the Epistle to the Hebrews," NTS 9 (1962-63), 66 f; Michel, *Hebräer,* 73 f. The problems of tension seem slighted in S. Lyonnet, "Expiation et Intercession," *Biblica* 40 (1959), 900 f.

The allusion in *8.1* is incorporated into a sentence which, along with 7.26-28, forms a bridge from the first part of the priestly argument (4.14–7.25) to the second (8.3–10.18). If 7.28 joins the themes of Jesus' priesthood and sonship, 8.1 joins his priesthood with the heavenly SESSION.[94] The reason for this combination of themes is not far to seek. 8.2-5 gives a foretaste of the great development of the two-sanctuary schema in 9.1–10.25. In contrast to the levitical priests, Jesus is said to exercise a heavenly office. How can believers be sure of this? Certainly their confidence stems from faith in Christ's ascension and in his death as the ground of forgiveness. But 7.28 and 8.1 attest that the author was also basing the conviction on the words of Ps. 110. The psalm's first verse is the only scriptural evidence which the author adduces to prove that Jesus is in heaven; and, if he were not in heaven, he would not be a priest at all.[95] Other testimonies attest the Son's exaltation, but only this one specifies the location beside God's throne (which is, of course, *en tois ouranois*).

In *Heb 10.12-13,* near the conclusion of the whole argument about priesthood, Ps 110.1 is cited once more and made to yield a last vital addition to that argument. Now, in company with Ps 40.6-8 and Jer. 31.34, it supplies testimony for the perfection and total sufficiency of Jesus' saving work (again set over against the sacrifices of the Aaronite priesthood).[96] From the psalm verse's *kathou* and its reference to God's subjection of foes, the author infers that Jesus' priestly task is finished with his death. The levitical priests stand day after day offering ineffectual sacrifices (10.11). The conclusion, argued chiefly from the psalm, is that Jesus' death has brought perfection for all time (10.14).[97] As in Heb 1.3, this citation of Ps 110.1*b* comes immediately

[94] Only here, and at Heb 10.12-13, is Jesus' heavenly SESSION linked explicitly with his priestly office. There may be a link with the tradition about Jesus' sanhedrin trial, where words about his heavenly SESSION lie close to the promise of a temple "not made with hands" (Mk 14.58,62=Mt 26.61,64). One recalls Rev 1.13, where "one like a son of man" wears priestly costume. See also above, pp. 132-33 n. 15.

[95] Heb 8.4. This axiom is (like 7.7) not obviously valid. Why could there not be two legitimate earthly priesthoods? Was not Melchizedek an earthly priest? The real necessity for Christ's priesthood to be heavenly lies in the need for priestly work to be performed regarding realities, not copies (8.5-6).

[96] Each of the three quotations has its special function in the passage. Ps 40 shows the superiority of obedience to Jewish sacrifices, Jer 31 the absoluteness of the new covenant. Only Ps. 110 is used to argue directly the adequacy of Jesus' priestly death.

[97] Because of this connection between sacrifice and SESSION, no substantial point hinges on whether *eis to diēnekes* in 10.12 is taken with "having offered a single

after a compendious reference to Jesus' death. Yet the link between cross and SESSION is shown to be more than one of mere chronological sequence: now the SESSION attests the enduring effect of the sacrifice. The author comes closer here than anywhere else in his epistle to exhibiting death and heavenly SESSION as a single theological event.[98]

Conclusions

Ps 110.1 is openly connected with Jesus as intercessor only in Rom 8.34. Probably the same association is implied in Heb 7.25; perhaps it is in Acts 7.55-56 and 1 Pet 3.21-22. Jewish sources do not offer any close parallels to such exegesis of the psalm verse, but they do present numerous traditions about heavenly advocates and priestly salvation. Early Christian writings, apart from Hebrews, offer only a handful of references to Jesus as a heavenly witness or priest.

Melchizedek, unmentioned by all but one Christian work preserved from the earliest period, is occasionally described in contemporary Jewish literature. (There *may* be a special relation between Hebrews and the community which produced 11Q Melchizedek, but the ancient priest-king was highly regarded in other sectors as well, and it is very doubtful that the epistle is a polemic against the specific doctrine of that Qumran text.)[99] The marvel about the argument concerning

---

sacrifice" or with "he sat down." The essential meaning of the phrase becomes clear in 10.14 (cf 10.1), and this meaning may already be in the author's mind when he uses the phrase in 7.3. Of course its virtual equivalence to *eis ton aiōna* (cf 6.20 with 7.3, 17, 24, 28) suggests that 10.12 is meant to recall Ps 110.4. Cf Spicq, *Hébreux* 1,296 n.1.

[98] Death and ascension are one event in which Jesus enters the heavenly sanctuary as priest (cf 6.19-20; 10.19-20). See Käsemann, *Gottesvolk*, 148. One need not, however, agree with Bertram ("Himmelfahrt") that Hebrews presupposes ascension directly from the cross.

[99] Since several scholars have seen large implications for the interpretation of Hebrews in 11QMelch (e.g., de Jonge and van der Woude, "11Q Melchizedek," 322), a summary comparison of the two may be useful here. Both emphasize atonement; perhaps both stress the day of atonement. In the Qumran document Melchizedek is a warrior savior; in Hebrews he is a priest-king but not a savior, and the saving work of Jesus is represented chiefly in sacrificial rather than military categories. In the Qumran document, Melchizedek is a heavenly angel or divinity; in Hebrews he seems conceived as an earthly and human personage (though one without parents or mortality). In 11QMelch he is directly related to levitical laws; in Hebrews stress is laid on his non-levitical status. Hebrews says nothing about him which is not connected with Gen 14 or Ps 110; 11QMelch never clearly alludes to either text. On the relation between the documents, see further Y.

Melchizedek in Heb 5-7 is not that the author has made so much out of so little, but that he has made so little out of so much. It is clear that at least within Judaism large clouds of speculation swirled about Melchizedek, and there can be little doubt that the author of the epistle knew more than he chose to elaborate (cf 7.1-3). With the most astonishing thrift, or resolute reserve, he determined to know nothing of him that could not be inferred from Gen 14.18-20 and Ps 110.4 (chiefly the latter). Perhaps he thought that his readers would suspect ideas not grounded on scripture texts. It is at least possible, however, that there already existed before him a tradition of interpreting Jesus in relation to Melchizedek and that he wrote partly to set limits on such interpretation. Melchizedek is mentioned to demonstrate the reality and superiority of Jesus' priestly office; he is not related to Jesus' priestly work and after 7.17 drops out of sight altogether. Plainly he has no independent significance in Hebrews; the author's description of his office and actions makes him not so much a parallel or prototype as simply a witness to Jesus' unique office.

The unusual significance which Ps 110 has for the author of Hebrews is shown by the frequency with which it is cited and by the pivotal assertions it is called on to support. The psalm's fourth verse is cited to prove that Jesus belongs to an authentic priesthood, the mere existence of which shows the futility of the levitical order. Its first verse is cited to certify that he is a priest in heaven whose perfect sacrifice is already consummated. No other scripture is cited to establish any of these critical points, and it is reasonable to suppose that the psalm influenced not only the defense but also the conception of the christology here set forth.[100] Obviously the single major christological idea which the author of Hebrews could not find in Ps 110 was that of the messiah's death. One can imagine his regret.

Yadin, "A Note on Melchizedek and Qumran," *Israel Exploration Journal* 15 (1965), 152-54; Higgins, "Messiah," 232-34, 238 f; Carmignac, "Le document," 371-78.

[100] It is probably too much to say, however, that Ps 110 was the most important source of that christology or that the epistle is essentially a midrash on the psalm. Cf Lindars, *Apologetic*, 51; R. Williamson, *Philo and the Epistle to the Hebrews* (Leiden: Brill, 1970), 446-49.

Conclusions

A summary of the details of the preceding pages would be both difficult and superfluous. Yet the main results of this investigation may be set in fresh perspective by consideration of certain general questions which have still to be answered. We need to inquire into the probable development of early Christian exegesis of Ps 110, hoping to gain insight into the remarkable diversity of the interpretations and into the interrelationships among them. Secondly, some discussion must be devoted to the factors which may account for the popularity of the psalm. Finally, I shall attempt to summarize the relationship between ancient Jewish and Christian interpretations.

Unity and Diversity of Early Christian Interpretations

This investigation has shown that almost every early Christian reference to Ps 110 has unique features. The meaning of each quotation or allusion emerges only through study of its literary context and the particular function or functions that it has there. Yet all these functions can be readily grouped into four major categories: expressions of the idea that Jesus or Christians sit at God's right hand, the use of the psalm to support particular christological titles, its use to affirm the subjection of powers to Christ, and its employment regarding his heavenly intercession or priesthood. Further, all these functions may be collapsed into one: early Christians chiefly employed the psalm to articulate the supreme glory, the divine transcendence, of Jesus, through whom salvation was mediated. It was primarily used as a symbol not of his saving work but of his ultimate status. Indeed, a brief reference to Ps 110.1*b* could simply mean: Jesus is God's messiah.[1]

---

[1] On the use of this portion of the psalm in model confessions of faith, see above, pp. 41, 76-77.

155

Many of the references to Jesus' SESSION do connect it with particular heavenly actions (ruling, judging, interceding, etc.), but many others do not. From Rom 8.34 to Sib Or 2.243, however, the SESSION regularly implies that Jesus determines mankind's destiny. A number of texts explicitly relate the SESSION to the empowerment or exaltation of Christians alongside Jesus; but these interpretations hinge on the primal conviction of his glory. The first clause in the psalm, "The Lord said to my lord," was sometimes taken as support for certain christological titles; but mainly it served as testimony to the supreme dignity of the one called "my lord." Again, Ps 110.1c, though associated with the subjection of powers, meant first and last the superiority of Jesus to every other power (except that of God the Father). The exact nature of the subjection and the particular objects of it were probably always of secondary interest. Although some early Christian documents connect Ps 110.1 with the intercessory activity of Jesus, the chief force of Ps 110.1 and 4 for the author of Hebrews lay in the proof for him of Jesus' status as heavenly Son and priest. He usually turned to other means when he wished to describe Jesus' saving work.

All early Christian references to the psalm connect it with Jesus' post-death glory. Some, like Acts 2.33-36, emphasize its relation to the past event of resurrection and ascension. Others connect it mainly with his present exaltation, and still others emphasize its connection with his parousia. The concrete imagery of the psalm could hardly lend itself to descriptions of Jesus' earthly life. Yet his exaltation as described by means of the psalm is often represented as his vindication by God (e.g., Mk 14.62; Acts 5.31); thus the psalm is indirectly linked with his earthly life and death as a token of their ultimate significance.[2]

No simple line of development can be plotted for early Christian exegesis of the psalm. Thus Eph 1.20 is certainly later in date than 1 Cor 15.25; but its interpretation of Ps 110.1 in terms of realized eschatology might well be earlier, one to which 1 Cor 15.25 is a reaction. Regarding the identification of the enemies mentioned in the psalm, one may wonder whether 1 Clem 36.5-6 (human foes) marks a relatively late interpretation by comparison with 1 Cor 15.25 (supernatural foes); Mk 14.62 also implies the defeat of human opponents. Our data simply do not permit firm chronological conclusions.

[2] Cf V. A. Harvey, *The Historian and the Believer* (New York: Macmillan, 1966), 274.

Further, it seems doubtful that early Christian understanding of the psalm ever developed stepwise along a single path. There are so many different patterns of interpretation that one is inclined to posit a kind of fission process producing bursts of exegetical energy in many directions. Sometimes the psalm is used to establish the truth of basic kerygmatic convictions (notably those concerning the resurrection—Acts 2.33-36). In Mk 12.35-37 par and Barn 12.10-11, it is the foundation of subtle argument, presumably for disciples and non-disciples alike, showing the inadequacy of conventional messianic ideas. Paul, in 1 Cor 15.25, uses Ps 110.1c to argue an eschatological point with fellow Christians. The author of Hebrews uses two verses of the psalm in a meticulous demonstration of the reality and potency of Jesus' priesthood. Elsewhere the psalm often seems to function as a kind of phrase book, supplying vocabulary and imagery to writers not obviously concerned to argue from it in strict exegetical fashion.

To the extent that rough dates can be assigned to primitive Christian writings, certain broad observations can be made about the history of Christian interpretation of Ps 110. It obviously began well before Romans or 1 Corinthians was written, probably in the pre-Pauline period, possibly (recalling Mk 12.35-37 par) in the pre-Easter period. The textual evidence suggests that our OG version of the psalm, or one very similar to it, was widely known in early Christian circles; it seems to be the form on which most or all of the extant quotations and allusions directly or indirectly depend. A number of passages which we have labeled as references to the psalm are probably based not directly on the psalm itself but on intermediary sources: early Christian hymns and confessions incorporating the SESSION image and collections of scriptural testimonies. From the absence of references to any part of the psalm but its first and fourth verses, it is a fair conclusion that early Christians did not find its other portions too meaningful. On the other hand, Justin Martyr applies the entire psalm to Jesus with an ease that suggests that this had become customary by the middle of the second century.

The frequency of allusions to the idea of Jesus' SESSION, as opposed to direct quotations of the psalm or allusions to other portions of it, suggests that the SESSION became a fixed theologoumenon in its own right. Perhaps, then, several early Christian references to the SESSION were written with no conscious thought of Ps 110.1. Yet the number of verbatim quotations of the psalm verse throughout the early period indicates that its connection with the SESSION image was not widely forgotten. Also, the SESSION image did not become so commonplace that it perceptibly lost appeal or power to suggest fresh inferences.

The similarities among the various interpretations of the psalm may be explained by several factors, the chief being its fundamental and persistent association with Jesus' heavenly glory. Its very popularity would tend to promote a certain homogeneity, since writers would naturally hesitate to deviate too widely from well-known conceptions. The use of the psalm in confessional or hymnic formulations must have contributed in a major way to the stabilizing of its meaning. Many early Christians must have been familiar with the psalm's ideas chiefly as these were mediated through such liturgical materials. The baptismal *Sitz im Leben* of some of these materials would go far to explain why in several different traditions Christ's SESSION is associated with his triumph over supernatural powers and the exaltation of believers.

The comparative unity within diversity of early Christian interpretations of Ps 110 cannot be accounted for by the hypothesis of a widely used testimony book. Nor can it be explained by positing a school or distinctive method of exegesis. Consideration of literary context may have encouraged agreement among interpreters. This can hardly have been a major factor, however, since every Christian user of the psalm before Justin Martyr seems oblivious to vss 2-3 and 5-7, and only the author of Hebrews refers to vs 4. Possibly many of the writers who quote or allude to only a small fragment of the psalm were familiar with the rest of it, but their exegesis usually does not betray such knowledge.

So the decisive influences controlling the progress of the interpretation of the psalm appear to have been basic christological convictions and loyalty to traditional formulas. But these were elastic bonds, and individual exegetes felt free to go separate ways as far as their ingenuity and particular purposes would carry them.[3]

Why Was Psalm 110 So Popular?

It has often been maintained that the popularity of the psalm within the early church stemmed from Jesus' own use of it in Mk 12.35-37

---

[3] Cf the contention of J. Barr (*Old and New in Interpretation* [New York: Harper, 1966], esp. 143 f) that in general early Christian interpreters of Jewish scriptures were guided not so much by fixed exegetical methods as by their concerns for content and results.

par and 14.62 par. In my opinion only Mk 12.35-37 par represents authentic tradition about Jesus. Yet both the debate-saying about the son of David and the trial confession were at an early date credited to Jesus, and belief that he had spoken about the psalm's christological significance must have encouraged Christians to study and appropriate its verses. Nonetheless, the early church did not produce interpretations of most of those verses, and only occasionally do we find passages preserving something like the interest in vs 1a manifest in the saying about David's son (Acts 2.36; Barn 12.10-11). Even what is developed from Ps 110.1b is often not closely akin to Mk 14.62 par. Although the church's interest in the psalm may have been stimulated by its ideas about Jesus' teaching, early Christian exegetes did not labor much to demonstrate connections between their interpretations and the words attributed to the earthly Jesus.

It is reasonable to assume that prior Jewish messianic interpretation of the psalm was a factor behind its popularity among Christians. Obviously not every representative of early Christianity felt constrained to conform his messianic views to those of the synagogue, but preaching to Jews would have been facilitated by references to texts on which some basic agreement could be presupposed.

It would appear that the primary reason for the psalm's popularity among early Christians lay in its meeting vital religious needs of which they were conscious. The moving cause behind the emphasis on Ps 110.4 in Hebrews seems plainly to be the author's desire for a scriptural basis for his priestly christology. Apparently this text suited his purpose better than any other. Likewise this author and Paul cited Ps 110.1c (Heb 10.12-13; 1 Cor 15.25) because they believed that it supported their eschatological arguments. Probably the authors of Acts 2.33-36 and Barn 12.10-11 cited vs 1a because they knew of no other prooftext which fitted their needs so well.

The crucial and most complex problem concerning the psalm's popularity is the question of why the SESSION image was so appealing. I have already suggested (above, p. 91) that one reason probably was that the image affirmed supreme exaltation without calling into question the glory and sovereignty of God the Father. Jesus' elevation was thereby defined in terms of unique proximity to God, and Father and Son were carefully distinguished. The phrase did not resolve the potential problems of ditheism or subordinationism, but it permitted Christians to confess faith in the absoluteness of Jesus before they had "solved" such issues. Over against expressions like

"Jesus is lord," this image intrinsically affirmed a continuing relationship between the exalted Christ and God, precluding any possibility of conceiving Christ as a new deity dethroning an older one.

It may also be significant for our question that the conception of a right-hand SESSION has an aura of definiteness about it, a quality which might have satisfied early believers perplexed about the post-Easter location or precise dignity of their lord. Some naïve Christians may have imagined or visualized (cf Acts 7.55-56!) the risen Jesus as literally(spatially) situated on a throne to the right of God the Father. Yet men accustomed to the dictum that "no one has ever seen God" will probably not have been guilty of crude anthropomorphism when they applied Ps 110.1b to Jesus. The psalm phrase provided language to state or evoke the ultimately unstatable and incomprehensible. Perhaps the very simplicity of the phrase reminded early Christians of the impenetrable character as well as the reality of Jesus' exaltation.

One may also speak of an attractive vagueness in the SESSION image. Even more than other elements in Ps 110.1 and 4, vs 1b could suggest or accommodate a wide variety of meanings. Also, one could declare Jesus to be at God's right hand without committing oneself to any particular idea about his present activity (or inactivity).

All this is not to say that Ps 110 was infinitely flexible and functioned in the church only to express pre-established dogmas.[4] It is clear that the church had other language, some of it scriptural, to refer to Jesus' exaltation. The high frequency of citations of Ps 110.1 suggests that early Christians not only spoke but often thought in terms of the psalm's wording and imagery. Normally there is a positive correlation between the ways people think and the language they habitually employ. Above all, the patient argumentation from the psalm in passages like Mk 12.35 par and Heb 5–7 suggests that the psalm generated some relatively fresh insights. This creative capacity of the psalm must have contributed to its popularity.

To return to the narrower question of the popularity of the image of a right-hand SESSION, it is of course relevant to note that that image could easily be shown to be of scriptural descent. The hel-

---

[4] On the specific question of whether Ps 110 molded early Christian thinking about Jesus' exaltation, see Vielhauer, *Aufsätze*, 174 f. The issue is one instance of the larger problem of whether early Christian exegesis of the Jewish scriptures may be considered "the substructure of all Christian theology" (Dodd, *Scriptures*, 127; cf Harris and Burch, *Testimonies* 1,25; Lindars, *Apologetic*, 17).

lenistic period saw many attempts, pagan, Jewish, and Christian, to describe the position of mediators between God and the world. For those early Christians who venerated Jewish scriptures (and they seem to have been a majority), Ps 110.1b must have seemed an inspired and hence authoritative means of articulating the glory of Jesus.

Finally, the very conciseness of the phrase "at the right hand of God" probably told in its favor. The words were simple and direct, did not require extended explication, and could readily be incorporated into hymns and confessions.

The Distance from Jewish Scriptures and Exegesis

Perhaps nothing better illustrates early Christianity's nearness and distance from the Jewish scriptures and Judaism than its use of Ps 110. Originally the psalm was a confession of faith that a particular Jerusalem monarch governed with the power and authority of God. Apparently Jews shortly before and during the period of Christian origins applied the psalm variously, sometimes to a future messiah, sometimes to the heavenly vindication of a righteous sufferer (T Job), perhaps sometimes to a reigning Hasmonean king or supernatural being (the son of man, the heavenly Melchizedek).

Early Christian exegesis of the psalm was conditioned by a general confidence that it was Jesus in whom all the promises of the Jewish scriptures had their eschatological fulfillment. That is, it was conditioned by a faith that could not be shared by any non-Christian. To a remarkable degree the particular ideas of heavenly position, vindication, and a distinctive priesthood which Christians associated with the psalm were anticipated within the traditions of Jewish exegesis. Yet Christian exegesis took a new path by referring the psalm to the invisible glory of one who had lived as a prophet opposed in part to Judaism and the Mosaic law itself, one who had been condemned by Jewish leaders and executed as a political criminal. Further, early Christian conceptions of Jesus' heavenly glory at God's right hand probably went beyond the limits of what most Jewish exegesis could tolerate just because these conceptions moved in the direction of affirming the full divinity of Christ. (It is significant that Christian exegesis from Justin Martyr to Nicea tended to extend precisely the psalm's implications of Jesus' status as lord and Son of God.) To some degree pagan conceptions of divine persons seated to the right

161

of gods may have contributed to the willingness of early Christians to view Jesus as exalted higher and more permanently than Judaism would imagine possible. The fundamental factor, however, was the general early Christian conviction that Jesus was and remained the absolute mediator between man and God. Beginning with that conviction, early Christians used Ps 110 to affirm both their sense of continuity with Jewish scriptures and their belief that Jesus transcended Jewish expectations and all human categories.

Appendix

Numbers and small letters indicate portion of Ps 110 to which reference is made. An asterisk indicates direct quotation. Underlining calls attention to wording different from OG of Ps 109 (110).

a) Texts of Early Christian Quotations of, and Allusions to, Psalm 110.1

MT	Ps. 110.1	OG
נאם יהוה לאדני	(a)	Εἶπεν (+ὁ) κύριος τῷ κυρίῳ μου
שב לימיני	(b)	Κάθου ἐκ δεξιῶν μου
עד־אשית איביך	(c)	ἕως ἂν θῶ τοὺς ἐχθρούς σου
הדם לרגליך		ὑποπόδιον τῶν ποδῶν σου

Passage	Reference	Text
Mt 22.44	1a-c*	Εἶπεν (+ὁ) κύριος τῷ κυρίῳ μου Κάθου ἐκ δεξιῶν μου ἕως ἂν θῶ τοὺς ἐχθρούς σου <u>ὑποκάτω</u> (ὑποπόδιον) τῶν ποδῶν σου.
Mt 26.64	1b	. . . ὄψεσθε τὸν υἱὸν τοῦ ἀνθρώπου <u>καθήμενον</u> ἐκ δεξιῶν τῆς δυνάμεως . . . .
Mk 12.36	1a-c*	Εἶπεν (+ὁ) κύριος τῷ κυρίῳ μου Κάθου (<u>κάθισον</u>) ἐκ δεξιῶν μου ἕως ἂν θῶ τοὺς ἐχθρούς σου <u>ὑποκάτω</u> (ὑποπόδιον) τῶν ποδῶν σου.
Mk 14.62	1b	. . . ὄψεσθε τὸν υἱὸν τοῦ ἀνθρώπου ἐκ δεξιῶν <u>καθήμενον</u> τῆς δυνάμεως . . . .
"Mk" 16.19	1b	ὁ μὲν οὖν κύριος (+᾿Ιησοῦς) . . . <u>ἐκάθισεν</u> ἐκ δεξιῶν τοῦ θεοῦ (πατρός).
Lk 20.42-43	1a-c*	Εἶπεν (<u>λέγει</u>) (+ὁ) κύριος τῷ κυρίῳ μου Κάθου ἐκ δεξιῶν μου ἕως ἂν θῶ τοὺς ἐχθρούς σου ὑποπόδιον (<u>ὑποκάτω</u>) τῶν ποδῶν σου.
Lk 22.69	1b	. . . ἔσται ὁ υἱὸς τοῦ ἀνθρώπου <u>καθήμενος</u> ἐκ δεξιῶν τῆς δυνάμεως τοῦ θεοῦ.
Acts 2.33	1b	τῇ δεξιᾷ οὖν τοῦ θεοῦ <u>ὑψωθείς</u> . . . .

163

Passage	Reference	Text
Acts 2.34-35	1a-c*	Εἶπεν (+ὁ) κύριος τῷ κυρίῳ μου Κάθου ἐκ δεξιῶν μου ἕως ἂν θῶ τοὺς ἐχθρούς σου ὑποπόδιον τῶν ποδῶν σου.
Acts 5.31	1b	τοῦτον ὁ θεὸς ἀρχηγὸν καὶ σωτῆρα <u>ὕψωσεν τῇ δεξιᾷ</u> (δόξῃ) αὐτοῦ . . . .
Acts 7.55-56	1b	εἶδεν . . . ᾿Ιησοῦν (τὸν κύριον) <u>ἑστῶτα</u> ἐκ δεξιῶν τοῦ θεοῦ . . . . θεωρῶ . . . τὸν υἱὸν τοῦ ἀνθοώπου (θεοῦ) ἐκ δεξιῶν <u>ἑστῶτα</u> τοῦ θεοῦ.
Rom 8.34	1b	ὅς (+καί) <u>ἐστιν ἐν δεξιᾷ</u> τοῦ θεοῦ, ὅς καὶ ἐντυγχάνει ὑπὲρ ἡμῶν.
1 Cor 15.25	1c	δεῖ γὰρ αὐτὸν βασιλεύειν <u>ἄχρι οὗ θῇ πάντας</u> τοὺς ἐχθροὺς <u>(+αὐτοῦ) ὑπὸ τοὺς πόδας αὐτοῦ.</u>
Eph 1.20	1b	. . . <u>καθίσας (ἐκάθισεν) (+αὐτὸν) ἐν δεξιᾷ αὐτοῦ</u> ἐν τοῖς ἐπουρανίοις . . . .
Eph 2.6	1b	. . . <u>συνεκάθισεν</u> ἐν τοῖς ἐπουρανίοις ἐν Χριστῷ ᾿Ιησοῦ . . . .
Col 3.1	1b	τὰ ἄνω ζητεῖτε, οὗ ὁ Χριστός ἐστιν <u>ἐν δεξιᾷ τοῦ θεοῦ καθήμενος.</u>
Heb 1.3	1b	. . . <u>ἐκάθισεν ἐν δεξιᾷ</u> τῆς μεγαλωσύνης ἐν ὑψηλοῖς . . . .
Heb 1.13	1b-c*	κάθου ἐκ δεξιῶν μου ἕως ἂν θῶ τοὺς ἐχθρούς σου ὑποπόδιον τῶν ποδῶν σου.
Heb 8.1	1b	. . . ὃς <u>ἐκάθισεν ἐν δεξιᾷ</u> τοῦ θρόνου τῆς μεγαλωσύνης ἐν τοῖς οὐρανοῖς (ὑψηλοῖς) . . . .
Heb 10.12-13	1b-c	οὗτος (αὐτὸς) . . . <u>ἐκάθισεν ἐν δεξιᾷ (ἐκ δεξιῶν)</u> τοῦ θεοῦ, τὸ λοιπὸν ἐκδεχόμενος ἕως <u>τεθῶσιν οἱ ἐχθροὶ (+αὐτοῦ)</u> ὑποπόδιον τῶν ποδῶν αὐτοῦ.
Heb 12.2	1b	. . . ὃς . . . <u>ἐν δεξιᾷ τε τοῦ θρόνου τοῦ θεοῦ κεκάθικεν (ἐκάθισεν)</u> .
1 Pet 3.22	1b	. . . ὃς <u>ἐστιν ἐν δεξιᾷ (+τοῦ) θεοῦ</u> . . . .
Rev 3.21	1b	ὁ νικῶν, <u>δώσω αὐτῷ καθίσαι</u> μετ᾿ ἐμοῦ ἐν τῷ θρόνῳ μου, ὡς κἀγὼ ἐνίκησα καὶ <u>ἐκάθισα</u> μετὰ τοῦ πατρός μου ἐν τῷ θρόνῳ αὐτοῦ.
1 Clem 36.5	1b-c*	κάθου ἐκ δεξιῶν μου ἕως ἂν θῶ τοὺς ἐχθρούς σου ὑποπόδιον τῶν ποδῶν σου.

APPENDIX

Passage	Reference	Text
Pol *Phil* 2.1	1*b*	. . . δόντα αὐτῷ δόξαν καὶ <u>θρόνον</u> ἐκ δεξιῶν <u>αὐτοῦ</u>.
Barn 12.10	1*a-c**	Εἶπεν (+ὁ) κύριος τῷ κυρίῳ μου Κάθου ἐκ δεξιῶν μου ἕως ἂν θῶ τοὺς ἐχθρούς σου ὑποπόδιον τῶν ποδῶν σου.
Apoc Pet 6	1*b*	. . . the angels of God . . . will sit with me on the throne of my glory at the right hand of my heavenly Father.†
Sib Or 2.243	1*b*	. . . ἥξει . . . ἐν δόξῃ Χριστὸς σὺν ἀμύμοσιν ἀγγελτῆρσιν καὶ καθίσει μεγάλῳ <u>ἐπὶ δεξιᾷ</u> βήματι κρίνων . . . .
Apcr Jas 14.30 f	1*b*	. . . it is necessary for me today to occupy (the) right side of my Father.‡
Heg (EH 2.23.13	1*b*	. . . αὐτὸς <u>κάθηται</u> ἐν τῷ οὐρανῷ ἐκ δεξιῶν τῆς μεγάλης δυνάμεως . . . .

† English translation from Ethiopic in H-S 2, 671 f.
‡ English translation from Coptic in Malinine *et al.*, *Epistula*, 128.

b) Texts of Early Christian Quotations of, and Allusions to, Psalm 110.4

MT		OG
נשבע יהוה ולא ינחם	(a)	ὤμοσεν κύριος καὶ οὐ μεταμεληθήσεται
אתה־כהן לעולם	(b)	Σὺ (εἶ) ἱερεὺς εἰς τὸν αἰῶνα
על־דברתי מלכי־צדק	(c)	κατὰ τὴν τάξιν Μελχισεδεκ.

Heb 5.6	4*b-c**	σὺ (+εἶ) ἱερεὺς εἰς τὸν αἰῶνα κατὰ τὴν τάξιν Μελχισεδεκ.
5.10	4*b-c*	<u>προσαγορευθεὶς</u> ὑπὸ τοῦ θεοῦ <u>ἀρχιερεὺς</u> κατὰ τὴν τάξιν Μελχισεδεκ.
6.20	4*b-c*	. . . Ἰησους, κατὰ τὴν τάξιν Μελχισεδεκ ἀρχιερεὺς <u>γενόμενος</u> εἰς τὸν αἰῶνα.
7.3	4*b*	. . . <u>μένει</u> ἱερεὺς εἰς τὸ <u>διηνεκές</u>.
7.8	4*b*	. . . ἐκεῖ μαρτυρούμενος ὅτι ζῇ.
7.11	4*b-c*	. . . τίς ἔτι χρεία κατὰ τὴν τάξιν Μελχισεδεκ ἕτερον <u>ἀνίστασθαι</u> ἱερέα καὶ οὐ κατὰ τὴν τάξιν Ἀαρων λέγεσθαι;

Passage	Reference	Text
7.15-17	4b-c*	. . . εἰ κατὰ τὴν <u>ὁμοιότητα</u> Μελχισεδεκ <u>ἀνίσταται</u> ἱερεὺς ἕτερος. . . . μαρτυρεῖται γὰρ ὅτι σὺ (+εἶ) ἱερεὺς εἰς τὸν αἰῶνα κατὰ τὴν τάξιν Μελχισεδεκ.
7.21	4a-b*	ὤμοσεν κύριος καὶ οὐ μεταμεληθήσεται Σὺ (+εἶ) ἱερεὺς εἰς τὸν αἰῶνα.
7.24-25	4b	ὁ δὲ διὰ τὸ μένειν αὐτὸν εἰς τὸν αἰῶνα . . . πάντοτε ζῶν . . . .
7.28	4a-b	. . . ὁ λόγος δὲ τῆς ὁρκωμοσίας τῆς μετὰ τὸν νόμον υἱὸν εἰς τὸν αἰῶνα τετελειωμένον.

Indexes

I A

Index of Quotations of, and Allusions to, Ps 110.1

(Boldface indicates pages containing primary discussions)

Mk 12.35-37=Mt 22.41-46=Lk 20.41-44: 24, 30, 34-37, 42, 45, 47, 66, 102, 104, 106-7, **109-18,** 119-20, 126, 146, 149, 157-58, 160

Mk 14.62=Mt 26.64=Lk 22.69: 41-42, 45-46, **64-70,** 74, 77-78, 90-91, 102, 108-9, 111, 113-14, 118, 123, 127-28, 130, 151, 156, 159

"Mk" 16.19: 17, 42-45, 71, **83-84,** 92, 102, 104-5, 123, 128

Acts 2.33-35: 17, 24, 35-36, 46-47, 69, **70-72,** 73, 76, 90, 92-93, 104-6, 115, 126, 156-57, 159

Acts 5.31: 35-36, 46, 69, **71-73,** 90, 156

Acts 7.55-56: 36, 41-42, 46, 59, 70, **73-76,** 77, 80, 89-91, 93, 101, 104-5, 108, 110, 123, 128, **132-33,** 152, 160

Rom 8.34: 35-36, 39-40, 42-43, 46, **59-60,** 90-91, 102, 123, 126-27, **131-32,** 133-34, 149, 152, 156

1 Cor 15.25: 35-38, 42-43, 46-47, 49, **60-62,** 88, 90-91, 106, 109-10, **123-25,** 126, 129, 156-57, 159

Eph 1.20: 35, 40, 42, 44, 46, **63-64,** 90, 97-98, 109, 123, 125, 127, 129, 156

Eph 2.6: 17, 40, 44, 46, **97-99,** 100

Col 3.1: 35, 40, 42, 44, 46, **62-63,** 64, 89-91, 97, **99-100**

Heb 1.3: 17, 35, 39, 41-42, 46, 71, **85-86,** 87-91, 109, 143, 150-51

Heb 1.13: 35, 38-39, 42, 46, **85-86,** 90-91, 109, 126, 144

Heb 8.1: 35, 44, 46, 71, 86, **87,** 89-91, 145, 150, **151**

Heb 10.12-13: 35-36, 38, 46-47, 49, 71, 86, **87-88,** 89-91, 95, 123, **125,** 126, 129, 150, **151-52,** 159

Heb 12.2: 35, 46, 69, 71, 86, **88-89,** 90-91, **95-96,** 100, 145-46, 150

1 Pet 3.22: 40-42, 44, 46-47, **76-77,** 90, 123, 127, 129, **133-34,** 152

Rev 3.21: 17, 44-46, **80-81,** 90, **94-95,** 96, 100-101, 123, 128

1 Clem 36.5: 35, 39, 42, 46-47, **82-83,** 90, 110, 123, **126,** 128-29, 140, 156

Pol *Phil* 2.1: 40-42, 44, 46, **81-82,** 90, 97, 104-5, 123, 127, 129

Barn 12.10: 35, 38, 42, 46, 47, 105, 108-10, 116, **118-19,** 120-21, 126, 146, 157, 159

Apoc Pet 6: 44-46, **78-79,** 90-91, 123, 128

Sib Or 2.243: 35, 44-46, **79-80,** 90-91, 123, 128, 156

167

171

III

Index of Modern Authors

175